WHAT PEOPLE ARE SAYING

What We Learned in the Rainforest is a monumental piece of work. All the knowledge we need to create sustainable, profitable businesses is right there in the forest, if only we can learn from it. Kiuchi and Shireman show us how.

—William K. Coors, Chairman of the Board,
Adolph Coors Company

A fascinating book bridging the chasm between business and nature by two people who have been there and done it. Immensely readable—a must for anyone who cares about profit or a livable world.

—Dee Hock, Founder and CEO Emeritus, VISA,
Author of *Birth of the Chaordic Age*

Business has much to learn from the natural world, and there are no better teachers than Tachi Kiuchi and Bill Shireman. Their book guides companies through the sustainability jungle, helping them see both the forest and the trees. Their message is clear and concise: To prosper in the 21st century, businesses of all sizes and sectors must heed not just the laws of governments and the marketplace but also the laws of nature.

—Joel Makower, Co-founder, Clean Edge, Inc.,
Editor, *The Green Business Letter*

Tachi Kiuchi and Bill Shireman offer a wonderfully fresh perspective on sustainable development. They explain potentially mind-twisting phenomena in a very entertaining, story-telling style that draws on, of course, what they learned in the rainforest but also sheds light on some things they couldn't possibly have learned there . . . such as what some very innovative companies are doing in Colorado, Minnesota, and The Hague. An important contribution to a rapidly moving field.

—Matthew Arnold, CEO, World Resources Institute

WHAT WE LEARNED

IN THE RAINFOREST

Business
Lessons
from
Nature

INNOVATION, GROWTH, PROFIT, AND SUSTAINABILITY
AT 20 OF THE WORLD'S TOP COMPANIES

Tachi Kiuchi

CHAIRMAN AND CEO EMERITUS,
MITSUBISHI ELECTRIC AMERICA

Bill Shireman

PRESIDENT AND CEO,
THE FUTURE 500

A Future 500 Book

BK

BERRETT-KOEHLER PUBLISHERS, INC.
San Francisco

Berrett-Koehler Publishers, Inc.
235 Montgomery Street, Suite 650
San Francisco, CA 94104-2916
Tel: 415-288-0260   Fax: 415-362-2512
Website: www.bkconnection.com

ORDERING INFORMATION

Individual sales. Berrett-Koehler publications are available through most bookstores. They can also be ordered direct from Berrett-Koehler Publishers by calling, toll-free: 800-929-2929; fax 802-864-7626.

Quantity sales. Special discounts are available on quantity purchases by corporations, associations, and others. For details, contact the "Special Sales Department" at the Berrett-Koehler address above.

Orders for college textbook/course adoption use. Please contact Berrett-Koehler Publishers toll-free: 800-929-2929; fax 802-864-7626.

Orders by U.S. trade bookstores and wholesalers. Please contact Publishers Group West, 1700 Fourth Street, Berkeley, CA 94710; 510-528-1444; 1-800-788-3123; fax 510-528-9555.

Printed in the United States of America

Printed on acid-free and recycled paper that is composed of 85 percent recovered fiber, including 10 percent postconsumer waste.

Library of Congress Cataloging-in-Publication Data
Kiuchi, Tachi, 1935–
   What we learned in the rainforest : business lessons from nature : innovation, growth, profit, and sustainability at 20 of the world's top companies / Tachi Kiuchi, Bill Shireman.
         p.   cm.
   Includes bibliographical references and index.
   ISBN 1-57675-127-9
   1. Sustainable development.   2. Social responsibility of business.   3. Symbiosis.   4. Rain forests
I. Shireman, William K.   II. Title.
   HD75.6.K577   2001
   658.4'08—dc21   2001043181

06   05   04   03   02   01   10   9   8   7   6   5   4   3   2   1

Copyeditor: Stacey Sawyer
Text design: Detta Penna
Compositor/production service: Penna Design & Production
Indexer: Joan Dickey

Table of Contents

Preface

How can business profit from nature? Here's what we used to think: Business can profit from nature by conquering it and bringing it under human control, where our machines can turn its resources into products that we can buy and sell.

This approach delivered enormous wealth to people in the industrial age. But in the emerging economy, nature is not an enemy to be conquered. It is not a bank of wealth to be withdrawn from until used up. The energy and materials we extract from nature now offer business less and less value at higher and higher cost.

In today's economy, nature's real value to business lies in the lessons it teaches. Nature is a source of knowledge; an R&D lab with 3.8 billion years of product development and demonstration behind it; a storehouse of powerful principles that humanity can tap to cultivate more profitable businesses, a more abundant economy, a richer culture, and more fulfilling lives. By drawing on the physical resources of nature—extracting trees from its forests, minerals from its mountains, and fuels from its crust—business can profit for a day. But by drawing on the *wisdom* of nature—the principles that enable it to create extraordinary abundance in the face of extreme limits—business can profit over many human lifetimes.

This, therefore, is a how-to book about business—how to improve the bottom-line performance of business, economically, socially, and environmentally, by applying principles of nature. As we move beyond the industrial economy toward a more knowledge-based economy, business is beginning to recognize that the real profit to be earned from nature comes from the principles by which it flourishes—perhaps because in a knowledge economy, businesses run not just on fossil fuels and raw materials but on ideas, information, and inspiration; they begin more and more to resemble the creative systems of nature—systems like the prairie, the coral reef, and the rainforest.

In *What We Learned in the Rainforest*, we discuss the principles by which businesses maximize performance in the new economy, principles that became clear to us in our visits to the rainforests of Asia, the Pacific, and the Americas, and our observations of their application by business. Our thesis is that the old model of business—the machine model that pitted business against nature—is growing obsolete. In the emerging economy, businesses excel when they emulate what they once sought to conquer. They maximize performance as they become like nature, like a complex living system. In the process, they are changing our society's relationship with nature. By moving beyond the industrial, machine model and applying the dynamic principles of the rainforest and all complex living systems, businesses can learn how to create more profit than ever, and to do so sustainably.

We use nature as our model for emulation *not* because the rainforest is always a place of gentleness and cooperation—it isn't—but because in the patterns and cycles of the rainforest we can learn how the less savory, destructive phases we see in nature can evolve toward more creative, value-creating, life-affirming patterns. The question is not *whether* we will change, but when and how and with what level of discomfort and pain. If instead of controlling nature we listen to and learn from it, we can find our way with minimal pain and maximal gain.

To teach the principles of business as a living system, we use a personal approach. Each chapter is structured in the same way. It begins with a short segment of a continuing story to highlight a single principle or method. We then illustrate the principle with a lesson from the rainforest. Then, through a business case study that walks you through the *business* rainforest, we show how the principle or method can be practically applied.

The book is divided into two parts. The first presents core principles that maximize the performance of living businesses: feedback, information, profit, design, diversity, succession. The second describes how to apply the lessons learned in the first part. It provides a tool set for business management, measurement, strategy, and tactics.

To start off the book, we jump out of an airplane high above the rainforests of Costa Rica and begin our descent to the ground, where we plan to join our colleagues and start our exploration of the forest. We continue the story of our descent at the start of each chapter. The fall to earth is a metaphor for the fall of the industrial economy toward ecological limits, in a manner similar to the way in which the rainforest is always falling toward its limits. What happens on the way to the ground is what happens in nature and the economy as they speed toward their limits. They can slow their fall, change directions, gain capacities, and occasionally even reverse directions, at least for a time. We can do the same.

TEN POINTS ABOUT OUR PERSPECTIVE

You can understand our message—and develop, improve, or depart from it—if we tell you ten things about our ideas right away:

- First, *we see humanity as a part of nature.* Some scientists insist there is a solid line of demarcation that divides humanity from nature. We disagree. Humans do have some unique characteristics, as do other living things—but being a distinct creation of nature does not cancel our family membership.

- Second, because humanity is a part of nature, we see *business as a part of nature, too.* Not everyone agrees. Some people point to the profligate waste perpetuated by business, the over-consumption, pollution, and destruction, and find it offensive to call this "natural." We take a different view. In nature, there are patterns of destruction and patterns of creation. Life learns to evolve from the former toward the latter; business can, too.

- Third, *at its best, business is a noble endeavor.* Some people believe that business is intrinsically amoral. Others insist that, because of its drive to maximize shareholder profit, business is not just amoral, it is selfish and *im*moral. A more enlightened understanding tells us that business is a living community: It exists to serve the whole as it serves its parts. Profits are a means to this end, not the end itself. The trick is to align the three parts of what John Elkington of SustainAbility calls the "triple bottom line": economic, social, and environmental gains.

- Fourth, *since business is a natural living system, the principles of living systems must apply to business.* If they don't, it doesn't mean business isn't natural; it means we don't yet fully understand natural systems. Science, not nature, needs to catch up. If human institutions such as business don't behave as the natural sciences say they should, don't change the definition of nature—improve the science.

- Fifth, *we are optimists.* Some people feel we should paint a gloomier picture, sound the alarms, pound the point home that if humanity is to survive, business must change in radical ways. We agree: We are at a point of crisis. If we fail to meet it, not only will our businesses die—we will. Because of this, our priority is to focus on positive solutions.

- Sixth, *we are pragmatic.* Some people believe we must advocate draconian changes. However, we don't believe change has to seem draconian to be fundamental. It's hard to build a tree but easy to plant a seed. Building a tree is draconian, desperate, and ineffective. Planting a seed is fundamental, serene, and easy. Where do we seek to plant the seeds? Why do we focus on big, successful, industrial-era companies? Haven't all these companies—Coca-Cola, Coors, Nike, VISA, Intel, Microsoft, Mitsubishi Electric, Weyerhaeuser, and so on—contributed to a system that perpetuates the endless growth-and-conquest cycle that epitomizes the industrial age? Absolutely. But we are all enmeshed in that system. We all contribute to its perpetuation. Those companies need to change. If they don't change, they will decline and eventually fail. If they do change, they can transcend their old forms and emerge in new ones. So can we. This book highlights the principles and tools we can use to change.

- Seventh, *this book is just a beginning*. We have not exhausted the range of actions businesses can take to profit in nature's way. The "to do's" in each chapter, especially in Part Two, are just a start. For example, although we do have much to say on the topic, in this book we say little about the laws and regulations of government. Interested readers can visit our websites and refer to other books and reports for our opinions on the flexible, incentive-oriented, market- and performance-based laws that could promote sustainable, profitable business.

- Eighth, *the "emerging economy," which we suggest can be more sustainable than the industrial economy, is in its earliest stages*. The Internet is much more than a shopping mall serving a billion online consumers. This narrow old-school vision doesn't represent the emerging economy, as we use the term—it's just an extension of the old economy. Today's economy remains largely industrial, *refined* by information but not *transformed* by it. An economy *founded* on information—one whose values and lifestyles reflect the idea that knowledge and design are the root source of value—is what we regard as the emerging economy.

- Ninth, *we share nature's secrets*. Many people have told us they fear that if business learns nature's profit secrets, it will have even more power to destroy the earth. We understand their concern. However, nature teaches that business will prosper more by protecting the earth than exploiting it. Indeed, as we learn nature's principles, we become less likely to damage the earth.

- Tenth, *we try to live our work*. Through the Future 500 and Global Futures, we resolve conflicts and forge partnerships between some of the world's largest corporations and its most impassioned environmental activist groups. With them we find opportunities, implement programs, and pass laws. The secret is to dig to the root cause of conflict. There you find ways to reconcile interests and to correlate economic, social, and environmental imperatives, so advances in one area serve others.

In the midst of our optimism, we still see causes for pessimism: business leaders and employees who believe they are powerless to make positive change; governments that hold on to ineffective policies, afraid to try anything new; activists conveniently wedded to old military models—essential for creating awareness and forcing action but useless without the second half of activism: change. These types of blindness sometimes make us frustrated and angry—but not for long. We prefer to focus on the opportunities that crisis brings. Our role is to point to the possible and to provide tools to get there.

Is our call-to-action drastic enough? We propose a radical departure from business-as-usual. However, to some people our steps may sound mild, easy, practical. Read carefully. They *are* straightforward and practical, yet they are fundamental. They lead us toward a whole new place.

To make our points, we mix business and ecological terms. To convey the concept of *gain*, for example, we use terms like *profit, net gain, synergy*, and so on. Those people who view profit merely in its monetary form or who see it as an evil product of base human activity may be put off by talk about "nature's profits." However, nature lives on profit, in the broad sense of the word. Without its extraordinary creative capacities, without the net gain that emerges with the exquisite diversity and complexity of its forms, nature would never have evolved a world that could challenge, fascinate, support, and inspire us as ours does. We also speak of nature as an entity that "chooses," "selects," "delivers," "sustains itself," and "has strategies," thus personifying "her." This is fairly conventional even in scientific discussions of topics such as genetics (for instance, *natural selection*). But this convention occasionally violates the scientist's code that forbids the use of language that even remotely suggests a purposeful or directional quality in nature—an often-exaggerated psychological fixation. However, we use such terms for the same reason scientists sometimes do—because they accurately reflect *effects* or *outcomes* of nature's processes and help us relate to and understand the phenomena. And we do see evidence that there is a subtle directionality in nature. The perfunctory line in the sand that writers on this issue are expected to draw seems more ideological, even religious, than scientific to us. But we don't mean to suggest that a typical ecosystem is willful or volitional in the way a human can be.

If our point of view differs from yours, then we have much to learn from each other. We hope that by offering a different perspective, we will stimulate your thinking, you will stimulate ours, and the gestalt will bring about new possibilities. We will all profit from the exchange.

As our economy speeds toward limits and we consume more of the earth's ecological capital than any species in the history of the planet, we are learning the principles by which we can transcend those limits, as nature does, and succeed to a more adaptive, resilient, profitable, and sustainable economy. These principles lie waiting to be discovered, in the rainforest.

Bill Shireman
Tachi Kiuchi

October 2001
San Francisco, California

In the rainforest,
where the soil is thin, minerals are scarce,
and resources are always in short supply,
life is extraordinarily rich,
more abundant and diverse than anywhere else on earth.

There is a simmering dynamism in the forest,
as organisms constantly chase the increments of sunlight, water,
    and minerals
that are always at a premium.
Yet through all their interplay with one another,
the plants and animals of the rainforest find their unique niches,
places where they fit better than any other,
where their specialized forms make them masters of skill and efficiency,
using just what they need of the scarce resources that are delivered to them,
"just in time,"
as those resources cascade through multiple stages of recycling.

Limits are a constant reality in the rainforest,
yet, paradoxically, scarcity is its own remedy.
It triggers constant feedback, learning, and adaptations
    that shape the organisms
and the relationships between organisms
so that an extraordinary richness of life is created.

On a constant flow of energy from the sun,
resources recycled continuously from the earth,
and nothing else but a complex and ever-changing design,
life flourishes in the rainforest in more concentrated abundance
than anywhere else on the planet.

Sometimes life departs from the rainforest for a time,
only to return there later,
for lessons that can be learned only at home.

We return there now.

Acknowledgments

We have many people to thank for shaping our thinking. In Bill Coors, the chairman of Adolph Coors Company, Doug Daft, Coca-Cola's chairman, and Dee Hock, the founding CEO of VISA, we found executives who had taken the theories of living systems and turned them into practice in the most extraordinary ways. Coors grew a series of product lines and companies; Daft applied the ideas to increase Coke's brand diversity, profits, and sustainability; and Hock created both the concept and the reality of a chaordic business organization, one that harmoniously blends chaos and order to serve the interests of all its members, as well as its customers and stakeholders.

William Ford championed the ideas of corporate sustainability and responsibility at one of the definitive companies of the industrial era, Ford Motor Company, to help it excel in the emerging economy. Paul Hawken also put theory to practice, first at Erehwon, then again at Smith & Hawken, and helped inspire us with his insights about *The Next Economy* in the 1980s and more recently with his focus on *Natural Capitalism*. Ray Anderson, founding head of Interface, pioneered those ideas at the world's largest carpet tile maker. Bill Green did the same in the chemical industry and proved its profit potential.

We would also like to acknowledge business and systems thinkers who have profoundly shaped our ideas: Tom Peters, Peter Drucker, Arie de Geus, Murray Gell-Mann, John Holland, Brian Arthur, Amory Lovins, Brian Tracy, Ichak Adizes, and Kevin Kelly.

Randy Hayes of Rainforest Action Network (RAN) and Michael Marx of ForestEthics provided the motivation and inspiration that got us to the tropical rainforest in the first place. Linda Coady of Weyerhaeuser and Chris Hatch of RAN introduced us to the temperate forests of British Columbia. Professor Ryoichi Yamamoto, the director of the Center for Collaborative Research at the University of Tokyo, and Peter David Pedersen, the president of E-Square Inc. in Tokyo, helped us to understand some of the principles at work in nature and in business. Joel Makower and Fritjof Capra turned systems theory into practical business ideas, each in his own way, at our Industrial Ecology conferences. Janet McElligott, a Republican environmentalist and exotic species in her own right, deepened our understanding of how to help developing economies leapfrog over the industrial stage to economic models that protect the environment and preserve local cultures. Together with Lynn Scarlett of the Reason Foundation and now Assistant Secretary of the U.S. Department of the Interior, one of the sharpest systems thinkers we know, they helped us integrate the ideas of systems thinkers from the often-antagonistic free market and deep ecology communities, a necessary synthesis whose potential is only beginning to be appreciated. And Drexel Sprecher of American Renaissance, an information age political philosopher, applied his innovative models and analytical tools to sharpen our discussions of the generic dynamics of change, information technology, and values.

For helping to shape this book, and believing in it, we thank Jeffrey Kulick, James Turner, Janet Coleman, Adam Davis, Mandy Blake, Karri Winn, Monica Bernardo, Cate Gable, Charlie Banks-Altekruse, Nikole Wilson, Steve Cassel, Aileen Ichikawa, Augustine Koh, John Van Gigch, Lou Capozzi, Joe Gleason, Jill Farwell, Christine Rosen, Bettina Murphy, Jay Harbison, Marti Kaplan, Sharon Maves, Molly Kicklighter, Alis Valencia, Sara Shireman, Eldee Stephens, Darcy Riddell, Don Yacktman, Morley Winograd, and Paul Wright. Julia Tindall planned some of our rainforest expeditions and helped make them adventurous, powerful, and fun. Peter Barnes, cofounder of Working Assets, provided a place for us to think and write at his Mesa

Refuge writers' retreat; Ward Mailliard and Brajesh Friedberg of Mount Madonna Center were equally generous with their site. Detta Penna and Richard Wilson gave the book its distinctive design. And Steven Piersanti and Jeevan Sivasubramaniam at Berrett-Koehler supported the project with enthusiasm and became our publisher of choice.

We greatly appreciate the contributions and support of all these people. Any errors or misconceptions in the work are solely our own.

Most of all, we thank our families and friends for supporting us during the five years—well, six years—it took us to complete this "one-year" project. From Bill to Aileen and Samantha, and from Tachi to Kyoko, who give us what we need more than anything, go our love and appreciation.

How Can Business Profit from Nature?

To profit in the forest, harvest the ideas.

Falling toward the limits of Earth, we learn how nature rises above them.

I n midair, we stepped out the open door of the plane, or, more accurately, were pushed out by our guides—"three, two, one, go"—and began the long, quick descent to the ground more than two miles below. We were traveling at 120 miles per hour, but oddly it didn't feel that way. We were so far above the ground at this point that we seemed almost to be lying motionless in the air, face down to the ground, the wind rushing up from below us, pillowing us in mid-air. Of course, we were free falling, through relatively calm air; the wind effect was generated by our descent through it, as gravity hurried us effortlessly toward the solid ground below.

As we looked around from our unusual vantage point, to the east we could see the mountains of Corcovado and to the west the vast expanse of the Pacific Ocean. Corcovado is an old-growth rainforest on the Osa Peninsula in Costa Rica, the one we would explore later that day. Far beyond our view, on the opposite (Caribbean) side of the country was another, younger forest that we would visit a few days later: Tortuguero.

Jumping out of the airplane marked the beginning of our expedition into the rainforests of Costa Rica, of our most recent exploration of the future of business and the principles by which it can profit, short term and long. Our adventures had previously taken us through Sarawak on the northern half of the island of Borneo in Malaysia; the Waipio and Waimanu Valleys of Hawaii and the volcanic northeast of the same island; the salt flats and wildlife sanctuaries of the Baja California peninsula; and the temperate forests of British Columbia, the Pacific Northwest, and the California Sierras.

Along the way, we also explored a different set of ecosystems, the industrial ecosystems of companies such as Hewlett-Packard, Coors Brewing, Xerox PARC, Coca-Cola, Nike, and Royal Dutch Shell. In both nature and business we began to discover the ecological principles by which living systems sustain themselves, as well as hints about how these principles can be applied to create more profitable, sustainable businesses.

What we learned became the thesis of this book: The machine economy is growing obsolete. A living economy is emerging to replace it. In this living economy, by moving beyond the industrial, machine model of business and instead emulating the dynamic principles of the rainforest, businesses can learn how to profit more than ever, not by consuming profit but by creating it.

IN THE RAINFOREST

NATURE TEACHES BUSINESS HOW TO PROFIT SUSTAINABLY

Before we set foot in the rainforest, we must cover some basic concepts that we will return to, again and again, throughout this book. We hope for your patience: These are not concepts usually found in a business book.

This is a book about ecology and economics—words with the same root and similar meanings. Both "ecology" and "economy" derive from the Greek *oikos*, which means "home." Economics studies the *management* of the home. Ecology goes beyond that, to study its underlying *logic*. For example, economics explores the interrelationships of producers and consumers in a marketplace, the dynamics through which supply meets demand and value is delivered to people. Ecology does the same but goes a step farther. It explores the interrelationships of *all* living things and all elements of their environments, the dynamic interconnections that animate life and create value, in business and nature alike. In studying ecology, we learn an advanced form of economics, more complex and dynamic than any conventional economic model.

Ecology is such a complex science that it cannot be easily understood using the simple cause-and-effect model most people use to analyze how things happen. A complex ecosystem encompasses so many causes and so many effects that isolating one from another is just about impossible. Only vast oversimplifications enable cause-and-effect analysis. Unless these oversimplified models are carefully matched to the crucial factors in the reality they describe, they are of limited use. As a result, it is often more useful to talk about the *principles* common to nature's complex systems. In a way, studying ecology is like studying business theory. Studying economics is like studying business management. You can't build sound management practices on flawed theory. Theory is fundamental; sound management depends on it. If you get the theory fundamentally wrong, you can't manage the business right. That is why, in each chapter, we focus on theory before practice—specifically, we focus on the systems principles and dynamics that create value in nature. Then, given this foundation, we can better understand how to leverage the fundamental principles of nature in ways that create profit for business.

Neither ecology nor economics studies living organisms in isolation. Both focus on the dynamics of living organisms with air, water, and other resources in a *community*. In ecology, these communities are called **ecosystems.**

What is an ecosystem? Is it a forest? A business? In this book, the term *ecosystem* doesn't mean just the natural ecosystems we usually think of; it refers to *any dynamic and interdependent community of living things.* A forest. A human family. A business. A city. All these are ecosystems, as natural in their own way as anything we find in what we usually mean by "nature."

The distinguishing characteristic of these ecosystems is their resilience. Arthur Tansley, the British ecologist who coined the term *ecosystem*, said that ecosystems *have the capacity to respond to change without altering the basic characteristics of the system.* They face the same limits that human economies do—finite physical resources and a limited flow of energy from the sun—yet develop and evolve continuously over time in a process that has carried on successfully for 3.8 billion years. Think about that: All the complex systems of nature are constantly falling toward ground zero, constantly consuming resources of limited supply, yet they continue to survive, evolve, and even advance.

How does nature slow its "fall"?

ON THE VERGE OF THE COSTA RICAN RAINFOREST

After less than a minute of our own fall toward earth, the ground was now just over a mile away, and we were approaching it a bit too rapidly if we desired to retain the capacity to explore it later. Of course, we planned to use our parachutes to slow our descent and make a soft landing. But, as we looked around us, we were reminded that in the forest, there were other ways, even better ways, to slow or stop a fall.

Stretching out for miles beneath us to the east was lush forest, in an extraordinary array of colors, mostly shades of green but every other color as well. From our bird's-eye view, the rainforest looked rich in resources. There was obviously plenty of water; a tropical rainforest receives at least 200 centimeters of rain a year. The temperature was high—25°C or higher—but it didn't vary much, so the climate was stable. Because the forest is near the equator, lack of sunlight doesn't seem to be a problem. Plants and animals must be abundant, and, as the result of the decay of dead and dying plants, the soil, we assumed, was rich. But this first impression was wrong. The Costa Rican rainforest—in fact, nearly every tropical rainforest—has thin soil virtually devoid of minerals. The forest floor is generally starved of sunlight and often of water, which is blocked and diverted by the forest canopy. And fallen vegetation seldom accumulates on the ground long enough to create humus to enrich the soil. It is immediately captured by fungi that tear it apart and deliver its nutrients straight to living things. Out of necessity, rainforests deliver resources to their populations "just in time."

How can this be? How can a region facing such immediate resource limits produce *more diverse abundance* than if the same region had richer soil, more sunlight and accessible water, and plenty of minerals? The answer is limits—and the feedback and adaptation triggered by limits. The scarcity of energy, water, and minerals means that every plant and animal species is continuously at the outer limits of its resource supplies, in danger of exhausting its reserves. In a very young, simple forest, this can be cataclysmic: Species that run out of fuel die. But species whose forms enable them to survive in the face of limits persist. Natural selection "chooses" them for another generation, and the attribute that gave them advantage tends to be passed on.

Over time, this process of natural selection leads to increasing variation. Every physiological advantage—every modification that gives an individual a reproductive edge—tends to be retained. As a consequence, species gradually adapt to define their specialties, the realms in which they compete better than in any other. These areas become their niches, the places where they are particularly adapted to excel.

If resources were abundant in the rainforest, these specialists would have no place. Faster-growing, more consumptive species would quickly outdistance them, and the forest would quickly be dominated by a monoculture of these—what ecologists call **r-strategists,** pioneer species that grow fast, produce lots of seeds, and die young. They are called "pioneers" because their growth and fertility enable them to quickly dominate an open field; they are "r-strategists" because their core strategy is mass *reproduction.*

Limits are, in fact, the platform from which innovation springs in nature. As each stage of development reaches its limits, new creativity emerges. If this innovation is adequate to the challenge presented by the limits, a more capable species or a richer ecosystem results. If limits are removed—for example, if fire is repressed—even a complex forest may be destroyed, because other limits that had been held in check finally impose themselves in force.

In the absence of seasonal fires, the trees of a simple forest may grow rapidly in size and number, closing off opportunities for young seedlings or more diverse species to take up niches. Eventually, without forces to hold it in check, the dominant species could overstep natural **boundaries** and exceed the **carrying capacity** of the forest. Because the trees would be of similar age, they would decline and die almost simultaneously, creating such an accumulation of deadwood that an inevitable fire's destruction could be total. The repression of fire, or the **overshoot** of any natural limit or boundary, places the whole ecosystem at risk of being destroyed. But if change is permitted, if co-evolution proceeds at a measured pace, the forest will grow more diverse. Its cycle of innovation, growth, improvement, and creative destruction will repeat over and over again. On this moving "platform," it will cultivate an increasing array of species and qualities of life, from the simplest to the most complex and self-aware.

So, despite its resource poverty—or perhaps because of it— the rainforest is extraordinarily abundant, with more life of greater diversity than any other type of ecosystem on the planet. Perhaps two-thirds of the earth's species reside in its rainforests.

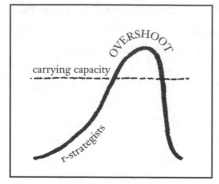

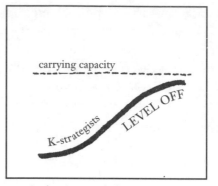

Pioneer species—"r-strategists"—
are so fast-growing and fertile that
they tend to shoot past the carrying
capacity of the environment, Then
they die off.

As the pioneers decline,
"K-strategists" move in. They have
lower fertility, but are more specialized to the local environment. Their
population is more stable around
local carrying capacity.

Pioneer species grow and reproduce so quickly that they tend to "overshoot" the carrying capacity of their environment. Their population and consumption can follow an
upside-down "U" curve. In comparison to r-strategists, K-strategists are more finely
tuned species who evolve into more efficient forms in response to environmental limits. Their population and consumption can follow an "S" curve.

CHANGE AMIDST STABILITY

All complex ecosystems possess **dynamic equilibrium,** whereby
change is constant yet conditions that support life are somehow sustained. In a simple ecosystem, one with very few organisms—such as a
lawn, a garden, or a young forest—one disruption can lead to total dev-
astation. So long as this ecosystem is loaded with growth-inducing
resources like fertilizer, it may excel for a while, almost unchanging
except in physical size. But then, if it is attacked by a fungus or a pest,
it may be quickly destroyed.

However, in a complex ecosystem with lots of variety, everything is
constantly in flux. This type of system tends to be **chaordic,** blending
characteristics of order and chaos. Every species influences every other;
every change fans out through a complex web of relationships to affect
everything else. Yet the whole remains healthy. Stresses to one part of the
system may be severe. Populations of individual species may fluctuate
greatly, or even die out. But changes in one area are compensated in oth-

ers. After a disturbance, an ecosystem will be drawn back toward a point of equilibrium, an ever-shifting target it never continuously attains.

Equilibrium is not a fixed point; it is a point of balance that changes as the conditions of the ecosystem itself change. For example, it might seem that, if people left the rainforest untouched, then 100 years from now it would remain pretty much unchanged. That's not generally true. Rainforests evolve continuously, sometimes changing in dramatic ways. We could see that in the two Costa Rican rainforests we visited, by comparing how dense their vegetation was at ground level.

Young forests, those cut in the last two or three generations, have very dense thickets of vegetation near the ground, in what ecologists call their **understories**. Tortuguero is one of these young forests. When we walked outside our cabins past the prepared trails, we faced an almost solid wall of vegetation. These fast-growing, fertile pioneer species, the r-strategists, are the first to settle in when a large space opens up in a forest. Penetrating that wall of vines and branches was almost impossible and a little intimidating, given the coral snakes and other deadly creatures there. Tortuguero reminded us of the old popular conception of the jungle—a dark and dangerous place filled with threatening creatures; enemy territory, waiting to be conquered.

Corcovado, by contrast, is an ancient primary forest, filled not so much with fast-growth pioneers, the r-strategists, but by **K-strategists.** Their survival strategy is to adapt to fit specific niches more perfectly, and consume resources more frugally, than the pioneers. This expands the *carrying capacity* (K) of the forest ecosystem; it enables more life to co-exist on fewer resources.

In these older growth forests, which represent the great majority of all intact rainforests, the understories are largely open. This was a surprise to us when we visited our first rainforest, in Sarawak on the island of Borneo. We found that, far from being a dense thicket of branches, vines and leaves, the forest floor was often open and easy to penetrate. That is because, while the ancient rainforest is brimming with life, you won't see it by looking ahead. Leaves and shoots, after all, take a major investment of scarce resources, and grasses and shrubs simply can't thrive in the shadow at the forest floor. Instead, to find life, you must look up, to the densely leafed **canopy**, which captures 90% of the sunlight, blocking it from the forest floor. Life has moved upstairs.

In the canopy of the rainforest, soil rests on the tops of tree limbs and between branches, held there by root systems, which form a kind of mesh. In the mesh sprout thousands of kinds of seeds, including more than 1,400 types of orchids, most of them epiphytic, meaning that they nest in trees and plants. The plants, leaves, and soil capture sunlight and slow the descent of rain, diverting it to local use. So tight is the mesh they form that, after the start of a rainstorm, it can take ten minutes for water to pass from the canopy to the forest floor.

It was also surprising how little direct competition was in the rainforest. We had imagined the rainforest filled with plants and animals in constant mortal combat, which may be true in a very young forest, or an open field, where species are in a free-for-all for suddenly abundant stores of resources. But in a more developed forest, species have adapted to fill an array of distinct but interdependent niches. In this respect, as species adapt, cooperation grows gradually more common than competition. Competitive battles, for the most part, are carried out not directly, species-to-species, but between species and the resources of their own narrowly-defined niches. This niche competition, while still demanding, causes a much more gradual and less destructive reallocation of resources than does direct combat to dominate a larger ecosystem. "Studies of competition among animal species usually find that they divide resources in a manner that allows each species to exist on a unique subset of the resource spectrum," say biologists Adrian Forsyth and Ken Miyata (1984).

Many scientists challenge the idea that cooperation may become more frequent than competition as species adapt. They often base their belief on a narrow view of cooperation. We view it this way: Every system comprises other systems—wholes and parts, and parts of parts. To make a coherent whole, the behavior of all the parts must be coordinated so the whole functions to their individual and collective benefit. For example, as a forest ecosystem grows more complex, it becomes divided into myriad niches, as species "get out of one another's way" and find sources of support they are most adept at tapping. This subdividing of forest tasks too is cooperation. The cooperation is not conscious, as human cooperation sometimes is; it is a consequence of specialization and interdependency. As they specialize, living things find it to their advantage to cooperate. Whether they like it or not, the parts come together, in cooperation, as wholes.

One reason parts in effect "choose" to join together as wholes is that they sometimes gain new qualities through the combination, qualities so valuable that the combination is reinforced. Through processes of **synergy,** the molecules in a cell, the cells in an organism, the organisms in a forest each come to express higher qualities when they join to form next-higher systems. In this sense they "profit" from their combination. **Complexity theory,** originating in the fields of natural ecology and biology, explores how and why whole systems behave in ways unexplainable by the sum of their parts.

In a sense, then, the organisms of the rainforest have divided their territories. Each species both defines and fills its own niche. Other species constantly jockey with it at the borders of the niche, and often conditions change in ways that destroy a niche and leave its species without a home base. But rainforest species are not solitary organisms fighting myriad others to be the last to survive in a hostile environment. They all depend on one another to collectively build an ecosystem, each defining an exclusive niche vital to and dependent on the other niches that border and overlap it.

Here is where we discovered the most valuable resources of the rainforest: not the trees or other physical resources but the *relationships,* the complex array of designs. Each of the millions of species is different from every other; each fills a particular niche more perfectly than the others in its locale. Through species relationships the forest sustains itself in the face of limits. Species' niche efficiency is a source of net gain in the forest, its source of "profit." To the extent that one species is able to fill its niche—that is, carry out its function—using fewer resources than another, it has slowed the fall of the rainforest toward its limits. As these specialists come to supplant pioneer species in the forest, more life of greater variety is able to excel in a given space.

Another way forests slow their fall is through **nesting, bordering,** and **overlap.** Ecosystems are not isolated entities with impenetrable borders. Every ecosystem is nested within, borders on, or overlaps with other systems. The mangrove plant, for example, thrives at the border between land and water. As it multiplies, it overlaps the water, eventually forming a mangrove swamp, which is nested within the local ecosystem. In these ways, ecosystems layer themselves inside, outside, and atop one another.

In fact, examine any one species and you will find that it is both a nest for, and is nested within, a sequence of interrelated systems. Bacteria are nested in organs, and organs in individuals. Families are nested in communities. Species are nested in ecosystems, ecosystems in the biosphere, the biosphere in the planet, and so on. Philosopher Ken Wilber, drawing on the work of Arthur Koestler, calls each successive whole a **holon**, a whole that is also part of a more encompassing whole. By drawing together in holonic organizations—**holarchies**—systems can be large and complex, yet efficient, resilient, and adaptable.

When ecosystems overlap without nesting within one another, they define an ecological verge on which they may engage in a kind of battle. A **verge** is a rich mixture of ecosystems that happens where two distinct forms meet with each other and begin to intermix. Often, two species seek to inhabit the same niche, but they will not be successful. According to the **competitive exclusion principle** developed by biologist Garrett Hardin, at least one of the organisms must adapt or die. Thus, while nested systems may in effect cooperate, overlapping ones often foster competition. The competition often leads to co-adaptations in which the systems become interdependent, one bordering on or even nesting within the other.

Costa Rica's species show many such combinations. Bordered on the north and south by the two great American continents and on the east and west by two great tectonic plates, the country is one of the hottest spots along the Pacific's Rim of Fire. Volcanic activity transforms it periodically from an isthmus to a peninsula to an archipelago and back again. That means it sometimes forms a barrier to, and other times provides a corridor for, the migrations of plants and animals from the north and south, first inviting new ecological and cultural combinations, then closing them off, forcing them to evolve. During times of overlap, some species excelled in their new environments. Some perished. But most evolved, taking on characteristics of both the north and the south.

Overall, the blending of the two continents, through their point of convergence, has led to increased biological diversity. Old forms found new homes within the array of microclimates now available to them. Others adapted into forms more appropriate to their new habitats. Thus Costa Rica is a cauldron of biological innovation. It makes up less

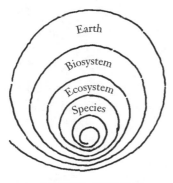

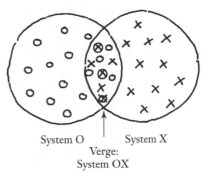

<table>
<tr><td>

NESTED SYSTEMS

Every system is both a nest for, and is
nested within, another system. Each
part-within-a-whole is called a *holon*.

</td><td>

OVERLAPPING SYSTEMS

When two systems overlap, they form
a verge. Verges are more diverse. They
can also set the stage for combinations
that create something new.

</td></tr>
</table>

than three ten-thousandths of the earth's landmass, yet it is home to
five percent of its species. Hectare for hectare, its species diversity is
hundreds of times the global average. Why is this important? Because
it shows what happens when two systems are brought together, over-
laid on the same territory—the mix of competition and cooperation, of
destruction and creation. Verges are places of conflict, but also of positive change. They bring together diverse systems and set the stage
either for their integration or for their destruction.

Our economy, too, is on a verge. We are living between two great
eras of civilization, between two ecological seasons.

IN BUSINESS

FROM BILL COORS TO DEE HOCK, THE CREATURES OF THE RAINFOREST ECONOMY AND THE FUTURE 500

In December 1995, we gathered 60 leaders of companies from both the
old economy and the new in Aspen, Colorado, to consider how we
could begin to run our companies in more sustainable ways. We agreed
on one point: The world was between economies—between an industrial economy founded on the use of machines to multiply human

muscle and a more information-based economy with the capacity to expand the human mind. Three forces were compelling this convergence: environment, technology, and values.

Environmental limits, from local air and water pollution problems to global concerns about climate change, species loss, and rainforest destruction were forcing changes in the way we do business.

New technologies, like the microchip, advanced materials, the computer, and the Internet, were beginning to make those business changes possible. By replacing fossil fuels and raw materials with knowledge, they created the seeds of an economy that offered a high standard of living, using a fraction of the resources once required.

New values were beginning to emerge, values that reflected these changes in technology and the environment. In surveys, most consumers said they no longer saw the interests of business and of the earth as intrinsically at odds. Most believed that the needs of people could be met with less effect on the earth, not more.

Yet, despite the new technologies and values, we weren't making the progress we needed to develop a rich and sustainable business culture. We seemed married to business models and methods of the last economy, not the next one. From that meeting emerged a new business network, an informal alliance of companies that came to be known as the Future 500. It included companies from the old economy and the new. Industrial and information-based; mass production r-strategists and niche-filling K-strategists. For the next five years, we met, made plans, held conferences, and developed tools that our member companies could use to begin to tap the potential of the emerging economy to profit sustainably. This book is one outgrowth of that effort, as well as a report card on some of our successes.

On the date we took our dive into the Costa Rican rainforest, October 10, 2000, some of the most innovative creatures in the business rainforest were just below us, on the ground—some of the unconventional corporate CEO's, technologists, executives, and activists who often joined us in our expeditions, the Future 500 leaders whose stories are woven together to tell the lessons in *What We Learned in the Rainforest*. They are characters in the truest sense. But what is most intriguingly similar about them may be this: They all gained business insights and inspiration from nature, and all have used what they learned to develop more successful companies.

PART ONE

The Principles That Maximize
Performance in Business

CHAPTER ONE

Feedback

LESSON ONE:
USE LIMITS TO CREATE VALUE—CLOSE THE LOOP

IN THE RAINFOREST, *nature uses feedback to "close the loop." In the face of limits, feedback triggers adaptations that lessen or make an end-run around physical constraints.*

IN BUSINESS, *companies like Coors use feedback to "close the loop," triggering innovations that lead to new products, processes, businesses, and profits.*

Skydiving is the perfect antidote for a high-stress job. It gives you total release. When you look down and realize that you are free-falling, straight for the ground, at 120 miles per hour, all your senses are fully engaged. There is little opportunity to dwell on corporate strategy, balance sheets, or day-to-day family issues.

When people skydive, all their five senses must be operating effectively. Imagine, for example, that during this particular dive over Costa Rica, we had no sense of sight or hearing—just a sense of touch.

With only a sense of touch, after we stepped from the airplane, we would feel the rush of the wind against our faces; we would sense great movement and exhilaration. It would be very exciting. The only problem is that we would not be able to see the ground, so we would have no way of knowing that we were descending rapidly toward it. We would not even know that we were falling. Thus the ground would have no impact on us at all, until we reached it. Then, it would have a significant impact.

In business, we are much like a deaf and blind skydiver. Business operates with only two senses: taste and touch. Our businesses have a

sense of taste in that we know what is going on inside the business—
what our immediate bottom line is. And our businesses have a sense of
touch in that we know the effect of what is happening directly to us
from the outside, we feel it right now, this quarter.

But think about it: Our businesses have no real sense of sight or
hearing. We do not know what is happening at a distance, until it is
directly affecting us, until we feel the impact. So we speed forward
blindly, feeling the excitement of commerce, the exhilaration of the
wind against our faces. But we do not know if we are ascending quickly into the sky or speeding toward the ground.

Ray Anderson, the chairman of Interface Carpets, says that modern
business people are often like the early inventors of airplanes, who
pushed their homemade planes off the edges of cliffs, confident that
once in the air they would fly. Many were surprised when they crashed
to the ground. Ray says that we have pushed our whole economy off a
cliff. We are rapidly consuming the earth's resources, cultivating a fast-
moving economy. We feel the wind against our faces. Gravity is pulling
us faster and faster, and we feel more excitement than ever. But now we
are approaching the ground.

Before we reach the ground, we need to wake up. We have work to
do. While we are in midair, falling, we must—as the rainforest has—
learn to slow our fall, or even to reverse it and fly.

IN THE RAINFOREST
FEEDBACK TRIGGERS THE CREATION OF VALUE

FEEDBACK IS NATURE'S WAY TO LEARN

In the rainforest, the evolution of every creature is shaped by feedback,
adaptation, and learning. Every species is sculpted in response to the
extreme limits that are a constant reality. These limits propel the creatures of the forest rapidly toward a "ground zero" at which they have
fully consumed the resources that had sustained them. However,
through feedback and adaptation, they develop a system that brings
new supplies of resources—the margin they require to avoid hitting the
ground—often just in time.

The rainforest delivers these resources through an extensive array of feedback loops that serve as the sensory system of the forest. These loops are extremely tightly bound, compared to those of temperate forests. In Pacific Northwest forests, for example, warm spring days signal plants to burst with buds, shoots, and leaves, creating an environment rich in protein. Animals conditioned by this protein pulse bring forth their young during this time; birds return to raise their newborn, insect eggs hatch, frogs awaken from hibernation. In summer, plants and animals tap the abundant food to grow in size and number. Come autumn, growth slows, trees drop their leaves, and plants produce berries, seeds, and nuts to reproduce again in the spring and to sustain life through the winter.

In the tropical rainforests we visited, by contrast, sunlight, rain, and warm temperatures are constant, and plants germinate, grow, flower, and seed year-round. Leaf fall is slow and continuous, rather than concentrated in the fall. As a result, there is no seasonal protein glut. Constant heat and moisture lead to fast decomposition. The humus that enriches the soil in temperate forests doesn't have time to accumulate in the tropics. The forest floor is a dark factory of decomposition. A leaf that falls in a North American forest may take a year to decompose; the same leaf in the rainforest will fully decay in a month. Bacteria, mushrooms, and insects are on it as soon as it reaches the ground, or before, tearing it into nutrient molecules, liberating them to be drawn up into roots or leached quickly from the soil by rain.

In Costa Rica, it seemed that at the base of every tree, along every fallen log, and in every crevice where forest litter could gather, wild mushrooms were flourishing, tearing apart the dying leaves and wood and returning their components to the soil as rapidly as possible. Here in the tropics, root systems find water and nutrients close to the soil surface, so these root systems are shallow. Roots may barely penetrate the soil, or they may even run along the top of the ground. Such shallow root systems can leave tall trees vulnerable to wind or weather that could topple them. To keep them upright in the absence of a deep root system, many tree species grow side buttresses—thin, hollow flanges that extend from the base of the tree to the ground like the legs of a Christmas tree stand. These supports sprawl outward across the forest floor, like a vacuum system that draws in resources and delivers them to the rich canopies of life above.

The processes of breakdown and buildup in living systems are called their **metabolism.** Within every living system, from a forest to a cell, raw materials are drawn in and broken down into simpler forms in a process biologists call **catabolism.** Then, inside each cell, enzymes, cellular factories, or other agents take the pieces and rearrange them in more complex forms—a process called **anabolism.** In this process, certain values are lost, traded for new ones that yield a new whole. In other words, new resources are gained as others are lost.

In the forest, resources are drawn up from the soil into the roots of trees and plants and delivered to a vast array of species. Biologists used to diagram this arrangement by relating species to one another in a manner so simple that they resemble linear **food chains,** each link reliant mostly on one or two other links. This simple kind of diagram has, of course, been used to depict the way we convert resources to industrial products. However, this approach, even when used in scientific journals, vastly understates the diversity and interrelationships of species.

If all forest forms of life were linked together in simple food chains, they would quickly run out of resources. Conversion rates are extremely low: Often 1 percent or less of the caloric content of one link is converted to calories by the next. For example, plants convert into energy no more than 2 percent of the sunlight that reaches them. Sheep that eat grass or cows that eat corn keep about 1 percent of that. People that eat the sheep or the cows keep 1 percent of that. This entire three-link food chain ends up "wasting" 99.9998 percent of the original energy of the sun.

How does nature overcome such extreme wastefulness? By drawing species together in complex **food webs.** Food webs offer major efficiency gains over simple food chains. In a web, energy "wasted" in one process isn't really lost. It just shoots off to the side, where nature tends to put it to its best local use, in whatever form it's in. Thus webs contain vastly more connections than classic descriptions of food chains. Most species eat or are eaten by ten to 1,000 other species. Resources cascade through the web as they are transformed back into their simplest forms and are drawn back through the web again as they meet and combine with other resources to take on more complex forms, in an endless nonlinear flow. The resources do not usually cycle back into the same forms, since that would require the consumption of more energy

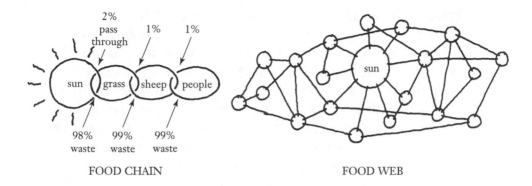

FOOD CHAIN   FOOD WEB

to transport and reform them. Instead, they are taken up in their present form, to fill a local need to which they are already suited.

MACHINES JUST DO IT— LIVING SYSTEMS ALSO IMPROVE IT

The strands in these webs aren't static like those in a spider's web. They are dynamic passageways that in effect draw all the organisms in a forest together into a single coextensive network, Tansley's **ecosystem.** Competition, which forced the adaptations in the first place, now undermines its own position and partially gives way to cooperation. Everything begins to rely on everything else for the efficient and effective operation of the whole.

As the linked strands in simple food chains branch off in all directions to form webs, feedback and adaptation accelerates. Food webs find ways to use all the resources consumed within them. With every new feedback loop, new arrangements are made, over time leading to the development of new relationships, even new species. With every adaptation, the information content of the ecosystem increases; in effect, ecosystems *learn.*

For example, in simple food chains, resources are taken in at one end, used in the middle, and discarded as waste out the other end—to the "outside," that is, to the next larger ecosystem. Food chains act more like **simple machines:** When they are receiving fuel, they keep performing the same task, repetitively. When the fuel runs out, they stop. They lack the options of a more complex system, so they are less able to adapt.

Food webs, in contrast, have lots of options. They act not as machines but as **complex adaptive systems** with the ability to sense resource supply levels and adapt to subtle shifts as they happen. In complex food webs, *all waste is food*. However, this **recycling** isn't direct. In the forest, nature doesn't waste energy turning leaves directly back into leaves. She takes them as they are. Leaves may become mulch, then break down into their chemical components, each of which is taken up in new processes. Like the organisms they previously constituted, they feed or are fed by many subsequent processes.

Nature also follows this strategy on much larger scales. Look, for example, at how nature recycles water through the **hydrological cycle,** the natural circulation of water between earth's surface and the atmosphere. Water evaporates from the oceans. From there, air moves the water to cooler realms where it condenses into clouds. Then the clouds drop the water back to earth through precipitation. Once it reaches the ground, it spreads out and joins rivers, streams, and soil. From there, it may be taken up into plants and animals, many of which are at least 95 percent water. Then, the water may be broken down into hydrogen and oxygen and reassembled with other atoms such as carbon to form carbon dioxide and other compounds.

Because water serves functions at every stage along the way, the "transportation costs" of water recycling are, in an important sense, zero. The entire contents of the world's oceans would take about one million years to pass through the water cycle, but this does not mean nature is slow—it means nature is thorough, complex, and yielding.

This fact points to a flaw in conventional wisdom about recycling. Often, environmentalists and business leaders seek to "close the loop" by recycling a given product back into the same product—a can into a can, a box into a box, a car into a car, for example. That's fine, but simple closed recycling loops can be inefficient. If a product is consumed far from where it is produced, for example, the energy costs of getting that product back to the point of production can wipe out the environmental gains of recycling. Yet when one product is recycled into a different one, especially a less valuable one, environmentalists sometimes criticize the process as "downcycling." Sometimes they are right: If a high-value application is locally available, then a low-value use of recyclables may be wasteful. But often "downcycling" is simply the most efficient way to use resources.

Consider, for example, the crude ways we have been recycling most plastics. Plastic bottles of milk or soft drinks are placed in recycling bins, transported to local service centers for sorting, transported to centralized facilities for grinding. Then they undergo three separate, energy-intensive processes to prepare them for remanufacture back into bottles. Each process imposes additional environmental costs, as the empties are shipped cross-country from one process to the next. The components of the bottle are of value only at the beginning and the end of the process. The entire chain that takes them from the home back to the factory imposes costs, both economic and environmental. It can take more energy and materials to recycle a plastic bottle back into a plastic bottle than to make a brand new one. By comparison, if plastic bottles are refilled or recycled as fabric for clothing or carpet, reprocessing steps are reduced, costs are lower, and less energy and pollution is created in the process. Plus, a handful of companies, such as C&A Floorcoverings, can recycle the end product yet again.

So, nature's strategy for recycling is to build local markets, using materials as it finds them, at or near the point where they are created. In this way, the path of resources through nature's economy grows more and more complex, less like a food chain, and more like a food web.

IN BUSINESS

TO CREATE VALUE, HARNESS FEEDBACK— CLOSE THE LOOP

BILL COORS AND THE CLOSED LOOP: BUSINESS-AS-LIVING-SYSTEM

The first step in turning an inefficient food chain into a rich food web and fostering a vibrant productive economy is to *close the loop*. In so doing, nature takes a simple *machinelike system*, one without the immediate capacity to sense costs and adapt, and awakens it gradually into a more adaptive and resilient *complex living system*.

Closing the loop is a core strategy that Bill Coors, Chairman of Adolph Coors Company, has used for many years to awaken machinelike companies and turn them into more adaptive, living companies, able to learn how to grow more efficient and innovative year by year. By feeding back the environmental costs and benefits of doing business, he has triggered a series of efficiencies and synergies that have enabled both his companies and their stakeholders to profit.

Feedback is a source of information, says Coors, and it takes two forms. Soft, gentle feedback cultivates easy adaptation. Hard, powerful feedback forces painful adaptation, or death. Coors prefers the soft, gradual path of adaptation. He has learned that by triggering early, subtle forms of feedback, he can stimulate both continuous and discontinuous change at his companies and keep them a step ahead of trends that buried most of his one-time competitors. Bill first met Bill Coors in 1985, in his office adjacent to his brewery in Golden, Colorado. We were supposed to be on opposite sides in a bitter environmental battle. I was CEO of the nation's largest recycling lobby at the time, fighting for a California "bottle bill" that would require deposits on beer and soft-drink cans and bottles. Coors was head of the nation's number-three brewery. I was preparing my organization to mount a second statewide initiative campaign for a bottle bill, an effort that Coors and his allies would have invested millions to stop.

Yet Coors turned out to be our most powerful ally, not for a *traditional* bottle bill but for a new, more effective form of the law that we designed and that California passed into law. The law has historically recycled nearly 80% of bottles and cans, according to Darryl Young, director of the California Department of conservation. California's version of the bottle bill applied a philosophy Coors had used to create profits at the brewing company and a host of spin-offs: "All pollution and all waste is lost profit."

Coors knows that in business, pollution and waste are stuff the company has paid for but can't sell. He also knows that the costs of pollution and waste extend far beyond those the company pays directly. Even before biologists described to him the ecological effects of can and bottle litter in the hills around his brewery, Coors had been on a mission to reduce waste and recycle everything the company made.

As can most industrial companies, Coors Brewing can be seen as a **value chain** of related suppliers and customers, a linear, industrial food chain. Raw materials are extracted or grown by producers, processed by a succession of suppliers, then purchased, processed, and packaged by

Coors to create and deliver its final product—beer in packages that are quickly used up and thrown out.

Being structured like a food chain can be highly profitable as long as you aren't stuck at either end of the chain, where resources are taken or wastes thrown away, where costs are externalized. Brewers and most other profitable companies enjoy their position in the middle of the chain. That is understandable: They get to pass those external costs on to the environment or society and keep many of the profits for themselves, as long as no one balks. But eventually, as those unaccounted costs rise, someone objects. While most other brewers saw in their success a sign that they could grow forever, by the late 1950s Bill Coors was convinced such growth was not sustainable.

The Achilles heel of the industrial economy, Coors says, is the linear system that is its principal profit driver. Industrial companies in essence take raw materials and fuels from nature, cycle them through the economy as products, then throw them away as garbage. Coors calls that an "open loop" system, a linear food chain that exploits nature's resources and leaves only waste at both ends.

Such open loop systems might work in the short term, but Coors believes no economy can last forever if it systematically depletes its sources of supply. In the end, Coors believes, the open loop will have to be succeeded by what he calls a "closed loop" economy, one where the full array of costs is accounted for within the system, quickly and gently. That way, companies and consumers would be rewarded for reducing them.

In a closed loop system, the costs of any action are fed back promptly to the person or company in the best position to reduce them, before they build up and impose great pain. Assigning blame isn't the point. Since resources flow in cycles, finger pointing always leads back to the accuser. Instead, each link in the system must learn to respond to soft, gentle forms of feedback, adjusting its behavior to reduce costs to the whole.

Of course, laws are sometimes needed to create incentives for this approach. The person responsible for a cost and the one best able to reduce the cost are not always the same. Because many still insist on assigning *blame* as well as *responsibility*, laws often take a punitive form. These are difficult to pass and often unnecessarily costly when implemented. Simply dropping issues of morality and focusing on practicality would do much to unify business and advocates.

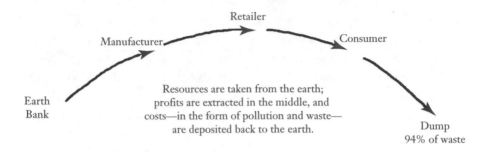

OPEN LOOP ECONOMY
Linear Value Chain

Retailer

Manufacturer   Consumer

Earth
Bank
                Resources are taken from the earth;
                profits are extracted in the middle, and
                costs—in the form of pollution and waste—
                are deposited back to the earth.
                                                        Dump
                                                   94% of waste

CLOSED LOOP ECONOMY
Single Value Web

Retailer

Manufacturer   Consumer

Earth
Bank

Here, all the outputs of business—including wastes—
are fed back to the business, so that it adapts
and learns to reduce or eliminate them.

Bill Coors wanted to create a closed loop system at Coors with zero waste as a goal, decades before it became fashionable, and he invested in programs to achieve it. Coors found the closed loop concept—through feedback—to be a powerful driver of two kinds of value that we will discuss at depth in a later chapter: efficiencies and breakthrough innovations. To create the new system, Coors decided simply to *target costs* and *enhance feedback.* As open loops were closed, the company's simple value chains would begin to take the form of innovation-inducing **value webs.** As in nature, these webs would stimulate a cascading series of effects to *increase adaptation, hone specialties, harness diversity, promote excellence amidst complexity, build cooperative alliances,* and *create emergent value through synergies.* How?

Driven by the closed loop ideal, Coors first stimulated a wave of innovations founded on efficiency. To control liquid waste from the brewery, Coors built Colorado's first biological water treatment plant in 1952. He offered to treat all sewage from the city of Golden as well, a partnership that endures almost 50 years later. The investment made little sense from the short-term profit perspective of Coors Brewing, but it was clearly the least-cost path for the community as a whole, so Coors took it. He could do that back then, he says. The company was privately held, so covering extra costs wouldn't run counter to their shareholder responsibilities. He also formed environmental task forces, set goals ("zero waste, zero emissions"), and launched a series of programs designed to eliminate waste from Coors operations.

No waste stream was spared. Spent grains became fertilizer and feed. Organic waste was sold as compost. An improved internal accounting system tracked every use of toxic materials, triggering new innovations that led to an 80 percent reduction.

Coors even found a way to eliminate the solvent-based inks that other manufacturers still use to decorate their cans. The company invented an ultraviolet process that cured inks in less than a second and cut ink consumption as much as 90 percent. That eliminated the energy-hungry ovens that previously took two minutes to dry solvent-based inks.

Among environmentalists, however, Bill Coors is best known as the father of aluminum recycling—and hence of much of the residential recycling that has blossomed over the past generation, since its costs are often largely borne by revenues from aluminum. His fascination with recycling was triggered in 1957 by a chance encounter with a local environmentalist, Dr. Beatrice Willard, who taught biology at the University of Colorado. Dr. Willard led Coors on a trail in the forest tundra surrounding Golden. She showed him the empty bottles and cans and explained the effect they were having on the tundra ecosystem.

That got Coors thinking: if he could buy back those cans and recycle them, not only would the litter problem be reduced, but he would have a continuous supply of packaging materials. Coors went back to the brewery and penciled out a program to offer consumers a penny for every Coors can they returned for recycling.

COORS INDUSTRIAL ECOLOGY
How Waste Reductions Trigger New Products, Companies, and Profits

Waste led to . . .	a new idea or process . . .	that turned into a new company, facility or partnership . . .	that reduced resource consumption, waste and costs.
Spent grains	→ Fertilizer and feed	→ ZEAGEN	→ $
Can waste	→ Aluminum can and recycling	→ Coors can manufacturing subsidiary	→ $
Aluminum can waste	→ Drawn and iron	→ Golden Aluminum	→ $
	→ Continuous casting and very high recycled content	→ Aluminum mill in Fort Lipton	→ $
		→ Aluminum mill in San Antonio	→ $
	→ Down weighted		→ $
	→ Recycling	→ BICS	→ $
Secondary package waste	→ Recycled content partnerships	→ Recycling agreements with suppliers	→ $
Solvent waste	→ Bio-T	→ New product for Golden Technologies	→ $
Wood waste	→ Compost (with spent grains)	→ New product for Coors	→ $
Plastic waste	→ Organic plastics	→ Future Graphics Packaging products	→ $
Ceramic technologies	→ Advanced materials	→ Coors Ceramics	→ $
	→ Lightweight engines better pollution controls; energy/materials, efficiency		→ $
Environmental research	→ New solar technologies	→ Golden Photon	→ $

The collection program was an overwhelming success. More cans came back than anyone had projected, millions more. The problem was that the aluminum companies wouldn't take them back, and Coors had no way to recycle most of them on its own. So, as millions of cans were stockpiled at Coors' Golden brewery, Bill Coors spent millions of dollars to launch his own development effort. He refused to buy aluminum from companies that wouldn't take it back for recycling. He end-ran the aluminum companies by developing a "continuous casting" system for can making that cut costs and could use almost 100 percent recycled aluminum. And he opened the nation's first aluminum recycling centers offering "cash for cans."

Coors even developed a concept for a national law requiring returnable beverage containers. Called the "Closed Loop System," it became the first draft of what we later used as our model when we designed California's beverage container recycling law.

But Coors found another source of profit that may be even more environmentally sustainable and financially lucrative than efficiency. That source is *breakthrough innovation*. Coors' source for these breakthroughs comes from the designs of nature. According to Coors, value doesn't come from physical resources per se, but from their design. All fossil fuels and other raw materials are made of the same fundamental components. It is the design of these resources, not simply their physical content, that gives them their value. Similarly, businesses don't create value by consuming materials but by combining them into forms that yield new qualities. Coors taps this kind of value at two of the other companies he founded: CoorsTek and Graphic Packaging. For example, CoorsTek—now the largest U.S.-owned manufacturer of advanced technical ceramics—uses smart design, not additional materials, to embed hardness, strength, insulation, and durability into its products. Graphic Packaging uses ingenious technology to cut ink use as much as 90 percent and solvent use 100 percent, at the same time producing bolder graphics.

CoorsTek and Graphic Packaging couldn't be more different from Coors Brewing. Rather than making one product for a mass market, they make 10,000 different products that fit very precise market niches in 23 of the 24 defined business sectors. In the past, they made everything from high-tech ceramics to solar cells to organic plastics. Products that found market demand were kept—*selected*, to use the genetic parallel. Those that didn't were eventually sold or dropped. Today, CoorsTek's engineered materials are used for everything from computer hard drives and mobile phones to on-board auto electronics, to fuel cells used in experimental hypercars. Graphic Packaging makes some of the most environmentally resource-efficient packaging in the consumer market. Both companies create value by following Coors' core philosophy: All waste is lost profit. Eliminate everything that doesn't deliver value, and you can maximize both economic and environmental performance.

FIRST, FORD'S MACHINES FOMENT A REVOLUTION: THEN, FEEDBACK TRIGGERS THE EVOLUTION.

Bill Coors credits Henry Ford with developing the open-loop machine model for business. At the time, it was a powerful agent for progressive change. Henry Ford, who founded Ford Motor Company in 1903, was not just a capitalist seeking to maximize return to shareholders. Uninspired routine goals like that would have bored him. He was a social activist, with a cause as elevated and progressive as any that motivates today's activists.

Ford had a mission. He knew that machines embodied human genius; they were ideas expressed in design. He saw the machine as a magnificent instrument, created by ingenious design, that distributed value widely throughout society. Because they could take the genius of one individual and deliver it to millions, they carried with them the capacity to create equal opportunity and eradicate ignorance and poverty. They would enable people, in the words of visionary designers Charles and Ray Eames, to "get the most of the best to the most for the least."

Value is created when an idea—a particular machine design: the printing press, the assembly line, the microprocessor—is formed in one's mind. That's *breakthrough innovation*. Once proven, the idea is like a bank into which a large deposit is made. All great inventions in effect put vast amounts of money in society's bank—and sometimes, of course, take money out as well.

How do you draw on the created value? First by applying the idea. Initially you may apply it in one big way. Later you create variations on your core idea—you refine it and apply it in many smaller ways. You design better printing presses; you customize the assembly line for many kinds of products; you embed computer chips in watches, daily planners, cars. This process of refining, varying, and improving an idea is *continuous improvement*. But the source of any gains is not in the materials, it's in the ideas. Obviously, once an idea is applied in a physical way, matter then embodies the idea; the materials contain the value, but they aren't its source. Matter is like paint to the painter; it is neither the source of value nor the inspiration, but only the medium to express it.

Ford's vision, his breakthrough innovation, was to use machines to make machines: Machines to make his parts, machines to run his assembly line, in a horizontal arrangement that substituted machine work for muscle. His workers too he used as machines. He even organized the workers in a machinelike institution, a top-down industrial hierarchy, with brainwork removed from the local level and centralized at the top, an approach that became the dominant model of industrial management for much of the 20th century. Through these efforts, Ford created a manufacturing system that radically reduced the costs and expanded the output of the early automobile industry.

Ford's crowning achievement is well known. The automobile assembly line, and all the innovations that enabled it, so streamlined the process of automobile manufacture that it led to the explosive growth of the product line; indeed, he triggered the industry's greatest period of growth. By using precision-made standardized parts and moving them to workers along an assembly line, Ford increased labor productivity by a factor of four or more. Because workers no longer needed to walk from car to car or file down individual parts to fit, the amount of labor required to make a car dropped from 12 hours to two and a half. Ford's economies of scale delivered a Model T to consumers for $360, compared to competitors' $850. By 1914, Ford was making nearly as many cars as his 300 competitors combined, with a fifth as many workers.

Thus Ford's breakthrough—his assembly line system—was so efficient that it drove down the cost of cars, leading to dramatic boosts in his volume, the economic equivalent of *replication*. Ford's sales success led in essence to the company's *selection* by the economy and forced his competitors to either adapt in response or leave the market.

Ford carried the genius of the machine to the structure of work itself. Instead of relying on trained craftspeople, he reorganized production so that each assembler had only a single task, one which required at most a few minutes of training. As a result, he could bring together workers from widely divergent cultures and backgrounds. The need for a common language among workers became irrelevant: They had no need to talk to one another at all.

Economically, Ford's assembly line was a breakthrough innovation.

It did not merely refine the craft of automobile making, shaving off a little waste here and there; it revolutionized the business and brought a huge gain in efficiency. But was Ford's assembly line itself efficient? Yes, but only by comparison to the craft system it replaced. It was far from the most efficient that an *assembly line* system of manufacture could be. As is any prototype, Ford's breakthrough was now ripe for its own series of improvements.

The relationship of breakthrough innovation and continuous improvement is an important distinction to remember. Breakthrough innovations often bring radical gains in effectiveness, much greater than incremental improvements in efficiency of an older process. But in their early forms, these innovations are like prototypes, crude and imperfect, requiring continuous improvement.

Ford's machines—and the machine style of management he championed—were powerful and progressive tools in their time. However, machinelike forms of management are neither unnatural nor undesirable in an absolute sense. They are a necessary (and perhaps universal) stage of industrial development. They play their roles as agents for mass production, but they are only one form of management. If not blended with others, they can be expensive.

One of the most significant costs of the assembly line was a human cost. By removing brainwork from the factory floor and centralizing it at the top of the machinelike structure of the business, Ford ultimately undermined the resilience of his design. His system lacked a quality essential to long-term sustainability: the ability to foster dynamic, continuous change and improvement. As a result, Ford was slow—very slow—to develop a manufacturing system with the capacity for learning and continuous improvement.

Ford's competitors corrected the imbalance. These competitors pioneered changes that took Ford's breakthrough and institutionalized within it a system of continuous improvement. Later, the leading proponent of the changed system, W. Edwards Deming, and his colleagues, such as Joseph Juran and Kaoru Ishikawa, became the champions of **quality management** and **learning organizations**, companies with the capacity to learn and improve by doing. Formal systems of feedback kept workers aware of how well objectives were being met. Formal and informal relationships among employees allowed them to identify and solve problems on their own. While most objectives were necessarily centrally set to meet the needs defined by the market and stakeholders, the methods used to meet the objectives were often selected by the workers who performed the tasks.

To Deming, this system of feedback was vital to improving quality and productivity. He believed that the workplace is a learning community, a campus, where people are motivated by the ability to apply their own intelligence and skill. Power in a Deming organization is decentralized; people work together in teams and networks. Hierarchies are relatively flat, and leadership is held by those able to facilitate functional relationships between formal and informal teams of specialists.

The most valuable forms of capital in the learning organization are knowledge, gained through *feedback and learning*, and changes in design—that is, *adaptation*. Workers are a vital, engaged part of the production process; they learn what's working, and what's not, and they apply their knowledge to continuously refine and improve products and processes. Achievement is motivated mostly by the recognition and appreciation one receives from colleagues and team members. Status is accorded by one's specialty and how it advances the performance of the team as a whole.

Toyota mastered Deming's methods and refined them using the ideas of Shigeo Shingo and Taichi Ohno, who developed the company's famed production systems in the 1950s and 1960s. Ohno thought, *why hire outside experts to reengineer production processes, as Henry Ford did, when you have workers who study and know the system through experience, every day?* Instead of just hiring outside experts, Toyota used their own home grown ones. By 1982, workers were making nearly two million suggestions a year, more than two every month per employee, and 95 percent were implemented.

Thus was developed *kaizen* (ky-zen), Japan's learning organization system that creates value through continuous improvement by everyone from executives to managers to workers. Kaizen identifies costs and inefficiencies before products even leave the factory and feeds that information back at the design stage, closing the loop. Machines multiply the worker's muscle; kaizen rediscovers the value of the worker's mind. According to management consultant Masaaki Imai, "Kaizen strategy is the single most important concept in Japanese management—the key to Japanese competitive success."

Today, Ford Motor Company is also applying the lessons of kaizen. Chairman and CEO William Clay Ford, Jr.'s strategy is to make Ford a "consumer-focused company," super-responsive to both broad and subtle consumer desires, by feeding marketplace information back to the design level. As devoted a social activist as his great-grandfather, Bill Ford's personal mission is for people to feel that the world is a better place because Ford is in it. When the company recalled 20 million Firestone tires because of safety problems in 2000 and 2001, Ford believed the company's best strategy was total openness. As former CEO Jacques Nasser played the leading public role, Ford worked with the board of directors and shareholders to carry out the company's response in full public view.

Bill Ford remains a step ahead of his colleagues, even at his own company. The result: "Ford is two companies," says Corporate Governance director Deborah Zemke, one of Bill Ford's designated internal activists. The first company is today's Ford, a main line automaker that makes low-mileage SUVs. The second Ford is the company it aspires to be, the one that makes the best-selling high-mileage car, the Focus, plus battery electric cars, closed community vehicles, and electric bikes. It is revamping its historic River Rogue factory complex using design concepts of ecological architect William McDonough. It rates its own performance on sustainability and publishes the results annually.

Bill Ford thinks electric vehicles are a better option, but their next generation won't just be traditional cars with electric engines. Ford thinks the new electrics may be strikingly different, redesigned from the ground up. Under the "TH!NK" brand name, Ford makes three types of electric vehicles: an electric bicycle, a neighborhood car, and a city car. The TH!NK traveler is an electric bicycle that folds so that riders can carry it on transit systems and into the office.

The brand name Th!nk gives a clue about Ford's approach to the future. The key to Bill Ford's success is the company's openness to feedback and its ability to learn and adapt in response to it. To stay ahead of the market, Ford must be a living company. And the core resource that can make that a success is *information*.

CHAPTER TWO

Information

**LESSON TWO:
REPLACE PHYSICAL RESOURCES WITH INFORMATION
—AND LEARN TO DO MORE WITH LESS**

Physical resources decline with use: The more you use, the less you have. But information resources are regenerative: The more you use, the more you have. That is why, in the rainforest and in business, information beats scarcity. As limits are approached, living systems adapt. Information becomes embedded in their structures, rendering them more efficient and effective. That is the advantage information has over fossil fuels: The more we use it, the less likely we are to run out.

The two of us—Tachi first, then Bill—exited through the open door of the airplane, and began our fall to the ground. As we did, our feedback systems—our senses of sight, sound, smell, touch, and even taste—were all operating at peak performance. It occurred to us that free falling from over two miles above the ground must not be, in evolutionary terms, a typical human experience.

At first, the ground seemed distant, and our approach to it slow. But after a minute or so, the ground seemed to begin rushing toward us, and we realized it was time to do something about it.

We didn't have too many options, apart from our parachutes. We were falling a total of almost 15,000 feet, at a speed of perhaps 150 feet per second. But what if other options were available to us? For example, what if, with a fair amount of ingenuity, and a lot of flailing, we could have slowed ourselves down gradually?

For example, beginning at 15,000 feet, falling at 150 feet per second, we would have 100 seconds before we smashed into the ground. If every second we could slow that speed slightly, by just one percent, then after the first second, we would have fallen to 14,850 feet. But we would have slowed our rate to 148.5 feet per second—so we would still have 100 seconds left before we hit. Another second later, we would have fallen to 14,701.5 feet and slowed to 147 feet per second, so would still have 100 seconds left. One hundred seconds later, still 100 seconds left. Ten years later—100 seconds left. If we could just put our quality management skills to work and achieve continuous improvement—that is, a slightly slower rate of fall—indefinitely, we would never hit the ground.

However, given our limited technological choices and the difficulties of conceiving of and implementing continuous changes while falling through the air at immense speed, about all we could do was to open our parachutes, slow our decline suddenly to around 10 feet per second, and prepare for a safe landing.

Interestingly, to slow our rate of speed from 150 feet per second to 10 feet per second in little more than an instant, we needed nothing more than the technology we had strapped to our backs when we started our descent. The key was not to get more stuff than we already had but to better use the stuff we already had. That meant unwinding the parachutes from their solid, bound-up form and allowing them to open into a more functional shape and structure, one that would catch the wind and harness it on our behalf. In this case—in every case—making technology serve us better meant changing its shape, so that it conveys meaning in a language that nature can hear and use—in ways that can bring us softly toward earth.

IN THE RAINFOREST

INFORMATION BEATS SCARCITY— IT'S HOW NATURE GETS MORE WITH LESS

In skydiving and every other human or natural endeavor, you can't do any one thing forever. There's no such thing as a perpetual motion machine—the laws of thermodynamics don't allow it. In Costa Rica, so dynamic and vibrant is the rainforest, despite the thinness of its soil, that it seems to be in perpetual motion.

In a way, perhaps it is. The continuing dynamism is a function of its ever-approaching limits, which are in turn the catalyst that drives the creation of new options, new tools, through diversity. In the rainforest, nature is constantly creating new kinds of parachutes—new physical forms that can be used to slow the approach of limits and create new possibilities for life in specific settings. For example, you can't walk far in the Costa Rican rainforest without encountering a fern. Not just one fern but dozens of varieties of ferns, each distinctly different. From a few original species that inhabited the area centuries ago, more than 800 species have now been counted.

Why so many ferns? Because the ecosystem is a demanding customer, with very particular tastes. Through the constraints and opportunities defined by its conditions, each region "chooses" the qualities it looks for and "rejects" the ones it doesn't. The conditions or choices vary from location to location. To primp itself for selection, each fern shapes, prunes, and adapts itself to better fulfill the precise conditions of each niche.

Of course, neither the ecosystem nor the fern actually *choose* anything in a conscious, volitional manner. Nor do they prune or primp themselves in the ways we might. All the apparent handiwork is a consequence of what Charles Darwin called **variation by descent,** a process of change caused by **natural selection.**

Darwin's view, based on his exploration of the rainforests of the Galapagos, was that variations within a species are caused both by spontaneous **mutations** and the genetic **recombinations** caused by sexual reproduction. These are analogous to creativity and innovation in the human economy. When these variations increase the chances that the organism will produce fertile offspring, they will tend to be passed along genetically and be reinforced in future generations.

Darwin's variations are shaped by local conditions. A region with high rainfall may cultivate one type of change; a region with particular insect populations may stimulate another. Thus a single species may adapt differently from place to place, in ways that mirror local conditions. Biologists call this **differentiation.** In Costa Rica, differentiation has resulted in the 800 different ferns in 800 separate niches spread throughout the rainforests.

The process of differentiation isn't linear. Variations tend to diverge in all directions, spreading out like the branches of a tree as they extend from the trunk to the outermost extension. Hence Darwin describes **branches of descent** from a common ancestor. When change on gradual change leads to offspring that can no longer mate with those from parallel branches, then a new **species** has emerged. The four primates we met in the rainforest, for example—spider monkeys, howler monkeys, sloths, and human beings—all share a common ancestor that lived 5-10 million years ago.

Since variation is reflected by a change in the **genetic code,** the information that defines the structure of the individual, every species—and every individual—embodies a specific **information set.** Quite literally, every creature in the rainforest represents a unique information set, a vast collection of points of differentiation, from which emerge the specific genetic characteristics of the individual. This extends to the heart of matter itself, where chemical structure defines unique information sets. For example, every living creature, and every physical resource, is made up of atoms. There are 112 types of atoms in the periodic table. Think of these atoms as constituting a natural language. Each of the 112 "words" in the atomic language conveys a different "meaning," a different information set from which emerges a unique set of qualities. It is as if nature were saying: *"If I combine two atoms of hydrogen with one of oxygen, then behave like water."*

Every distinct pattern of atoms, or molecules, or cells, creates a new and distinct type of **resource.** A resource is a material building block with a set of functional capacities—in other words, it does things. Different kinds of resources do different kinds of things. When atomic elements like hydrogen, carbon, nitrogen, and oxygen join in specific combinations, they become **natural resources**: anything from air to water to fossil fuels and more. Resources that are replenished quickly by nature, such as energy from sun and wind or trees from forests, are called **renewables;** those that take well over a human lifetime to regenerate—for example, coal, iron, or petroleum—are called **nonrenewables.** Materials no longer needed are called **waste.** Waste is a temporary phenomenon: Every element of waste is a resource-in-waiting, ultimately taken into the system to serve a different role.

As these building blocks come together in more elaborate combinations, their behavior becomes more complex. It is as if nature were saying, for example, *"Combine these sets of information on this molecule of DNA, in this environment at this time and they will behave like Tachi Kiuchi."*

None of this is to say that human beings lack the capacity for spontaneous change or for conscious choice. The point is that *information forms the basis of every capability expressed in nature. Every atom, every molecule, every cell, plant, animal, and human being, is ultimately made of and dependent on information.*

Moreover, if Darwin's theories of natural selection are more or less correct, then the information sets that are passed along tend to be either those that enhance the capacity of an individual to survive and reproduce or those that don't diminish it in any significant way. That is, *almost every new information set is a new parachute—a new resource or technology that can extend, just a little bit longer, the fall of the skydiver toward earth, the fall of life toward a limit.*

In this sense, the rainforest—and nature as a whole—is not a perpetual motion machine, but for all intents and purposes, it is a *perpetual notion* machine. It generates a continuous stream of new ideas, new information sets, each creating a new resource, a new set of qualities, stretching the duration of its fall just a little bit more, in a process that so far has lasted 3.8 billion years. Absent a sizable misstep on our part, it may last for billions more.

THE CURIOUS QUALITY OF INFORMATION: THE MORE YOU USE, THE MORE YOU HAVE

As a resource, information has a curious quality. If I give you a physical resource, then you have it, and I don't. But if I give you information, then you have it, and so do I. Moreover, if you take my information and combine it with your own, you create new knowledge. Then, if you give that back to me, I can combine it with mine and create yet more.

In fact, new growth theory, built on work done in the 1950s by Nobel laureate Robert Solow and more recently championed by Stanford University's Paul Romer, points out that because of this iterative process, information—particularly about technology—is crucial to the process of economic improvement. A classic example is India's automobile industry. Tariff walls long protected it, on the theory that high prices would be plowed back into investment, fueling more growth. Instead, high profits discouraged Indian automakers from modernizing. In the 1960s they made bad copies of British cars, and decades later nothing had changed. The absence of feedback from the market increased profits in the short run but, because it failed to encourage the use of information, it stymied progress and led to decline.

Information can be expensive to create, but it is cheap to reproduce and distribute. Copying it is just a mouse click away. Incremental costs are often close to zero. Numerous companies assemble data into valuable databases and sell them repeatedly. And companies like Adobe develop Photoshop image-editing software once and then sell it over and over again.

The power of information is reinforced, for better or worse, by information networks. These networks grow in value as more people join them, just as graduates of large business schools have more business contacts than do graduates of smaller ones. A fax machine is worth very little if you have the only one. It is worth more if all your colleagues have one. It is worth a lot if millions of people have one.

Metcalfe's Law says the value of a computer network grows exponentially with its size. So a network twice as large will have perhaps six times as many connections and be much more valuable. Thus the whole adds to the value of each of its parts.

For example, a network of two means each member can communicate with the other. Doubling the network to four triples the number of people each can communicate with. Doubling it again means each can communicate with seven others, plus many different combinations of others.

That multiplies the value of the network, with no change in the technology that enables it. So, if a new technology comes around that is vastly superior, people still won't switch, because the value they receive is based on the size of the network, not the quality of the technology.

Does it make sense to place this network under the ownership of those who happen to have popularized the first generation of a technology? Doing so means that they get a disproportionate share of the value of the network, without contributing to that value through better technology. In fact, their incentive is to block the entry of better technologies, to keep control of the network.

Metcalfe's Law
Networks increase value, but they can discourage innovation

For a company that wants to gain a monopoly in its market, Metcalfe's Law is a powerful tool. For example, a word processor is more valuable if others can read the files you create. Microsoft has leveraged this to great profit. First, it rode the IBM PC monopoly to dominance in the operating system market. Then, it used that advantage to turn Microsoft Word into the leading word processor. Now, it uses proprietary file formats to lock competitors out of the word processor market. It is difficult to read a Word file in Word Perfect or read an Excel spreadsheet file in Lotus 1-2-3. These proprietary file formats add no value to the files users create. In a competitive market, developers of word processing software would ensure that their products would be able to read and edit files created on any other word processor. The only reason to keep them proprietary is to exclude competitors, who must continuously "reverse engineer" their programs to interoperate with Microsoft—until Microsoft changes its formats again. In this way, a company can hijack "network effects," privatize the commons, and pervert these potentially beneficial effects into a one monopoly after another.

Microsoft maintains that the world needs standard products. But what it actually needs is standard interfaces, communication protocols, and file formats. Not private property, but a commons under the self-regulating, noncoercive control of users.

This highlights a key distinction between physical and intellectual infrastructure. Common ownership of physical property often breaks down, because each user has an incentive to exploit the resource. If cars were free to taxpayers, then I might as well choose the most expensive car, since other taxpayers will pick up most of the cost. But if everyone does this, it bankrupts the system.

But intellectual property isn't limited in this manner. Information can be endlessly reproduced. Network effects are virtually free to create. Locking them up in private hands encourages the owner to restrict access to them, simply to boost profits.

In technology, when a first mover's product becomes a *de facto* standard through network effects and momentum, it co-opts what should be a public protocol to force people to either give up the benefit of the public network or to give up the choices of product. All the benefits of the standard can be extracted as monopoly profits or market power that can be used to exclude competitors and suppress innovation. The tens of billions of dollars taken from the

> hands of individual owners might have been used to accelerate the rate at which the commons develops and innovation occurs.
>
> There is an answer to this dilemma: standardized track, not standardized trains. In the 1800s, railroads attempted to persuade the world that only their trains would run on their tracks, when anyone who knew the gauge width of the tracks could build trains to run on them.

Information resources are fundamental to physical ones. Structure defines matter; without structure, matter would cease to be. That is why, in business and nature, complex living systems can create more value than simple machines. Machines run on fuel—energy and materials, which degrade with use: The more you use, the less you have. But systems run on information, which is generative: The more you use, the more you can have. As we move beyond the machine economy, we begin to tap this successor to the fossil fuel economy, information, a source of economic well-being vastly more abundant than oil, and growing in supply.

That is not to diminish the unique and critical importance of physical resources. Without them, we can't clothe, house, or feed ourselves. But at the genetic and subatomic level physical resources are themselves made up of information, in the form of structure and design. The more information-rich a physical resource is, the more service it can provide in clothing, housing, or feeding people.

The Achilles heel of physical resources is that as you use them, they decline in value. They are limited by the laws of thermodynamics. These include the laws of conservation and of entropy: Matter cannot be created or destroyed, yet every time you use a physical resource, it loses some of its capacity to do work—its structure or information content. It never loses all its structure; matter can never fully come to rest. But all physical resources continuously run down with use. They undergo entropy. In this sense, they *lose* value as they are used.

Pure information, however, follows a different set of laws—what we call the laws of system dynamics. Information is generative; it can be created as well as destroyed. It is never complete; there is always more to learn. And while matter runs down, information builds up; every conversion of information can lead to more information, every variation can lead to another variation. In these ways, information resources are synergetic. They have the capacity to *create* value.

THERMODYNAMICS VERSUS SYSTEM DYNAMICS

Matter degrades with use, losing its special capacities. Burning oil, for example, turns complex hydrocarbons into simple hydrogen and carbon. Information does the opposite. It improves with use, growing more complex and elaborate. Practice, for example, gradually improves one's skill, as knowledge is refined. Yet neither matter nor information reaches absolutes. No matter how much matter you spend, you never spend it all; you never reach a temperature of absolute zero, where there is no movement of energy. Similarly, no matter how much information you draw in, you never get it all. These countervailing qualities—one resource declining as the other advances, one approaching zero and the other approaching infinity—give insights into the interplay between matter and information that helps keep nature running.

THERMODYNAMICS VERSUS SYSTEM DYNAMICS	
Matter and Energy— *the "Hard" Resources— Are Limited by the Laws of Thermodynamics*	**Information and Knowledge—** *the "Soft" Resources— Are Limited by the Laws of System Dynamics*
Conservation Energy and matter can be neither created nor destroyed.	*Generation* Information can be created, replicated, or destroyed.
Entropy Matter runs down. Order tends to disorder.	*Synergy* Information builds up. Disorder tends to order.
Dynamism Matter can never fully come to rest. It can never fully dissipate its energy.	*Dynamism* Information can never be complete. There is always more to gather.

In the industrial economy, we tend to take resources that are highly complex in form—those with elaborate information content, like hydrocarbons—and we spend them. For example, we explore the planet in a global hunting-and-gathering expedition for everything from petroleum to bauxite to mahogany. Then we extract these ready-made resources from their natural settings, where they may provide useful ecological functions, and apply them in the human economy. In the process, we spend them. When we burn fossil fuels, we dissipate their structure, spending their information content, depleting them of their capacity to provide service to us. *They* don't go away, physically, but the only thing about them that "matters"—their knowledge content—does.

Gradually, however, by applying the scientific and technical knowledge we have gained from our industrial culture, we have begun to shift to a different set of resources. Rather than taking complex resources out of their places in nature, and using them up, we are just beginning to take simpler resources, substrates for our designs, and *adding value* to them. We are building them up structurally, into forms that offer us the services we want.

Examples of this process range from the simple to the complex. We take a strip of metal and bend it to make a paper clip, and it suddenly gains the capacity to fasten paper. We take ink and press it to paper to form words, and we convey information. We take a manufactured base made of pure silica and inscribe on it a design, and it gains the qualities of a solar cell, or a semiconductor, or an integrated circuit. Or we draw together 10,000 individually designed parts, metal and plastic and rubber and glass, and form them into an automobile, and through their combination we gain powers that transport us.

---

yCsPl fsgA lrt. eiir tDd oieaeBn

All Profit is Created By Design.

Letters mean nothing unless arranged in the right order. Bring together material resources in the right structural combinations, and something valuable can spring forth. The value isn't in the matter; it's in the design.

In each case, the source of capacity is somehow latent within the laws of physics or chemistry or biology that are revealed to us as we experiment and apply them. But, in a sense, we do not really know how to make a paperclip or a microchip or a car. We simply learn that certain capacities emerge when we get the design right. We put together the universe as if it were a puzzle, from its unassembled self, piece by piece. Each whole becomes a part in something new to come, a successive emergent whole.

IN BUSINESS

INFORMATION IS THE ULTIMATE RESOURCE, THE NEW FOSSIL FUEL—THE MORE YOU USE, THE MORE YOU HAVE

In 2001, California's economy was suddenly set back by a major shortage of energy, mostly electricity, that brought rolling blackouts, factory shutdowns, and unscheduled holidays for thousands of students and employees throughout the state.

To solve the crisis, U.S. Vice President Richard Cheney proposed a "more with more" strategy: Extract more fossil fuels, build more power plants, consume more petroleum to create more growth. Like a poor man who says, "the solution to my poverty is to spend more money," he proposed that the nation use more of what it was running short of.

Cheney belittled the notion that a "more with less" strategy—founded on innovation and efficiency—held any significant promise. Yet in so doing, he overlooked the entire information sector of the U.S. economy, which is founded on doing just that. Efficiency and innovation—not fossil fuels and raw materials—are what make information economies vibrant and healthy.

But a Vice President may be excused for overlooking the knowledge economy. There is another group of people who cannot be so easily excused. These are the CEOs and executives of information-based companies, who should worry greatly about demands for fossil fuels subsidized by taxpayers and the environment. Subsidized energy is a direct threat to every information-based company—from its biggest competitor: the fossil fuel industry.

We learned this from the previous energy crises, in the 1970s. The 1974 energy crisis slowed growth even at information-based companies for a time. But within a few years, the electronic and computer sector was growing more explosively than ever before in history. High energy prices helped boost demand for technologies that enabled us to do more with less.

They also taught a valuable lesson. Those technologies enable us to do more with less. When energy is in short supply, there are two ways we can respond: by consuming more energy, resources, and time, or by using our energy, resources, and time in smarter ways.

The first way means more pollution, more waste, and less opportunity. The second means more innovation, more creativity, and more opportunity.

The conventional wisdom in the 1970s was that we take the first strategy: Consume more energy, spend down our fossil fuel savings account. But that strategy largely failed. We found a faster, better, cheaper alternative: We harnessed the information sector. In thousands and thousands of ways, we used computers, electronics, microprocessors, advanced materials, smart products, learning organizations, and living companies to create value that we used to get by extracting and burning fossil fuels.

The result was extraordinary. From 1973 to 1990, we learned how to create more real economic value from every unit of energy we consumed. In comparison to 1970, by 1990 almost a third of our energy and material services were "supplied," in effect, through innovation and efficiency. Instead of more megawatts and materials, we used more *negawatts* and *immaterials*, and these became our biggest new source of supply. To deliver them, we tapped the information sector and created more jobs, more profits, and more value—even as our ideas and technologies were reducing the need for fossil fuels.

By 1990, because of the efficiencies we created, the world had so much excess fossil fuel that prices were near historical lows. It was innovation and efficiency, not increased supply or demand, that created cheap, abundant energy.

But by 2001, many people had forgotten that lesson. Some Silicon Valley executives demanded that the state use tax dollars to increase power supplies. They gave lip service to innovation and efficiency, but few saw much potential in that course. They had huge, energy-intensive chip-making plants to run, and they needed power. They forgot that the world's biggest "oil fields," the world's most powerful electricity-generating stations, were in effect located right in their backyards.

Think about it this way. Say you use 10 gallons of gasoline this year, which you draw from a 100-gallon tank—a ten-year supply. Now say you improve your efficiency 10 percent per year. How many years' supply will you have next year? You'll be down to 90 gallons—but you'll need only 9 gallons a year, so you'll still have a ten-year supply. In five years, you'll be down to around 60 gallons, but you'll need only six per year, so you'll still have a ten-year supply. In ten years, fifty years, 100 years, you'll still have a ten-year supply. So long as you improve your efficiency at a rate equal to or greater than your rate of depletion, you will never run out.

Can that be possible? Consider the nature of innovation and efficiency, which occur when we replace physical raw materials with better designs, and do more with less. Innovation is the *doing more* part; efficiency is the *with less* part. We don't just take physical resources *out*— we must put a better design *in*. We replace matter with information, and create value not by consumption but by design. For example, when Intel builds a better microchip, it doesn't add more silica. It adds more information, via design. It designs smaller and smaller transistors. This change allows its engineers to etch more and more transistors onto the same size microchip. The result is a microchip that does more with less. The energy consumed by each generation of Intel chip is shrinking more quickly than computer power is increasing.

Is there a limit to gains in efficiency? Each technical process has its own limit. Of course, the efficiency with which fuel can be converted to power cannot exceed 100 percent. However, scientists often end-run these limits by designing whole new technical processes, thus redefining the limits. At Intel, for example, cofounder Gordon Moore in 1993 predicted that, Moore's Law notwithstanding, the smallest possible transistor might be 0.25 microns. Less than five years later, his own company blew past that limit. By switching to new technical processes no one had foreseen, the company used information to design transistors that may soon be one-fifth the size of the once-supposed absolute limit.

How much further can innovation and efficiency be pressed to go? Are we close to the wall? That depends on whether information itself is limited. If it is—and we have learned almost all there is to know— then perhaps we are approaching the limit. But that seems unlikely. Nature has replaced consumption by design for billions of years. We have just begun to do so.

We are doing it in two ways. By evolution—gradually improving the efficiency of our existing technical processes, products and services, branching out into greater varieties and qualities. And by revolution—replacing today's processes with whole new ways for delivering value to people.

But while evolution and revolution make the industrial and information sectors fierce competitors—whether they realize it or not—in another way they make these sectors totally dependent on each other and make them cooperate for mutual gain. As the following examples from Shell, Dow, Dupont, Xerox, and Apple show, the injection of information into traditional industrial processes boosts productivity in both the old and the new economies and in the 1990s yielded a productivity revolution that raised every sector. Just as three centuries ago industrialization increased the productive capacity of agriculture, information technologies will ultimately be a boon to industry.

ANITA BURKE, SHELL OIL, AND THE NEW FOSSIL FUEL

No one would suggest that Royal Dutch Shell, one of the world's largest oil companies, is eagerly leading the world toward a post-petroleum future. Yet Shell has not grown to be one of the industrial age's longest-lived companies by being averse to change. As deeply committed as it is to the industrial economy, Shell is learning how to profit from a whole new source: the new fossil fuel, information.

Anita Burke is one example of Shell's valuable nonpetroleum assets. She uses profit to help drive improvements in the company's environmental performance, but she has learned that isn't always enough. Most companies are averse to change—even profitable change. To make progress happen, both profit and passion are often required.

Anita combines technical prowess with passion. We first met Anita on a Global Futures river-rafting trip for business and environmental leaders in 1997. After we hauled in our raft, we caught a ride back through the Sierras in Anita's car. That is when the real thrill began. It wasn't just *what* Anita told us; it was *how*. When she expresses herself, she often gestures wildly to make her points and looks you straight in the eye. This is generally a good thing, but then she was driving hastily down the road, making precision turns and lane changes seemingly timed to give *uumph* to her assertions, while rushing to get somewhere, trying to make up for lost time. Exactly what deadline we were trying to make was unclear.

Anita lives with a sense of constant urgency. She is on a mission. Based on her work as an industrial ecologist at Royal Dutch Shell,

Anita thinks that, just as the rainforest can create its own resources and operate sustainably, business too can be a perpetual notion machine. But the old machine model of business won't work. Business has to take on the adaptive capacities of life. She first learned how as head of environmental affairs for a jointly held Shell-Texaco refinery in Bakersfield, California. The company was getting feedback in the form of higher environmental costs that should have told it times had changed, that new priorities were in order. But as does any machine, it was ignoring the feedback. It was accepting the costs, not adapting in ways that reduced them. The result was more pollution, waste, and liability than was necessary.

"I was very young, 24 or 25, and I had in a burr in my saddle. I wanted to change the world," she says. "This marketing guy wouldn't let me spend any money on preventive maintenance at our retail service stations so that the gasoline wouldn't spill into the ground anymore and cost us a couple million bucks per station to clean up."

Despite the bottom-line cost, the message still wasn't clear. So Anita found a more graphic way to teach. "I had a $5 bill in my pocket. I took it out, and I lit it on fire, right in front of him.

"He was appalled. Not only that, it's a federal offense. He said, 'What are you doing?' I told him, 'I just want to hang around somebody who's making so much money they can just throw away refined product right into the ground. Never sell it to a customer and get your return on investment, and then spend another couple million cleaning it up. You've got so much money, you might as well be burning it.'"

Today, instead of a $5 bill, Burke channels information into the company through the use of Return on Investment analysis. At the award-winning Bakersfield Refining Company (BRC), for example, her team saved millions of dollars by redirecting waste into new products and profits. They got the go-ahead by using metrics that showed the savings they would generate.

Rather than a single refinery, BRC is actually three formerly independent refineries that Texaco and Shell bought and tied together to operate as a single refinery with a processing capability of 67,000 barrels of crude oil per day. Once combined, the diversity and history of the three refineries provided Burke and her group with a kind of puzzle: How can the three facilities gain from the synergies of their combination?

To find the answer, Burke has had to learn effective methods of persuasion. Burke uses two sources of information to teach the company how to stretch its resources: money and experience. Money is a powerful teacher. It conveys information. It tells people what we value—sometimes accurately, other times not. If we reward an activity with money, we are saying, "this is valuable." If we don't, we are saying, "this is not valuable." At BRC, money got Anita's programs off the ground. Then, experience deepened commitment to them. "Before there was this concept of sustainability being the right thing to do, it was about money. It was the only tool we had." Burke used that tool to develop Return on Investment (ROI) data showing that much of what BRC was shipping off as hazardous waste could be turned into another product, at a profit. The ROI data turned out to be more than a motivator. Measurement systems like that were *teaching tools*, in Anita's view.

"Example: We had sludges and waste streams that were costing us millions to load into barrels and haul off for safekeeping. Then we looked at the facility chart a little more closely, and we said, 'hey, we've got a coker over there that's got an appetite for that kind of stuff.'" It turned out that by using the coker, BRC could divert its waste without causing additional emissions. "So we stopped loading it into barrels, and we bought some processing equipment and fed it into the coker, and now we're selling that as fuel for other facilities."

Injecting knowledge into the operation as a substitute for fuel and a remedy for waste. Smarter engineering. The savings: $1.9 million a year. Later, when the U.S. Environmental Protection Agency (EPA) was about to slap new equipment mandates on the plant under the 1990 Clean Air Act Amendments, Burke calculated it would be cheaper to invest in equipment to turn the emissions into a new product. That eliminated the control mandate and created a new profit center. Again, smarter design meant lower consumption, less red tape, and higher profits.

After more successful projects, Burke's whole group started coming up with more ideas. The more information they used, the more they had. They shared their technologies with other plants and generated yet more ideas in return—for example, the idea to recycle tank bottom residue back into crude production. "We found a way to mix up the tank residuals, get the solvent suspended, and turn the rest back into crude and then into gasoline, instead of just hauling it all away as waste."

Eventually, Burke's initiatives made Shell enough money to convince the company to take her out of Bakersfield and make her a global industrial ecologist, helping to tap new supplies of information at facilities all around the world. Seeking to transform an oil company into a more sustainable company is a challenge many other environmentalists would be afraid to take on. But to Anita, "it's my dream job."

Anita Burke created value at Shell by injecting small increments of information into a petroleum-based business. What if a similar company, instead of simply augmenting its energy and materials with a little information, were to make a full commitment to information as its primary resource?

Dow and Dupont have taken steps along that path. Xerox has covered it by leaps and bounds.

ECO-EFFICIENCY VS. ECO-EFFECTIVENESS

Each time you consume physical resources, you end up with less. But each time you use information, you can have more. Information grows as you use it. That is true not just in the information sector but in the industrial sector as well. Dow and Dupont, for instance, use information to create value in two ways. First, they use it for continuous improvements, refining the efficiency, variety, and quality of their products—the business equivalent of natural selection and variation by descent. Second, they use it for breakthrough innovation, inventing whole new products and processes and unleashing whole new kinds of value—the business equivalent of synergy in nature.

The first formula—continuous improvement—means *making products better*, often called *eco-efficiency*. The second, breakthrough innovation, means *making better products*. That is often called *eco-effectiveness*, a term popularized by designer William McDonough.

For the past generation, Dow and Dupont have been competing aggressively with each other, often gaining or losing advantage by virtue of their comparative capacity to profit from information in these two ways.

In 1982, Dow began a famous program to encourage employees to find ways to reduce pollution. The first year, 27 ideas were implemented. These incremental eco-efficiencies paid a return on investment of 173 percent, which means that every dollar they spent gave them a $1.73 return in its first year.

Many people assumed that Dow had found the biggest sources of waste. Therefore, they thought, the 173 percent return would decline as the company tackled more difficult opportunities. Instead, just the opposite happened. Every idea led to another idea. People found more and more ways to improve. After 10 years and 700 projects, the program was not paying returns of 173 percent anymore. Now it was paying 300 percent. Every dollar brought $3 in savings the first year—*and every year thereafter.*

Dow's people didn't run out of ideas. Just the opposite. They discovered that information grows as it is used. It follows the laws of system dynamics.

Now let's look at Dupont. They knew that to stay competitive with Dow, and also to earn the support of the public and of regulators, they needed to match or beat Dow's achievements in eco-efficiency. But they took a different approach. Under the leadership of then-Chairman Edgar Woolard, they didn't focus only on eco-efficiency; they focused also on eco-effectiveness. Instead of just making the same products more efficiently, they focused on making *better* products—products that performed the same functions as the old ones but in new ways that were radically more productive.

Let's review our terms again. Dow's approach, continuous improvement—making a product better—means making the same product as before, except making it smarter, to contain more information and less stuff, as when we add a computer chip to a car to regulate its fuel use and improve mileage. We call this *eco-efficiency.*

Dupont's approach, breakthrough innovation—making a better product—means making a *different* product from before, one that provides the same service in a smarter way, as when we use a computer to work or shop at home, instead of using our car at all. We call this *eco-effectiveness.*

One of Dupont's biggest breakthroughs was in herbicides. At the start of their eco-effectiveness program, Dupont was the world's #7 herbicide manufacturer. They invented new herbicides that were 100 times less toxic than the old ones and that cost less to use. This innovation moved Dupont from the #7 to the #2 position in the market.

Don't forget, however, that Dow and Dupont are still fundamentally industrial companies. They are refining industrial processes with information, but they aren't replacing them. They have too much capital trapped in the old economy. Their competitors in the information sector, however, face no such barriers. By inventing technologies that enable people to do more with less, they compel yesterday's industrial giants to either adapt—sometimes in radical ways—or die.

XEROX MAKES TWO-SIDED VALUE, BUT THEY OFTEN USE ONLY ONE SIDE

If in the 1970s and 1980s Silicon Valley became, in effect, the world's largest supplier of energy-through-efficiency, then Xerox must have discovered its most productive fields. We think of Xerox as a copier company. But Xerox has also had its hand in a few other products you might have seen around the office lately. It designed the Alto, the prototype of all modern personal computers, as well as the word processor Bravo that later morphed into programs like WordStar and Microsoft Word. They developed e-mail, one of the phenomena that powered AOL's growth, and the GUI (graphical user interface) that Apple used to create the Lisa and the Macintosh and that Microsoft attempted to copy for Windows. They also developed Ethernet, which enabled PCs to tie into high-speed networks, populated the Internet, and made billions for 3Com and Cisco Systems.

Perhaps no company in history has created such a profitable series of products as has Xerox. Unfortunately for Xerox, none of those products carries the Xerox name. Back then, Xerox was earning comfortable profits on copy machines, so it didn't pursue these more exotic opportunities when a handful of its employees were literally inventing the new economy.

The source of these revolutionary innovations wasn't one of the company's big production plants or product development centers. It was a little factory in Palo Alto that created nothing but information and the technologies that were spawned by it.

The Palo Alto Research Center—Xerox PARC—was for decades a playground for some of the world's most creative scientists and engineers. Ostensibly PARC was Xerox's defense against the advent of the always-imminent-but-never-actual "paperless office" that computers were supposed to inaugurate.

But while Xerox continuously improved the efficiency, quality, and performance of its copiers, it was not so adept at taking advantage of breakthrough innovations, even its own. As a consequence, Xerox missed its opportunities while profits were strong; then it found itself unable to capitalize on them when recession struck and lean times ensued. "Xerox could have owned the entire computer industry today," says Apple CEO Steve Jobs. "But it didn't think it had to. In the years when those innovations appeared, Xerox copier sales were soaring, revenues climbed ten-fold in 12 years, and the company had neither a recognizable incentive nor any system for transferring its breakthrough innovations into new business units. So it didn't."

APPLE MISSED IT, TOO

What Jobs doesn't say is that he too could have owned it—if he had not made a similar error twice or even three times. Just as Xerox lived off the high margins from copier sales when it could have invested in its creations, Jobs protected Apple's high-margin computer hardware and missed the long-term opportunity to maximize the size of the network using its operating system. Back in the 1980s, before Microsoft had a lock on the market, Jobs refused to license the Macintosh operating system. That pushed up the company's short-term revenues, which peaked in 1991, but also eventually drove market share down to less than five percent. Then fate gave Jobs a second chance—and again he missed it. After he was forced out of Apple, Jobs formed a new company with a superb team and developed the superior NeXT operating system. When IBM offered Jobs $60 million to license NeXT as the standard operating system for PCs, Jobs first agreed to the deal and then undermined it to protect short-term sales of his $10,000 NeXT workstations. Microsoft was more than happy to build a monopoly with a lesser product in the niche Jobs twice abandoned.

Jobs' error was that, like Xerox, he based his business models on the illusion that the value was in the hardware rather than the software— on selling atoms instead of bits. Thus only the most zealous users stayed with his companies, while others drifted to manufacturers who offered lesser operating system software but didn't demand loyalty to exclusive and overpriced hardware.

The NeXT operating system finally appeared to have found a home when Apple acquired NeXT to replace the aging Macintosh and, more important, pursue a software-centric cross-platform strategy to compete with Microsoft and others. Apple promised a computing Eden with a modern computer that would make the Apple-faithful want to abandon the Macintosh; they promised an open-hardware specification to encourage third-party development and build market share and NeXT-based platform software that would allow applications written for the new Apple operating system to run on Windows and on other platforms. But after Jobs turned Apple's acquisition of NeXT into a de facto takeover of Apple, he made the same mistake a third time, canceling the cross-platform strategy to concentrate on maximizing short-term revenues from the Macintosh. Despite NeXT's superiority to Windows, it may now be too late for it to succeed. NeXT has become little more than a vehicle to extend the life of an increasingly irrelevant Macintosh line.

Like mangrove trees in the Costa Rican rainforest, who fashion an ecosystem in which other species flourish and then find they have failed to provide a secure place for themselves, Xerox and Apple may serve as textbook examples of how *not* to invent breakthrough products, and of the failure to take advantage of them. Like a fallen mangrove tree whose scattered remnants are torn apart and taken in by the hungry creatures in the rainforest, the decline of Xerox in the mid-1970s liberated its most valuable ideas. High-tech executives such as Scott McNealy at Sun, Bob Metcalfe at 3Com, and Sandy Lesner at Cisco will be forever grateful.

Many of today's information technology executives seem to be copying Xerox's and Apple's mistakes in a broader way. Their response to the energy crisis of 2001 was just one example. Because of environmental limits, the economic rewards for using technology to substitute information for renewable resources will only increase. The information sector has an economic opportunity not merely to refine the machines of industry but to replace them and invent a whole new economy with a whole new way to profit.

CHAPTER THREE

Profit

LESSON THREE:
CREATE MORE THAN YOU CONSUME—
USE LIMITS AS A SPRINGBOARD TO ABUNDANCE

IN THE RAINFOREST, *limits are a positive force.*
They trigger innovation and set in motion a sequence of
changes that lead to the creation of abundance—net gain.

IN BUSINESS, *too, limits are a disciplining*
force that channel action toward
the creation of value—net profit.

As we continued our fall and reached a point about one mile from the ground, all we could do with the technology we had on our backs was use the parachute to slow our fall. This was just fine for us—getting to the ground and walking away were our top priorities.

But we noticed that the birds could do more with less physical equipment than we had on our backs. They could not only slow their fall, they could reverse it and increase their elevation. They had learned to fly.

This observation became particularly interesting a few moments later. Tachi's parachute caught the wind, opened into a full canopy, and began carrying its passenger gently down. By contrast, Bill's parachute started to flip wildly in the wind, failing to catch the air or slow his fall in the least. In an instant, Bill passed Tachi in the race to the ground, but it was not a race he really wanted to win.

At that moment, we would both have felt more secure if, in addition to our parachutes, we had the ability of the birds that flourished in the rainforest around us—to simply spread wings and fly.

IN THE RAINFOREST

THE TEN DOMINOS OF VALUE CREATION —HOW NATURE PROFITS

PIONEERS MAY FOUL THEIR OWN NEST,
BUT THEY CREATE A HOME FOR THEIR SUCCESSORS

Hours later, we saw the birds up close, from our boats. In the mangrove swamps, they perched, as if on display, as we passed by and took an endless number of pictures. But while the birds captured our focus, it was the mangroves that we later found more interesting.

Mangroves grow like machines, with no feedback except "taste"— the taste of their fuel, the ready supplies of sunlight from above and water at the edge of land. Fueled by abundant resources, they grow explosively, drop the seeds of their successors, and expand. In so doing, they create a mangrove swamp rich in a diverse array of species. Oddly enough, though, a mangrove swamp isn't a very healthy place for a mangrove shrub. In fact, it is ultimately deadly. In building the swamp, the mangroves create the conditions that later starve them of resources and lead to their own destruction. But in the process, they create a habitat for something new: more resilient species, with whole new qualities, designed to excel in that niche.

In Costa Rica, mangrove ecosystems thrive at the verge between land and water. The irrepressible mangrove shrubs, pioneer "r-strategists" that grow fast on ample water and sunlight, send out interlocking stilt roots that hold soil in place, fighting tidal erosion and reclaiming land from the water. Mangroves thrive where no other tree can.

Once established, mangrove swamps form myriad niches where other plants and animals begin to thrive, each producing food or habitat for others. For example, the mangrove shrubs and aerial roots provide a safe haven for the water birds we saw along our route—cormorants, frigate birds, pelicans, herons, and egrets—that nest there by the thousands. They, in turn, deposit guano that makes the mangroves grow faster. Below the waterline, oysters and sponges attach to the roots, and stingrays flap slowly over the bottom. Tiny fish school by the thousands. Larger fish like the black-tipped shark begin their lives among the roots of the mangrove, using them as a shield against predators. Just beyond the mangrove roots, crocodiles move between their nests and the pond along a series of trails, which they keep open and clear of vegetation. Enriched by the crocodile's droppings, the waters around the crocodile's path support a healthy growth of algae and higher plants, which take root in the soil held in place by the mangrove's roots.

Through these processes, the mangroves establish a foothold, build a swamp, and gradually fill it in. As the plants of the mangrove swamp die and decay, they help to build more soil, held in place by the expanding mangroves, which act like a net. Eventually, as they continue to build the soil, the mangroves literally strand themselves on land too high and dry to support them. They die on the very land they created. But the death of a single mangrove is of little consequence to the species as a whole. Like other pioneers, the mangroves are aggressive colonizers. Even as individual trees perish, the seeds they have borne are beginning new colonies, building new forests elsewhere.

Throughout nature, fast-growing pioneers sow the seeds of their own destruction—literally. Every species in nature serves a "purpose" in this sense: It is fashioned as an adaptation to local limits. It is "selected" because its adaptation increases the likelihood that it will survive to reproduce.

This quality is not limited to individual species. Two species may join in mutualistic combinations that benefit the long-term survival of both. The two broad reproductive strategies—the fast growth and high fertility of r-strategists, and the specialized survival skills of the K-strategists—form such a mutualistic team. The r-strategist pioneers invade an open field and stitch it together into a series of niches. Within each of these niches, new environmental conditions invite specialists adapted to excel there. These specialists in turn create the efficiency gains—the profit margin—that support future generations of both r- and K-strategists.

HOW NATURE PROFITS: THE TEN DOMINOS OF EVOLUTION

What is profit? In the industrial economy, it's the difference between our costs and our revenues. If we think in traditional zero-sum terms, if I am a seller and you are a buyer, my "profit" is whatever I get to keep after taking money from you and paying the bills. Profit seems, at best, selfish, and, at worst, exploitive.

Because of this perception, when we think of profit and the environment, we usually think of the two in adversarial terms. "Profit," we assume, happens by extracting stuff from nature—land, food, minerals, trees. Every*thing* we use in our economy. So, as we expand the economy, we shrink nature; every profit to us is a loss for the earth. That is the conventional wisdom, anyway. But much of what we call profit is not the *creation* of profit at all. It is the *expenditure* of profit. In the industrial economy, we take complex resources from the earth—information-rich resources in the form of complex hydrocarbons, or living plants and animals, or diverse forest ecosystems. Earth's profits. Then we spend down their information content, the form that defines their capacities, the work they can do for us, the value they contain. Finally, we discard them and look for more. That's not creating profit; it's consuming profit.

Nature does the same thing, to a point. Every creature consumes resources, takes complex resources in and then processes and simplifies them. And many creatures seem almost exclusively predatory or parasitic—their gain is everything else's loss. But if we look deeper, we notice that most organisms take these simple resources and build them up, adding complexity, information in the language of structure. At the end of the process, they create something new—a net gain, not just consumption. The net gain might be an efficiency, or it might be a whole new quality, a breakthrough innovation. For example, mangroves create a place for efficiency, as a home for life forms that can excel with less sunlight and water than the mangroves. And they also create a place for more complex creatures, like the birds, and for the whole new quality that distinguishes the birds, their breakthrough innovation, the capacity to fly.

The process of evolution, leading from simple consumptive forms toward more efficient and creative ones—and often back again—can be distilled into a series of ecological principles. These principles are all related to one another, in a sequence of causes-and-effects. Think of them as dominos, the ten dominos of evolution, each falling and toppling the next and often in the process leading to the creation of net gain—that is, profit.

The first domino is *entropy*, the imposition of a loss or cost. According to the second law of thermodynamics, entropy means that every conversion of matter or energy leads to a net loss of potential energy. Bill Coors' cans and their impact on the tundra, and Anita Burke's oil and its impact on the bottom line, are just two examples. Every use of a resource creates a cost. Without new infusions of fuel, systems will quickly expend all their energy and run down.

It often takes a long time for the cost of an action to induce change in the system that created it. In the forest, for example, pioneers like mangroves quickly grow past the limits within which their own local environment can sustain them. To them, the forest is an abundant storehouse. They draw from it with abandon, sensing no effective constraints.

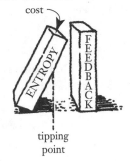

COST TRIGGERS FEEDBACK

tipping point

When entropy—cost—is high enough, it passes a threshold, a tipping point beyond which change becomes unavoidable.

The second domino is *feedback*—the effect of the action. Entropy triggers feedback, and the system begins to learn. It is the signal Bill Coors received when he noticed the effect of cans in the environment and later when he incurred the costs of retrieving them. It is the signal Anita Burke sent when she burned a $5 bill in her marketing boss's office and later when she introduced Return on Investment analysis to institutionalize change.

Feedback imposes a **forcing function** that ultimately prevents past behaviors from recurring, either because a customer changes a buying habit, an employee changes a production decision, an executive is fired, or a company goes bankrupt. The more effectively soft-feedback signals work to cultivate change gradually, the less likely more extreme changes are compelled later.

So feedback closes the open loop, helping turn a chain into a web, imposing a forcing function that induces change. That topples the third domino.

The third domino is *adaptation.* In the open forest floor, when resources are abundant, pioneers like the mangrove or pine are designed to have the competitive edge. Some have broad leaves that act like super-size solar collectors, feeding them fuel for fast growth. Others have fruit jam-packed with seeds that animals distribute throughout the forest.

Meanwhile, in the shade created by the r-strategists, the K-strategists now come to the fore. They don't need the vast sunlight and open space in which their predecessors flourished. K-strategists are slower growing, able to germinate in the shade beneath the deepening canopy.

Thus, the fourth domino falls: *specialization.* As organisms adapt to the imposition of environmental changes, they grow more refined, different from the pioneers. They become specialists, able to excel in more narrowly defined ecological niches, or places with particular types of soil, slope, sunlight, elevation, and moisture, for example. Because niches vary greatly, especially as pioneers and specialists divide the forest into more and more of them, the forest selects an increasing variety of species, previously held in abeyance. Over time, successive waves of limits and adaptations create an ever-greater array of specialists within the forest, each matched to the niche opened up by predecessor species.

Every appearance of a specialist triggers a succession of further changes in the forest. Not just one part of the system adapts; they all do. Every action has not just one reaction, but myriad reactions. Actions diffuse along every strand in the system's web, changing not one thing but every thing, and changing them in different ways.

Now the fifth domino falls: *diversification.* Remember the unique quality of information resources? Every time you trade information, you can get more in return. Similarly, each increase in diversity can lead to more diversity, as emerging species create space for myriad smaller plants and animals that fit into the niches among them. Since each specialized organism is a specific information set, each represents a new tool—a choice. Since diversity means choice, this increase in diversity generally increases the resilience of the forest.

Why are diverse systems often more resilient in the long term? Simple ecosystems have limited information content and limited choices. In the short term, they might seem to offer greater stability, but that's because they have no choice. They rebound *only so long as the system is not stressed too severely.* When a fire or other crisis is mild, a simple system remains as is, rock-solid, enabling individual species to rebound to previous population levels. But when a crisis is severe, the simple ecosystem can't flex, so it may in effect crack, break down, and collapse completely, often with catastrophic results for all its species.

The system grows more complex, and with it **the sixth domino falls:** *complexity.* So long as change is regulated but not repressed, a complex forest can adapt to it continuously. Small, frequent fires can wind through the living trees feeding only on deadwood. They leave behind them a healthy, diverse forest with a mix of young and mature plants, in a fractal structure that renews itself on many levels simultaneously. At the level of individual plants, even individual species, the change may be catastrophic. But for the system as a whole, small fires clear the way for the development of a richer and more vibrant ecosystem. If we look at the whole, the number of different parts becomes greater; there is greater variety.

And with every thing affecting every other, the relationships among them become ever more complicated. Diagram them, and what you see might resemble a computer-generated fractal, where simple yes/no instructions lead to the gradual emergence of recurring patterns. Since every niche is shaped and sculpted according to its relationship to every other, all the elements of the complex whole are dependent on one another, creating **the seventh domino:** *interdependence.*

In a system of increasingly interdependent parts, every thing is related to every other, dependent on every other for its very definition. Lines of relationship are drawn from everywhere to everywhere. Chains become webs. In a sense, each element of the whole becomes more unique, more individualized, as it grows more specialized and focused on its particular genius, its core competence. Yet through this individuation, it becomes more drawn into a larger whole. It is more individualized and yet less complete. Specialized to one place and purpose, it loses its capacity to fit other niches and relies on others better suited. Like it or not, **it falls into a condition of** *cooperation,* **the eighth domino.** Not by choice, not necessarily because it "desires" to or is drawn to by some sense of altruism, but by nature.

Ultimately, parts join as pieces of a larger whole and find that in serving the whole, they serve themselves best. As this larger whole becomes defined, something astonishing often happens: New properties often emerge, not just in the forest but in all complex systems. Not by an individual alone but by individuals in the context of their times and their whole communities. **This is the ninth domino—***emergence.* Something new is created—a parachute is unbound from its pack. This is a potential, a choice, a source of power, a bank account of new value.

Hence *synergy,* **the tenth domino,** the principle in nature that accounts for its extraordinary ability to end-run entropy.

HOW NATURE CREATES PROFIT
The 10 Dominoes

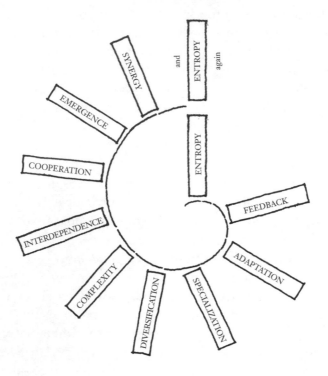

In complex systems, more is created than was spent to get there—not just quantitatively, but qualitatively. The "more" may include greater efficiency—a continuous improvement in our capacity to carry out an existing function. But its most compelling form is breakthrough innovation, the creation of a new resource containing a new capacity not present in its parts. Thus nature creates net gain—a profit. So can we. We use this profit to create greater distance between ourselves and our limits, our ground zero. And in using it, we find that we have toppled the first domino again and begun a new process of creation that can lead to the creation of profit in a whole new form.

As the dominos fall, change is inevitable, but the path it takes is not determined. Unlike physical dominos, these dominos can fall in any direction. The future is created by the actions we take in the present; and every action taken, no matter how small and inconsequential it seems, can change wholly the shape that emerges.

IN BUSINESS

THE TEN DOMINOS OF PROFIT
—AND HOW INDUSTRY TOPPLES THE FIRST

THE ENERGY CRISIS, THE TEN DOMINOS, AND THE EMERGENCE OF THE INFORMATION ECONOMY

We see the dominos falling each day in the emerging economy. In the machine economy, business is a pioneer system that often takes more than it gives. But like the mangroves, it creates a structure that can foster innovation.

Similarly, as we reach the limits of machine-style business, we are creating a framework of feedback loos that enable us to more quickly adapt to the costs we impose on the earth and on one another. In the process, we are learning to not merely consume profit, but to create it.

One thing hasn't changed in the information economy. The **entropy** domino falls—waste is created—each time a barrel of oil is burned and carbon is released to the atmosphere. The **feedback** from that can't be avoided, but the degree we feel it depends on how quickly and intelligently we respond to it. We can respond to its initial, soft and quiet forms. Or we can wait, as the signals become gradually more severe, until we notice them and then adapt.

For example, in the 1970s both the U.S. and Japanese economies were staggered by the Arab oil embargo. But in the years immediately following, Japan proved quicker at **adaptation.** Machinelike U.S. corporations lacked the flexibility to adjust instantly to the change. Japan's learning organizations were expert team-builders schooled in continuous change. They knew how to cultivate continuous improvement— gains in efficiency—and so proved much more resilient in the short term. By the late 1980s, Japanese autos accounted for two-thirds of all auto imports, and Japan's share of global semiconductor sales almost doubled, from 28 to 50 percent.

But while Japan excelled in continuous improvement, the free market forced U.S. companies to make more fundamental structural changes. Japan shielded its economy from much of the feedback that would otherwise have forced more basic shifts. It repressed the small fires that were forcing U.S. companies to make structural changes. Japan's efficiencies became almost meaningless as whole industries were transformed at their roots. U.S. industries leapfrogged past economies of scale. Instead of following the old formula and getting bigger, they tapped *ecologies* of scale, flattening hierarchies, restructuring, joining in strategic partnerships, and responding to feedback from everywhere in their web of relationships. Not because companies wanted to, but because they had to, the U.S. economy surged ahead in the 1990s and became more flexible and resilient.

The energy crisis also led to a wave of **specialization.** Mass markets began to subdivide into more narrowly defined niches. Products began to diversify. Generic giants like General Motors, Standard Brands, General Foods, and Standard Oil—the pioneer species of the industrial forest—fell on hard times and were forced to downsize or decentralize. The number and array of distinct brands, flavors, packages, products, offices, firms, industries, and technologies began to expand, as the imperative to specialize compelled producers to capitalize on comparative advantages and seek refuge in niches they could dominate. Instead of three dominant U.S. breweries—Budweiser, Miller, and Schlitz—three thousand new micro brews emerged, undermining the premium allure of the nationals, and squeezing margins. Only the most efficient mass market systems could survive. Budweiser prospered, Miller hung on, and Schlitz was destroyed, replaced in the number three spot by Coors.

Why does any of this matter? What happened, for example, as the shock waves from the energy crisis spread out through the economy? Companies began to shift from r-strategies to K-strategies, from mass production pioneers that operate blindly toward K-strategist specialists tied into a broader community of interests, to which they will gradually be held accountable.

This wave of specialization wasn't limited to a few markets. It spread across the economy, leading to a broad **diversification** of not just products and brands but companies and industries. Commodity product manufacturers found themselves locked in horrific competition from which only one or two real winners could emerge. Many collapsed and were absorbed by low-cost leaders. Most found ways to adapt, filling specialized niches in which they had a key advantage.

Diversity assumed just as much importance in the workforce. Success in the past came from consumption, and conformity and hierarchy sped it along. Now success emerged more from the ability to adapt in the face of challenge and change. The doctrines of workplace conformity so profitable in past industrial hierarchies made companies too rigid, and denied them the intellectual and cultural resources of a diverse workforce. They could no longer afford to treat their employees like mechanical parts—all the same, interchangeable. The economies gained were often less valuable than the human qualities lost. Companies needed on-the-job creativity. That required diversity. But diversity required that people work together, in cross-functional teams, formal and informal, to get whole jobs done. Employees grew **interdependent.**

Interdependence happened not just among employees but also among companies. While competition was the chief threat to businesses in uniform industrial markets, change became far more threatening as the economy grew more diverse, chaotic, and unpredictable. Unprecedented economic dynamism led to a paradoxical mix of instability at the local level and resilience for the system as a whole. Individual companies might grow terrifically, then suffer sudden declines. Whole subsectors like the dot-coms might explode forth, then collapse. Workers might be hired on in a growth phase, then find themselves searching when times suddenly became lean. A persistent population of the structurally unemployed and underemployed was abandoned except in times of especially intense employment demand. Workers without the basic skills needed to capture and retain a high value-added job fell out of the system as their jobs were moved overseas, increasing the need for policies to keep these workers in the job market. But on the whole, new jobs emerged quickly for those with sufficient education and training, and unemployment remained low.

In the face of change, there is safety in diversity. Company-to-company competition was thus tempered by increasing examples of **cooperation.** At first it looked like the opposite was happening. Long-time unions broke down. Corporate conglomerates such as ITT, Beatrice, AT&T—accumulations of dissimilar businesses under uniform machinelike management—fell apart, or they were torn apart in the 1970s and 1980s in leveraged buy-outs orchestrated by firms such as Kohlberg Kravis and Roberts.

But the breakdown of the conglomerates was just the first sign of change. Soon companies began to reassemble themselves into new, more flexible forms of cooperation. Conglomerates proved unmanageable—

the economy was too fast changing and performance driven to accommodate their rigid command structure. But strategic alliances prospered. Latter-day *keiretsu*, or informal business alliances, they brought together companies whose operations are complementary. Combined, the companies gained the ability to profit from innovation. They could seize on **emergent** opportunities, and gain the benefits of **synergy.**

Political philosopher Drexel Sprecher says that business alliances and strategies in the Internet age have already changed the nature of competition, in both positive and negative ways. On the one hand, as large firms disaggregate, the lower transaction costs enabled by the Internet make it easier for small firms to develop distinctive core competencies and put these together to create superior products, gaining the advantages of specialization, synergy and scale. On the other hand, the network effects of Metcalfe's Law create an open invitation for abuse, since first movers lacking any core competency can limit competition through alliances that exist for the purpose of excluding competitors, allowing them to dominate key sectors with lowest common denominator products.

Examples of synergetic corporate alliances are everywhere. Sometimes the alliances are intentional and formal, although carefully planned alliances often lead to completely unintended consequences. But most of the time, in business just as in nature, the alliances are a mixture of opportunity and affinity, springing into being as one innovation meets another, morphing into a third phenomenon. Thus Dee Hock assembles together a network of independent banks to form VISA, and the result is a new industry and, in effect, a global currency. Bill Coors works with European technologists to invent the aluminum can, and creates the economic foundation that births the community recycling industry.

THE EMERGING ECONOMIC REVOLUTION

The energy crisis was the forcing function that toppled the first domino in the decades-long wave of change just described. Drawn by higher oil prices and an almost universal belief that they would stay high, companies made huge investments in high-cost sources of fossil fuels and alternative energy—everything from oil shale to solar. These investments essentially collapsed when oil prices failed to stay high. Why?

Information was much cheaper. The energy-price shocks stimulated a drive to find efficiencies. As it turned out, the cheapest alternative to fossil fuels wasn't another energy source—it was information. People and companies soon found it was cheaper to save energy than to extract new supplies. This contributed to the explosion in demand for information technologies that powered the growth of the information economy in the 1980s and beyond.

So down the dominos fell, specializations triggering efficiencies triggering diversification, interdependence, cooperation, and the gradual emergence of what could become a whole new kind of economy.

What is this emerging economy? How far along is it in its development? What barriers remain to its full expression?

The global spread of information technologies has enabled important gains in industrial efficiency, powering a decade of sustained U.S. economic growth through the 1990s. The Internet now connects and informs hundreds of millions of people, using a fraction of the resources that would once have been required. In fact, the worldwide conversation now underway would not have been possible without the Internet, at any resource cost. People and cultures that would never have directly met are spontaneously organizing themselves around areas of interest, using the Internet as their means of connection. Instead of the one-way information flow of media like television and radio, on the Internet feedback is easy and automatic. People can work directly with other people, end-running the entrenched corporations and governments that used to regulate their interactions. The popularity of file sharing software like Napster and Gnutella—and the fear those technologies triggered in the industries they threatened—suggests that peer-to-peer communications has the potential to shift power from unresponsive businesses and governments to individuals.

So where is this process going? Industrialization swept away old forms of government, commerce, religion, and profession. Has the information economy—microchips, computers, the Internet and the World Wide Web—brought change nearly so vast?

Not yet. The next decades have the potential to bring changes more striking than those that accompanied the shift from agriculture to industry. But this new economy has just begun to emerge. And while its momentum is powerful, there is no assurance that it will fully develop. Why? Because flaws in its technical foundation may interfere with the realization of its potential. This is of no small consequence. Nature dictates that in the face of limits, species must either adapt or die. The industrial economy today faces an absolute limit. It cannot continue to develop along the consumptive, depletive line it has in the past followed. That is a physical impossibility. The economy and the environment cannot remain in competition for the same resources. Hardin's law of competitive exclusion dictates that if both reside in the same niche, only one can survive. A new path of development is essential, one that breaks the causal link between economic advance and environmental decline and aligns the interests of the economy and environment.

What would characterize such an economy? It must do two things at once: increase quality of life and reduce extraction and pollution. Scientists calculate that will require as much as a Factor 10 improvement in resource productivity. In other words, we will need to draw ten times as much value from every unit of energy and material we consume.

That is not as unreachable as it may sound. During the last century, machines improved *labor* productivity 40-fold. Now, in the beginning years of this century, the challenge is to improve *resource* productivity ten-fold.

The next generation of digital-age computing platforms and applications is an essential part of the next economy. While these breakthrough innovations offer no guarantees, a globally prosperous and sustainable economy is probably impossible without them. Just as machines replaced much physical labor, computers and software can replace many traditional machines, along with their massive appetite for materials and energy. They can create more value, using a fraction of the resources required today.

Michael Vlahos, Senior Policy Analyst at the Johns Hopkins University Applied Physics Laboratory, says that the successor to today's World Wide Web is what he calls the "Infosphere." This more fully developed information economy can emerge through the integration of the world's networks, libraries and other sources of information sources in a new virtual meeting place. This vast and heterogeneous tapestry of electronic interchange will draw the world's people and cultures together into a diverse yet cohesive commons—not a global monoculture replicating the features of American culture, but a rich mix of coevolving cultures.

The Infosphere will be as different from the World Wide Web as the Web is from the hard-to-use command-line Internet of the 1980s. It will enable people to join together in new communities for economic and cultural interchange, without many of today's constraints of time and place. Imagine broadcasting television-quality video from your home. Or designing a software agent that conducts research on the Web and organizes the results into categories you define—then offers the results for sale to others over the Web. Or meeting in three-dimensional virtual space with people on four continents—all speaking their native languages, simultaneously translated. Or replacing your monthly business trip to Singapore with virtual meetings, and investing a portion of the savings to take your family on a pilgrimage to Tibet.

Even these possibilities convey little of the potential of the Infosphere. Just as industry liberated people from the economic, political, and social structures of the feudal economy and led to the emergence of cities, commercial centers, and nation-states, the Infosphere can liberate people from the barriers that divide one place from another and lead to forms of cultural development impossible to predict.

Anything is possible, nothing is certain. To realize the tremendous potential of the Infosphere and to enjoy the economic and intrinsic benefits of a highly diverse, integrated global civilization, citizens will need access not just as consumers but as producers of content and culture. They will need to engage freely in the Infosphere without being regulated by intermediaries. Without this freedom, the potential of the Infosphere to shift power from giant industrial age enterprises to individuals and promote diversity instead of uniformity will be lost.

BARRIERS TO THE EMERGENCE OF THE INFOSPHERE

What stands in the way of such a fundamental shift? Certainly, time. But other factors could also slow or stop the transition. Entrenched interests will attempt to protect their position. Consumers comfortable with familiar technology and not aware of what they are missing may resist change.

In nature, breakthrough innovation is often disruptive, yet its benefits are essential to the evolution of life. Billions of years ago, the earth's first life support system had no free oxygen. Only extremely primitive microorganisms could survive. When they died, they left an accumulation of carbon, which became food for blue-green algae, which consume carbon dioxide. The algae paid back their anaerobic forebears by killing them *en masse*. By dispensing oxygen that eventually accumulated in the atmosphere, they killed off 99 percent of the earth's species and created conditions that made advanced life forms possible.

Earth's primitive anaerobic life support system could not evolve advanced forms of life. Free oxygen was required. Continuous improvement of anaerobic life was not a viable strategy. The limiting force—the life support system—had to be replaced by a breakthrough innovation.

Drexel Sprecher sees a parallel in today's information economy. The Wintel computing platform—a hybrid of Microsoft's Windows operating system and Intel's Pentium and earlier microprocessors—is inadequate to enable the emergence of the Infosphere. "Operating systems and microprocessors are to applications as the carbon-oxygen cycle on earth is to its life forms. They enable or limit diversity. While the carbon-oxygen system may seem rather ordinary at first glance, if it were less evolved the diversity of life forms as we know them would be greatly diminished. In technology, as in nature, the degree of flexibility, diversity, and stability at the most fundamental levels has consequences at higher levels. A variety of advanced computing platforms competing with different features and benefits will permit a virtual rainforest of advanced digital age applications, with a richness of capabilities beyond what most users of present platforms can imagine."

So what is a computing platform, and what could it *possibly* have to do with enabling the emergence of the Infosphere, much less a sustainable economy? A platform is a technology that converts people's requests into machine output. It consists of two familiar parts: a microprocessor and an operating system. An advanced platform enables development of applications with breakthrough capabilities with minimal coding.

The emergence of the Infosphere will require an array of new applications to conduct research, create and share content, bring people together, and manage resource usage. These will rely on the computer's life support system: its operating system and microprocessor architecture, as well as the abundance of its bandwidth. Since the design of these fundamental layers has immense power to constrain or enable the Infosphere, breakthrough innovations in operating systems and microprocessors are crucial to realization of its potential.

In the early 1990s, a widespread recognition that the basic architecture of existing platforms was inadequate to meet emerging needs led to a wave of extraordinary innovation in computing. Visionary business leaders, engineers, marketers, and venture capitalists brought together their resources to create a wave of new products and possibilities: New operating systems from IBM, NeXT, and Be. The PowerPC microprocessor and its Common Hardware Reference Platform. Internet software such as Netscape Navigator. OpenStep and Java cross-platform application environments that enabled developers to write an application once and run it on multiple platforms. And the promise of a new generation of digital media applications.

By the late 1990s there was tremendous investment in network infrastructure of the type required for the Infosphere. Then the computing market was overwhelmed by Wintel, a classic r-strategist, a generalist that does many things adequately but none particularly well. Wintel market share exceeded 90 percent, and the market shares of other platforms declined rapidly. Investment in new platform technologies declined with them. As a result, the next generation of digital age applications needed to fully take advantage of the Infosphere will not be ready when the bandwidth is in place.

Of course, most users have no idea what they are missing. You can't regret the loss of something you never imagined. With Microsoft continuously adding more and more features to Windows and its other products, consumers are easily misled into confusing incremental improvements with breakthough innovation. And, for the moment, the ever-increasing speeds predicted by Moore's Law hide many of the deficiencies of the Wintel architecture.

But while Wintel is enabling continuous improvements in mass market software products such as word processing and spreadsheets, a host of specialized applications—many that enhance human creativity and connection or drive radical reductions in use of energy and materials—are being held back, and perhaps prevented altogether, because Wintel is not an adequate foundation for such applications. Breakthrough innovations in operating systems and microprocessors are crucial to the emergence of the Infosphere and its enormous benefits.

Wintel will not be the source of these innovations. It is widely agreed that the basic architecture of the Wintel platform has been obsolete for more than a decade. Even the much-heralded Windows XP and Pentium IV are built on archaic foundations inherited from the 1970s. Yet Wintel has repeatedly rejected breakthrough innovation for continuous improvement of this obsolete platform.

Wintel Weaves a Web
But will it advance or impede a sustainable new economy?

Wintel is like a fast-growing mangrove, at home weaving the first strands of the new economy's web. It cannot replace the monoculture it has created. It is not in its nature—r-strategists are uniform, fast-growing species whose survival is tied to replicating themselves without limits.

So why hasn't Wintel been replaced in the market? Unlike pioneers like the mangrove, or Ford, it has the market power to shut out competitors.

A car is a complete product. Even though a few owners will add third party components to improve performance, most will drive it as is. But there has not been a "whole computer" since the days of the mainframe. A computer absolutely requires third party applications to be adequate for most users.

This dependency on third party investment means that computing platforms are subject to an insidious kind of network effects. For a platform to attract users, it needs a critical mass of existing applications. Yet software developers need a critical mass of existing users to write applications for it. This vicious circle enables first movers to create an "applications barrier to entry" that excludes competitors and claim almost all of the profit potential of the computing market.

Wintel's monolith exists because it hijacked these network effects before society recognized them and persuaded the world that Wintel is a "standard." But a "standard" computing platform is a myth. No single enterprise can have all the core competencies, resources, and market knowledge to create computing platforms with the diversity of capabilities needed for the digital age. Computing platforms are to software developers as soil and climate are to farmers. If every acre of farmland had identical soil and climate, farmers could grow only a narrow range of crops. If every computer platform had the same architecture, software developers could create 100,000 applications and all of them would inherit the constraints of that architecture. Civilization does not require a "standard" platform. It requires diversity.

And diversity requires interoperability so a variety of platforms can contribute to the digital rainforest. Interoperability enables applications and software components to run on multiple platforms and ensures that information and files may be exchanged across platforms. This allows new platforms to enter the digital ecosystem, fill niches, grow, and add valuable choices. Interoperability will promote the specialization, interdependency, and synergy necessary to create the large factor improvements necessary for a sustainable economy.

But interoperability threatens the Wintel monopoly. So Wintel has turned the rainforest into an orchard, converting essential habitat into its private preserve. By destroying market feedback processes and denying K-strategists the habitat they need to thrive, it has caused much more damage than typical r-strategists.

Consider the many tactics employed by Microsoft, Wintel's dominant partner, to genetically re-engineer itself to preempt competition and innovation. It pressures partners and competitors to prevent introduction or use of competing products. It punishes computer makers and Internet providers for using competing products. It acquires cross-platform technologies, makes them proprietary to Windows, and gives consumers initially "free" products until they are dependent on them. It interferes with the proper operation of competing products on Windows. It uses proprietary file formats. It commingles code and uses proprietary interfaces to lock distinct products together. All of these tactics are part of a comprehensive strategy to block interoperability and make the unit of competition the entire ecosystem, so neither software developers nor users can replace anything without replacing everything.

When IBM, a Microsoft partner, invested $10 million to add Windows application interfaces to its new OS/2 application environment so OS/2 could run the installed base of Windows applications and compete on a level playing field, Microsoft gratuitously changed its interfaces to thwart this process and threatened IBM with loss of its Windows license. Microsoft also used unnecessary interface changes to thwart competitor Sun's implementation of Windows application interfaces on the Solaris operating system.

Then Microsoft began locking its products together. Faced with superior productivity software like WordPerfect and Lotus 1-2-3, Microsoft used unpublished interfaces to create dependencies between Windows and its word processor, spreadsheet, presentation, and daily management software, placing competitors at a disadvantage. It solidified its hold by packaging these distinct applications into a single "product"—the Office productivity "suite," forcing competitors to offer complete suites instead of focusing on their core competency. Office applications also used unpublished interfaces to exchange information with each other, making it difficult to replace any one with a superior product. Competitors survived for awhile. Then Microsoft threatened computer makers with higher prices for Windows if they offered these products instead of Office. Frustrated computer makers and users resigned themselves to an "all Windows, all Office" world.

When Netscape created a browser that might ultimately have enabled people to switch from one operating system to another, Microsoft acquired the rights to another browser, renamed it Internet Explorer, and locked it together with Windows operating system. It claimed to give it away for "free," a good deal compared to Netscape's "selfish" desire to charge for Navigator. Microsoft then extended its reach to media streaming in the same way. In reality, the "free" Internet software was subsidized with monopoly profits as an investment in consolidating its market power on the desktop and extending it to the Internet.

When Sun developed a cross-platform Java application environment that also could have enabled people to switch operating systems, Microsoft added proprietary extensions to its Java implementation so that applications developed with its Java developer tools would only run on Windows. Microsoft then forced computer makers to ship computers with its implementation, sabotaging the cross-platform potential of Java.

In 1997, Microsoft even invested in Apple, the one company that, with newly acquired NeXT technology and tens of millions of zealous users, could have marketed a viable competing operating system. Apple promptly abandoned a cross-platform software strategy that would have enabled applications written for the new Apple platform to run on Wintel and other computers, and an open hardware strategy that would have made it easier to switch operating systems.

Microsoft is now extending its Internet Explorer monopoly with Web development tools that add proprietary extensions to the open languages of the World Wide Web and replace them with a de facto standard it can control. These extensions will add proprietary features to Web pages and compel users to have web sites hosted on servers running Windows. This may enable Microsoft to extend its monopoly to the server market and lock Web browsing and Web commerce to Windows.

Whenever a new technology emerges, Microsoft repeats the same tactics, acquiring it, locking it in with commingled code and unpublished interfaces, and using its monopoly power to ensure adoption by a critical mass of users. This bypasses the normal standards process and creates an endless stream of new de facto standards, all under the Microsoft mantle. Microsoft provides access to these secret standards to software developers who agree not to compete with its core products, and denies this information to those who do not. Microsoft thus determines which developers survive. It is virtually impossible for a software developer to replace a Microsoft product, or even product component, with superior technology. This precludes the niche-by-niche evolution that occurs in a healthy ecosystem. This enables the company to hijack network effects and extend its private commons into one monopoly after another.

This pattern has become so embedded in the Microsoft corporate culture that best practices, value added, and innovation are regularly sacrificed to strategies that extend the monopoly. Resources that could be invested in product improvement or breakthrough innovation are consistently diverted to prevent developers from substituting superior components and raise the "switching costs" for users who wish to replace Microsoft products with preferred alternatives.

This relentless pursuit of lock-in is promoted in the guise of "integration." But this purported integration makes software components neither run faster nor work more seamlessly together than they would with proper interfaces. Indeed, the commingling of code from so many components into the foundations of the operating system makes the entire system subject to instability and security breaches and, like any monoculture, vulnerable to viruses. The Infosphere requires a better foundation.

No organism in nature has this capacity to mutate at will to block the entry of superior competitors. There is no incentive for any software developer to create a new operating system, word processor, browser, or other common program. To compete with Microsoft, it would have to create an entire ecosystem of its own. At minimum, that would include a new operating system, a superior productivity suite, including word processing, spreadsheets, all its components, and even a user base. Even then, Microsoft could render these innovations moot with a few adjustments that prevent them from interoperating with the Microsoft monoculture. This has a chilling effect on research and investment.

Windows, Office and Explorer are just the beginning. Microsoft may be able to leverage its triple monopoly to capture the nascent Infosphere. The company is currently implementing ways to rent these monopoly products as a set of services over the Internet. After users connect, keystrokes will be monitored and fees charged for use of various features. This is a first step toward turning the information superhighway into a toll road.

Microsoft is already creating proprietary implementations of next generation Internet standards. This will inevitably lead to another set of secret de facto standards eliminating competition for the architecture for distributed Internet computing and the advanced networking applications so essential to the Infosphere. The ocean of innovation on the Internet will become a stagnant backwater. Developing third party software to compete with Microsoft to provide services like authentication, digital rights management, and Internet telephony will be forever foreclosed.

These new de facto standards will also make many essential services dependent on databases that store private data at Microsoft data centers and run user interactions through them. At this point we will have a client/server world that embodies the worst of industrial bureaucracy and discourages peer-to-peer computing. Microsoft will then be able to create an ever more powerful monoculture on the web and gain control of cyberspace in the same way it gained control of the desktop.

Intel behaves in similar, though less aggressive, ways. Any Intel innovations that would benefit consumers using alternative operating systems would also make it easier to switch to non-Intel microprocessors. So Intel embraces strategies and technologies that favor Windows at the expense of hardware innovations that would benefit superior operating systems. Locking Windows and Intel together locks others out of both markets.

The effect is to warp competition. Instead of rewarding value and niche innovation based on core competencies, competitive success is assured through the abuse of network effects by large monoliths. Regrettably, the current rules of competition provide few ways to contain this sort of runaway r-strategist until the damage is done.

Wintel is like the pines that outmuscle more efficient upstarts in a pioneer forest, too broadly dominant to give way quickly to better competitors. But the restrictive monoculture it has created offers neither the technical capacity nor the variety to grow a rich, diverse Infosphere.

Sprecher and Vlahos emphasize that while the benefit to Microsoft and Intel is monopoly profits, the cost to society from the misalignment of profit and innovation exceeds those profits many times over. This wholesale extraction of monopoly profits from the computing sector deprives investors and innovators of the incentive to take risks. That could destroy the promise of an abundant and sustainable digital economy. If digital age computing platforms cannot enter the market, then the digital age applications needed for the Infosphere may never be developed. This could significantly slow or even close off the emergence of the Infosphere, Sprecher and Vlahos say, and impede the transition to a truly new and more advanced civilization.

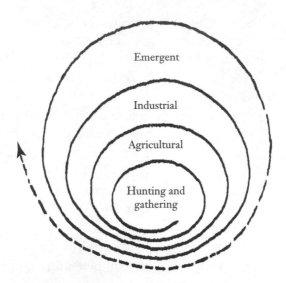

The toppling of the industrial dominos has created a nest in which a new economy, born of the industrial economy, is now just beginning.

Eventually the old way will yield to superior competitors or collapse to make way for its successor. But when? If change in a forest is repressed, deadwood accumulates, and sets the stage for a fiery transformation. Change appears to halt but is only delayed. When it is finally set loose, it happens more quickly and painfully than if it had been allowed to proceed gradually.

CHAPTER FOUR

Design

**LESSON FOUR:
CREATE PROFIT BY DESIGN**

IN THE RAINFOREST, *innovation emerges from the complex relationships that bind together the physical resources and living things that constitute it. Each design in nature yields specific qualities unique to that design. Net gain is created, in essence, by structure, by design.*

IN BUSINESS *too, profit is created by design.*

Wings would be useful at this point, we thought, when Bill's chute failed to open. Or at least, we might have thought this had we been in a reflective mood. But we were too highly focused to permit much broad introspection, at least at first.

To slow our fall and land softly on the ground, or even to reverse our fall and fly through the air, we needed nothing more than what we had with us, physically—which was more than the birds needed. The birds were smaller and lighter than us; their brains were less developed, and they would not have comprehended in the least what we pretended to know about aerodynamics. Yet they had a capacity that we envied.

What we lacked was not the physical resources to save ourselves; we had all the material we needed—Bill just needed it in a different shape. A canopy would have been a nice shape, for example. If Bill's parachute would just open up like Tachi's and take the form of a canopy, it would catch the wind and slow Bill's fall.

Wings would have been even better. With wings, we could have stopped our fall and propelled ourselves freely through the air. To do so, we didn't need any more stuff than we had. We needed only to arrange our stuff the right way. We needed the right design. Quickly.

IN THE RAINFOREST

ALL NET GAIN—ALL PROFIT— IS CREATED BY DESIGN

In the rainforest, we learned earlier, mangrove shrubs grow quickly to create and fill a mangrove swamp. Yet, paradoxically, mangroves are not adapted to endure in the environment they create. Their design is right to create a mangrove swamp but not to survive in one. Their feedback is direct and powerful. Upon filling the area available for a swamp, they hit their limit, and they die.

But they have served a purpose. In the nest they created, a thousand new species will thrive, species whose form and structure give them a host of capacities absent in the species that gave rise to them. The secret to the success of these K-strategists, these specialists, is their shape, their structure—their design.

Look deep into the mangrove—and into every species in the swamp, the forest, and beyond—and you will find that each is made of the same parts: cells, which are made of molecules, which are made of atoms, which are made of subatoms, and so on. The value of every thing in nature is defined not by what it is made of but by how its parts are arranged—again, its structure, or design.

Nature follows three strategies to create value by design. The first strategy is **integration**, when dissociated parts come together in a new design, creating a cohesive whole. Integration leads to synergy and *breakthrough innovation*—the emergence of new qualities, such as when atoms come together to form molecules, or molecules to form cells.

The second strategy is **replication**, when identical copies are made of the design that produced the successful innovation. Replication leads to *growth*—an increase in size or number, such as when cells reproduce.

The third strategy is **differentiation**, through variations of the successful innovation, often as an adaptive response to the demands of the environment. Differentiation leads to an increase in variety, efficiency, or quality, such as through sexual reproduction and natural selection.

These three strategies work in business, too. But in a machine-based industrial economy, the dominant strategy for wealth creation is strategy two: replication. Machines take in raw materials, tear them apart, and reconstitute them as identical copies of a prototype design,

HOW NATURE GETS MORE FROM LESS
It Creates Profit by Design

Natural systems generate two types of capital:
HARD CAPITAL—physical resources
SOFT CAPITAL—design and embedded knowledge

HARD CAPITAL	SOFT CAPITAL
Physical	Design or
resources—	arrangements
building blocks	of building blocks
	that exhibit
	emergent properties

while discarding nonproduct pollution and waste. So long as replication is balanced by a heavy emphasis on the other two value-creating strategies, it can be a sustainable form of value creation. But because replication relies on the transformation of physical resources from one form to another, extensive reliance on it can lead to destructive, nonsustainable levels of consumption.

The heavy emphasis of the industrial economy on replication tends to cultivate false beliefs about the source of value. According to the machine model of business, it is natural to think we create value by taking in resources and churning out products, plus pollution, plus waste. But a business does not create profit by consuming raw materials. Never. It may *realize* and *privatize* profit that way, but it does not create it that way. *All profit, all value, is created by design.*

Trees are made mostly of air, cars mostly of rock, computers mostly of dirt. What makes them trees, cars, and computers rather than air, rock, and dirt is their design, their structure, the way their parts are arranged. The Japanese language has two terms to describe this: *omote* and *ura*. *Omote* is the surface or front of an object. *Ura* is its back or invisible side. *Omote* and *ura*—external reality and underlying reality.

We are beginning to learn the value of understanding these two realities in business. A microchip's *omote*—its physical content, mostly sand—isn't very valuable. But a microchip's *ura*—its shape, structure, and hidden design—is extraordinarily valuable. It comes from a source that seems almost unlimited—the knowledge we draw from nature and the human mind. This knowledge is the most valuable resource, and the most abundant one.

To review: Design is information; information adds value. Every unique design creates a unique resource, a unique form of value. Because of this phenomenon, every one of nature's system designs is synergetic, meaning that its whole is more than the sum of its parts. Furthermore, by taking one of nature's designs and combining it with another, we create a third design, another new resource, with a new set of qualities and capacities. Sexual reproduction follows this principle, but the principle also applies at smaller and more fundamental levels. One proton and neutron together yield the simplest form of atom—hydrogen—and chemical reaction. Three protons yield the simplest metal—lithium—and conductivity. The marriage of common elements in new combinations yields unique qualities.

Throughout nature, things are continuously broken down and built up in new forms. Plants and animals consume the air, water, and minerals around them, as well as one another, breaking everything into pieces they can use and spending their capacities. Then, they take those pieces and make them into a part of their own body or body system, building them up into more complex forms. The physical parts lose the capacities of their previous form but gain others in their new form. In the forest, nature is ever destructive, imposing costs every time any resource is used. There are tearing-down and building-up processes, destruction and creation, constantly at play.

No designer or conscious entity is required for this design process to be carried out. The ten dominos of value creation fall on their own. Actions lead to feedback, adaptation, and specialization; specialists, dependent on one another, must join to form new wholes; these new wholes are new designs, from which emerge new kinds of value.

But, necessary or not, consciousness can be a handy strategic advantage. As skydivers falling to earth, we can unconsciously smash to the ground, one life after another, until by process of selection, an alternative strategy is encoded in the genes of our more sensible coun-terparts. That's adaptation by force. Or we can consciously apply our good sense, and adapt by choice.

DESIGN	WHAT IT IS	EMERGENT PROPERTIES
•	Point	Location
•——•	Two points Line	Distance
△	Three points Triangle	Area
◿	Four points Tetrahedron Carbon 60	Volume

IN BUSINESS

MAXIMIZE PROFIT BY DESIGN

Mark a single point on paper, and you define a new dimension: *location*. Now mark another point. That gives you two points, plus a second dimension: *distance*, defined by the invisible line connecting the points. Mark another point not on the same line. That gives you three points plus two more lines in between them and a third dimension: *area*, defined by the three lines of the triangle. Mark another point not on the same plane. That gives you four points plus six lines, plus four triangles, and another new dimension: *volume*.

Each time you add a new point, you get more than a point in return. Your gain is both quantitative and qualitative: In the example above, a single point can yield as many as three new lines and three new triangles, plus a whole new quality not present in the previous form— a new dimension.

This last observation bears emphasis: *The gain comes in two forms, quantitative and qualitative.* You get greater efficiency—a greater measurable output for a given input. With the third point, *two* additional lines emerge. But you also gain a new quality, a new dimension that can't be measured according to pre-existing qualities. With the third point, you get *volume*.

Nature generates value in much the same way. Break down any *thing* in nature, and you find that it is made of the same stuff: subatomic particles like quarks that have no mass, no weight, no location, no dimension. Value emerges as these component parts are brought together in unique combinations. These combinations yield something new—a new quality or dimension not present in the parts, only in the whole.

Combine quarks to form protons and neutrons, for example, and matter is born. Combine protons and neutrons to form atoms, and elements are born—more than 100 distinct elements, each with unique qualities defined by its structure. Combine atoms to form molecules, and water and air are born, along with thousands of chemical compounds, each again with unique qualities defined by its signature structure. Combine molecules in the proper relationship to form cells, and life is born. Combine simple cells with simple cells to form prokaryotes, and consciousness is born.

Bring all these together—air, water, bacteria, plants, animals—and communities, forests, ecosystems are born. In all these combinations and conversions of matter, both entropy and synergy are evident; something is lost and something is gained. When nutrients enter a living cell, energy is spent to break them down into their component parts—**catabolism**. Then, the components are arranged into new structures—**anabolism**. In these new, more complex forms, with a greater concentration of interconnections, new qualities emerge. Loss leads to gain, entropy to synergy.

The industrial economy and all effective pioneer species are very good at the first half of this process—catabolism, entropy, breaking down resources and spending them. For three centuries we have consumed vast quantities of fossil fuels and raw materials, hunting and gathering them across the globe, tearing down mountains and forests in the process, and building new mountains of waste in their place. But pioneers are just that: They lay the ground for something to follow, something that arrives only when the pioneers have approached the limits to their growth.

MATTER, INFORMATION, AND THE MICROCHIP

Recently, as we have begun to approach the limits to consumptive growth, we have begun to tap a more sustainable source of value: design. Intel cofounder Gordon Moore suggests how in a parable about the invention of the microchip:

We needed a substrate for our chips. So we looked at the substrate of the earth itself. It was mostly sand. So we used that. We needed a metal conductor for the wires and switches on the chip. We looked at all the metals in the earth and found aluminum was the most abundant. So we used that. We needed an insulator and we saw that the silicon in sand mixed with the oxygen in the air to form silicon dioxide—a kind of glass. The perfect insulator to protect the chip. So we used that.

If only chip making—hugely consumptive of energy and dependent on layer after layer of toxic material were environmentally benign. But Moore is right in a larger sense. He understands that when we bring together simple, abundant materials in unique combinations, new value emerges. The microchip is just one example. The Internet economy it spawned is just the beginning of a new era. Within our reach is an economy that could leave behind many of the chemical toxins, strip mines, clear cuts, and sweatshops of the industrial era—even the toxins required to make chips the way we do today. An economy with advanced materials made of simple, safe ingredients that enable everything from superefficient cars to the communication nodes of the Web. Organic plastics that grow from corn. Solar cells that turn sunlight to electricity. Computers, software, the Internet, smart manufacturing, new forms of agriculture, and nature-inspired technology.

How does information make it possible to enhance both the economy and the environment? How can we design products and processes that use less energy and fewer materials and produce fewer toxins? There is only one way—by being smarter.

When Toyota or Honda makes a car that is just as good as a Chrysler but is cheaper, safer, cleaner, and more fuel-efficient, that company has found a smarter way to design it. It has replaced fossil fuels and raw materials with knowledge.

We have said that there are two ways to use knowledge as a substitute for resources in a product. One is to make a product smarter—continuous improvement. The other is to make a smarter product—breakthrough innovation.

Breakthrough innovations create whole new seeds, which can then be replicated over and over, creating even more value. Breakthrough innovations include Ford's first assembly line, Intel's first microprocessor, Xerox's first PC, CoorsTek's advanced ceramics. When a breakthrough proves successful in the marketplace, it is replicated, each time reproducing the value by the breakthrough design. Continuous improvements increase the efficiency, quality, and variety of these innovations. They are the succeeding generations of Intel chip, the new features added to the PC motherboard, every process improvement that improves the ceramic.

The two work hand-in-hand. Breakthrough innovations create products like the plant and the eye, the steam engine and the microchip. Continuous improvements refine them in ways that improve efficiency and adaptiveness. The leaf enables photosynthesis, the eye improves adaptiveness. Industrial machines improved the productivity of agriculture, computers the productivity of industry.

CREATIVE COMBINATIONS

Species use the power of design even to foster new creative combinations. Whether to attract a victim, customer, strategic partner, or mate, plants and animals seduce one another with what we call **concentrated attractors**—colors, odors, and tastes that appeal to the target species, offered up in concentrated form so their allure is irresistible. For example, a Costa Rican orchid has a nectar so intoxicating that no bee can stay away. Like an addict, the bee just keeps coming back. Each time, after the slightest taste, the bee becomes so inebriated it slips into a small bucket of liquid. The only escape is to wiggle out beneath an overhanging rod, which showers the bee's back with pollen. So specific is the hybridization that the shape and structure of insects and plants co-evolve so that pollen attaches to a position on the insect's body that allows it to be later deposited to a precise receptor on the plant.

Other species use **concentrated repellants** to ward off threats. The poison dart frog is an example. In Costa Rica we could hardly miss them, brightly colored in green, red, and black, and moving slowly. We didn't know better, but potential predators do: The frogs' bright colors warn them that their mucous glands produce a bitter poison that can immediately paralyze a bird or monkey.

It doesn't take a marketing genius to see how humans have used concentrated attractors and repellants to sell products: foods decorated with bright colors and filled with sugar and fat, with the nutrients squeezed out; people decorated with flashy clothes and cosmetics, implying inner qualities they may not have developed. In modest proportions, concentrated attractors add spice to life. But in the long term, the overuse of concentrated attractors to drive profits—the strategy of a pioneer species of economy—can diminish business as an institution and discredit the efforts of business leaders to assert their commitment to social responsibility. Although concentrated attractors have their place, they are best used as a spice to entice, rather than the main course.

As we leave the machine economy behind and cultivate a living economy, we discover new drivers for business profit that nourish and renew the whole of society—not the exploitation of existing accumulations of value, which spends down our riches, but the cultivation of new value and the continuous renewal of our economy and culture through innovation.

CHAPTER FIVE

Innovation

LESSON FIVE:
MAKE PRODUCTS BETTER,
AND MAKE BETTER PRODUCTS

IN THE RAINFOREST, *there are two paths to innovation:*
The first, breakthrough innovation, creates prototypes to be
replicated. The second, continuous improvement, adapts
designs to meet local conditions.

IN BUSINESS *too, the two paths to innovation are linked,*
one leading to the other. Breakthrough innovations reveal
new synergies—new capacities that were beyond our reach
before. Continuous improvement hones these capacities
toward perfection, and creates the diverse parts that can
combine in new, breakthrough wholes.

Because the parachute slows our fall without fundamentally changing our direction we could call that *continuous improvement.* The ability to fly, if we could develop it quickly, would be a *breakthrough innovation.* However, if the ground were not below us, we would have no need for either. We could continue to fall through the sky forever, never bothering to pull our ripcords to slow our fall or look to the birds and wish we could fly. So, in a way, it's good that the ground is beneath us. Limits are essential catalysts to evolution and change.

Like babies in the womb, innovations lie in wait, *in potentia*, until called into use by need. Necessity may not always be the mother of invention, but it is the midwife. It births ideas and inventions buried deep within us, often at the moment they become vital to life.

IN THE RAINFOREST

THERE ARE TWO FORMS OF INNOVATION— BREAKTHROUGH INNOVATION AND CONTINUOUS IMPROVEMENT

In the face of impending demise, nature experiments and tries, in every way she can, to survive. Her attempts often fail, but occasionally they succeed. When they do, she "takes notes" and keeps records. Through the process of natural selection, she encodes the how to's of survival in the DNA of her organisms; in more complex species she records them in the memories of individuals or the patterns of culture, so that successful qualities are passed along to future generations.

Nature's two basic forms of innovation—breakthrough innovation and continuous improvement—function throughout many of her systems. Cells reproduce in two ways, for example: Mitosis creates occasional, sudden discontinuities; meiosis creates continuous variety. Planets seem to evolve through **catastrophism,** sudden change caused by catastrophic events such as asteroid collisions and volcanic eruptions, and through **uniformitarianism,** continuing everyday processes that operate slowly. Even the evolution of species seems to happen both incrementally, through adaptation and natural selection, and by more sudden transformations. Evolutionary scientists point to long periods of gradual change, punctuated by sudden transformations, a process some call **punctuated equilibrium**.

Charles Darwin is famous for focusing on one of nature's two strategies: continuous incremental change. He was also fascinated by the second strategy—breakthrough evolutionary leaps—but was confounded by it as well. What exactly were breakthrough changes? Was a different process at work? And are incremental and breakthrough changes related in some way?

What puzzled Darwin was how advanced physical adaptations, those breakthrough innovations that led to whole new *qualities*, emerged. His favorite example was the eye, whose intricate combination of lens, iris, and retina seems to defy the plausibility of incremental development. Given that half-an-eye would be more a hindrance than a help to survival, how could the complete mechanism of the eye have come about through gradual variation? "About the weak points [of incremental natural selection] I agree," Darwin wrote to his American friend Asa Gray. "The eye to this day gives me a cold shudder" (Kelly 1994, 367).

Evolutionary biologists debate the point endlessly. In the 1990s, a new theoretical framework called **intelligent design** began to emerge as a consequence of the debate. Adherents such as Dr. Michael J. Behe, biology professor at Lehigh University in Pennsylvania, argue that various biochemical structures in cells could not have been built in the step-by-step Darwinian fashion.

Some systems theorists argue that breakthrough innovation is a consequence of **downward causation.** In their view, "suprasystems," such as the human body, reach down and effectively regulate the actions of subsystems within them, such as our individual organs and their components, so that their actions collectively serve the survival interests of the whole. Billions of bacteria reside in every cell; billions of cells reside in every organ. These, in turn, are incremental parts of our bodies, regulated in ways that enhance our survival. Humanity in this view, rather than being at the outermost edge of nature's creative endeavors, may be part of a much larger, more encompassing whole, which only gradually comes into our view as we approach limits.

In the rainforest, one sees the suprasystem model in play. Young rainforests with relatively few species are born, grow, and gradually differentiate into more complex, ancient rainforests. In the process new species emerge that fill in a growing array of niches. Over time, new capacities emerge in which the freedom experienced by individual species expands. In a sense, the fully developed rainforest "exists" in the ura, the underside of the simple rainforest, as its potential. Perhaps the ura can be seen as a kind of cast, which is gradually filled in with an array of capacities as the forest and its species evolve.

Look again at the ten dominos of evolution. Pioneers, in the face of certain limits, are forced to adapt. Adaptations lead to more specialized plants and animals, which together fill the multiplying niches of a more diverse ecosystem. A single pioneer species is succeeded by a rich array of specialists. A single fern differentiates into 800 varieties. An embryo differentiates into male or female; then in adulthood, male and female join together to form a new whole. And in these wholes emerge new qualities. A new forest, a new genus, a new embryo. Later these wholes, too, face new limits, and the process repeats.

In this way, nature is always breathing out and breathing in, segregating and integrating, creating a wider array of species from the realm of the possible. Systems scientists call this process *synergy*, by which the whole system is more than the sum of its parts.

In the rainforest, synergy creates a new whole from every new combination of parts—soil, water, air, products of decay, and so on. In business, synergy does the same thing, but with information as a substitute for physical resources; information is the "more" that enables us to use "less." It creates the profit, the surplus, that keeps everything running. It's what happens when we get the design right.

In life, synergy is, for example, the meaning that springs from the words on this page; the taste of sugar from carbon, hydrogen, and oxygen melting together on your tongue; the power that drives you to work, when hydrogen and carbon join to form a fossil fuel; the beam of the laser that reads your CDs and provides you with music.

Nature forms a vast continuity that stretches from the simplest toward the most complex. At every level, synergy plays a part. This continuity is often described as a hierarchy, not in the sense we use the term in business, connoting domination and control, but in the sense that simple structures form the foundation for ever more complex ones, all related. At each level of the hierarchy—or the **holarchy**, to use philosopher Ken Wilber's term—new qualities emerge that are not present lower in the hierarchy: energy, matter, life, consciousness, choice. Each is a step along a path; each forms the foundation for the next; each harbors qualities revealed only with the next combination, at the next level.

IN BUSINESS

BREAKTHROUGH INNOVATION AND CONTINUOUS IMPROVEMENT ARE LINKED

Gordon Moore, the cofounder of Intel, suggested a link between incremental and breakthrough change four decades ago. In 1965, Moore published an article projecting the future of semiconductors. "Taking the little bit of data then based on the first few generations of integrated circuits, I postulated that the complexity of integrated circuits was going to double every year for the next ten years . . . (and that) the cost of doing things electronically was going to continue to decrease dramatically."

"Moore's Law" was the result. Moore's Law is usually paraphrased to say that performance doubles and price halves about every 18 months. In semiconductors, that overall two-times-two, or "factor four," gain has happened at least every two years.

Moore's prediction was borne out. In 1968, Intel's chips held 1,024 bits of information. By 1994, that had grown 1000-fold, to 1,024,000. The first Pentium chips processed that information with 3.1 million transistors per chip. By 2000, the Pentium 4 had 42 million transistors. Designs completed for commercial production by 2007 could have a billion.

Each time storage and processing capacity rises, breakthroughs in performance are made possible. Microprocessors enable PCs. PCs enable the popularity of the Internet. The Internet revolutionizes teaching, learning, and global communication. New possibilities spin out in ever-widening spirals, changing everything.

But the most promising possibilities of advanced microchips may not be realized for a very long time. Let's explore why.

APPLYING MOORE'S LAW: HOW TO MEASURE QUANTITATIVE AND QUALITATIVE GAINS

It's easy to measure continuous improvement. But qualitative gain is tougher to measure, because it's new and different. How much greater is the computing power of a microchip, compared to raw silica? How much greater is one than zero? Infinitely greater, since the latter lacks the quality of the former.

One way to illustrate the relationship between quantitative and qualitative gain is through a measurement tool called the *Power Function*, a measure of resource productivity any company can monitor. The Power Function doesn't measure qualitative change, but it helps showcase the relationship between incremental and breakthrough change.

The Power Function is output over input. Performance over price.

Innovation over improvement. Qualitative gains over quantitative efficiencies. Or, if you like, performance multiplied by savings.

The Power Function is a measure of resource productivity that
helps illustrate a curious feature of the new economy and of all
complex systems—the same feature Moore highlighted. As efficiencies
improve, thresholds of complexity are surpassed, creating *tipping points*
at which new capabilities emerge. Reductions in cost trigger increases
in benefits. Reductions in entropy yield gains through synergy. Each
half of the Power Function reinforces the other.

Here's how it works. The Power Function is a simple ratio of
inputs to outputs that allows us to measure the combined effects of
breakthrough innovations and continuous efficiency improvements.
You can express the idea using different terms, depending on what
community you come from. If you're an economist, it's benefit over
cost. To a systems scientist, it's synergy over entropy. To an industrial
ecologist, it's outputs over inputs.

You can also play with the numbers lots of ways. For example,
divide the cost reduction by the performance gain and you get
Resource Intensity. Over time, improvement gives you a downward-
sloping curve, good if you're trying to illustrate to environmentalists
that you're reducing harm to the earth. Or turn that ratio upside down,
and you get Resource Productivity. That gives you an upward-sloping
curve, excellent for reports to investors. Or multiply the cost reduction
by the performance improvement and you get the Factor Gain. Amory
Lovins's book *Factor Four* takes this approach.

Too conceptual? Here are some examples. To understand the
cumulative effect of the Power Function, follow it through two streams
of development—the PC and the Internet—including the point around
1975 when they converged in a torrent.

This is important: Note that in every example, part of the gain can
be measured, and part of it can't. That's because part of the gain is a *continuous improvement* of a capacity already established, and the other part
is *a whole new capacity*, a breakthrough innovation that can be measured
only once it actually comes into existence. Thus, each new capacity creates a new, irreducible baseline and a unit for future comparison.

THE PERSONAL COMPUTER
AND THE INTERNET

INTERNET, WEB, IBM, APPLE, MICROSOFT, INTEL, AND CISCO

Packet-switching yields a Factor 10 gain—and Arpanet. Back in 1960, UCLA computer science professor Len Kleinrock proposed in a paper that AT&T could dramatically boost the speed and volume of data transmission over its wires by switching from circuit-switching to what he called packet-switching technology. Assuming a ten-fold improvement—a conservative estimate given later performance—that's an initial Factor 10 gain.

AT&T wasn't interested in packet-switching. It was happy with circuit-switching and saw no reason to change. But Larry Roberts and Bob Taylor at the U.S. Department of Defense's Advanced Research Projects Agency (ARPA) liked the concept and decided to try it. In 1969 ARPA commissioned a small Cambridge engineering firm, Bolt, Berenek, & Newman (BBN), to build ARPAnet, the first long-distance computer network, to tie together computers at ARPA and leading university research centers.

Arpanet yields a Factor 3 gain—and the router, and the LAN. Ten months later, on October 1, 1969, ARPAnet sent its first message—"LO," hello—from UCLA to Stanford. Researchers found that with ARPAnet, they no longer needed their own battery of mainframe computers to do their work. They could tie in easily to other computers on the net.

By 1973, computer networking was so successful that it allowed Taylor to cut ARPA's computer budget 70 percent, more than paying the costs of ARPAnet. The enhanced communication among research labs yielded plenty of performance gains—after all, that was the objective of the technology. No one foresaw that it would cut equipment costs, too. But assuming zero performance gain, the computer cost savings alone brought a better than Factor 3 gain.

One of ARPAnet's innovations was the invention of an early router, which reduced the data load on host computers. That yielded another unexpected gain: Host sites could hook not just one but any number of

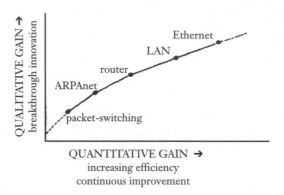

Now the stage was set for what we now call the Internet, the vast network connecting smaller networks including PCs that by the end of the century was the world's fastest-growing communications system. When did the personal computer enter the picture?

computers to the net. That led to a further gain. The centers soon realized their own computers could now talk to one another. Before that time, different models and brands of computers weren't on "speaking terms," but ARPAnet changed that. The same technology that enabled them to communicate long-distance also allowed them to tie in locally. That improved local performance and set the stage for the rapid expansion of another computer innovation, local area networks, or LANs.

The router and LANs yield Ethernet—and a Factor 1000 gain. One of the leaders in LAN development was Xerox Palo Alto Research Center (PARC), a playground for scientists and engineers set up by Xerox to develop products for the always-imminent "paperless office." By 1974, PARC was one of 64 sites linked to the ARPAnet. There, PARC connected it with one of their many home-grown innovations, Ethernet, which allowed them to tie not just mainframes but personal computers into the net—and increased speed one thousand-fold. Factor Gain: 1000 or more.

Intel's microprocessor yields a Factor 100 gain—and the personal computer, and a Factor 1000 gain. In 1970, IBM was the dominant computer maker of the day, and much like AT&T and packet-switching, it was satisfied with what it had, the mainframe computer, and it had no reason to change.

When Intel launched the 8080 microprocessor, or "chip," in 1974, it inadvertently pulled the rug—slowly—out from under IBM's stable platform. The 8080 replaced thousands of vacuum tubes, each about three times the size of a standard light bulb. Yet this microprocessor was faster, cheaper, more efficient, and more reliable. Assume conservatively that, by mass, the efficiency gain was 100-fold and that performance was equal. The Resource Intensity baseline improvement is 1/100: The chip consumed 1/100th the resources of vacuum tubes per unit of service. The Resource Productivity is 100/1, or 100: The chip was 100 times as resource productive as the tube. The Factor Gain was 1 x 100, or 100.

Intel's 8080 chip also improved the *performance* of computers, while it made them cheaper, true to Moore's law. It brought enough power to enable Ed Roberts to invent the Altair, the world's first personal computer. The Altair reportedly worked up to ten times as fast as the mainframe computers of its day and, at $500 versus $50,000, was 100 times cheaper than the typical research lab computer of 1975. That's 10 x 100, or as much as a Factor 1000 gain.

The PC was (to borrow a software term) the "killer app" innovation that eventually handed Intel its most lucrative market. Interestingly, when an Intel engineer proposed that the company build a personal computer, Gordon Moore thought it impractical. Steve Jobs and Steve Wozniak knew what Intel had. They formed Apple Computer, and Wozniak built the Apple II. Unfortunately, the 8080 cost $175 and was too expensive for their price point. So Wozniak used MOS's 6502 chip, which cost $25 and offered four times the performance per clock cycle—an edge that helped earn Apple a promising foothold in its niche. Jobs packaged it in a user-friendly unit that looked less like a lab instrument and more like a toaster oven, and Apple was off and running.

The Altair PC yielded the Apple II—and a Factor 2 gain. Once again, the Power Function opened the door. The Apple II seemed to be an impossible dream. To make it work required too many chips to make it affordable. But Wozniak didn't know it was impossible, so he designed his way around it. "Why have memory for your TV screen *and* memory for your computer, make them one," he figured. "That shrunk the chips down. And all these timing circuits—I looked through manuals and found a chip that did it in one chip instead of five, and reduced that. One thing after another after another happened."

Wozniak's ingenious use of chips gave the Apple II at least a Factor 2 to Factor 5 gain over the Altair, *on top* of previous gains. Jobs' user-friendly additions added further performance gains, hard to measure because the Apple II was qualitatively different but extraordinarily important because it busted the microcomputer out of the hobbyist niche and made it attractive to a mass market.

Each new generation of chip yielded a Factor 4 gain—and eventually, the Internet. In the years that followed, Intel—initially to equip IBM's new machines and what were called "IBM-compatible" machines—created new generations of chip: the 8088, 186, 286, 386, 486, Pentium, and so on. Each new generation of Intel chips roughly followed Moore's Law: double the performance, half the price. So, each generation yielded an additional 2 x 2, or Factor 4 gain.

Performance, however, can be measured quantitatively—increase in speed or accuracy, for example. Or it can be measured qualitatively, in terms of gains that are strikingly different in nature. Once Intel's 386 chip arrived, people could buy a desktop PC with a whole new set of qualities. It could, for example, tie into the Internet, and then—new world. Hence the two streams of breakthrough innovation and continuous improvement merged and created a torrent of connectivity. In 1969, there were two hosts on the Internet. By 1977, 100. By 1984, 1000. Three years later, 10,000. Two years later in 1989, 100,000. In 1992, one million. And just a year later, by 1993, the World Wide Web, the multimedia component of the Internet, was growing 341,000 percent per year.

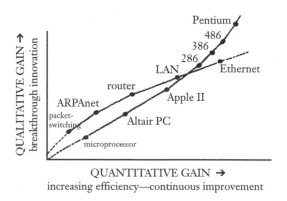

The Internet yielded Factor 10 gains in commerce—and a global economic web. The synergetic explosion set loose by the convergence of the PC and the Internet created a new world of instantaneous global communication, and commerce, accessible almost free to anyone with a computer and a phone jack. That broke down elitist gateways and drew millions into the cyberworld of self-generating information brokered by—after the introduction of the first Web browser software, Mosaic, in 1993—organizations like Yahoo! and America Online. The Internet began to hint of its power.

Soon Amazon.com, eBay, and others showed that the Web could be a consumer marketplace, eliminating the need for stores. Buying books from Amazon, instead of driving to the bookstore, yields up to a Factor 10 energy gain if you use ground shipping. eBay enabled people to trade directly, eliminating middlemen. And for people who wanted content alone, Yahoo! and Google delivered a global library of free information. Commerce without stores, content without cost.

That final point is critical. The Internet culture drove the creation and delivery of easy-access content by insisting that content be free. That changed after eBay and others proved the potential of the Web for direct peer-to-peer commerce. Their success drew thousands of would-be successors, as new dot-coms vied for market niches that had not yet even been defined. No one could implement a viable business model until everyone else's venture capital pretty much ran dry. Early dot-coms like Amazon and eBay were often refinements of the old industrial model, not whole new forms. They mimicked a bookstore or garage sale, but retained many of the costs of the industrial model, including warehouses, trucks, and products.

That contributed to the dot-com crash of 2000. The *competitive exclusion principle*, as always, held: If two or more species seek the identical niche, only one can survive. Thus the dot-coms collectively brought about their own early collapse.

But the fall of a few thousand dot-coms is not a sign of failure of the industry. Henry Ford, after all, put as many as 300 early automakers out of business. For any one pioneer firm, the odds of success are long.

The emergence of the Infosphere. The Internet remains young and constrained both by its own youth and that of the emerging system of which it is a part. The Internet is just one aspect of what we now call the *information economy*. It is one part of a just-emerging *Infosphere*, still a few more Factor leaps away.

The Infosphere, says Michael Vlahos, will have emergent qualities much greater than those of the networks it connects. The integration of these networks into one suprasystem will change the character of each individual network. "Networks will no longer serve simply as the medium through which people in different places can communicate, enhancing their *in situ* activities," says Vlahos. "The global integration of networks creates a network ecology—literally, a place in which people can gather, conduct business, share ideas, and build relationships. People will be able to conduct their activities increasingly in the global network ecology—the Infosphere."

The proto-Infosphere is already beginning to offer a taste of these benefits. People are finding that they can do business there, while happily pruning overhead and travel, and freeing their geographic reach. As the Infosphere becomes essential to commerce, it will become essential to most people as well. It will then be ratified in the life of society.

The real potential lies in the shift from an industrial economy *refined* by information, as exemplified by Amazon, toward a truly new economy *founded* on it, one that creates value dynamically and synergistically in the Infosphere—a place where industry plays a supporting role in a new system that transcends it, just as agriculture plays a supporting role in the industrial world today. This is what sets the Internet apart from past systems of communication, this extraordinary flow of information-on-information, extending not in linear form but through a web, not in one direction but all directions, not with static content and reruns, but with dynamic, living content that changes as it's used.

If all goes well, the Infosphere will not be under the control of any centralized institution; instead, it will be emergent from the actions of millions of engaged participants. The Internet is like an enzyme that speeds the pace of global communication, learning, and change. It isn't solid, it isn't physical. It's information, communication, relationship, an ever-evolving design, whereby the design itself, not the observer, is primary. It can access information in such vast quantities. It can create new information without direction from anyone. It can self-organize the information and make it available like never before. And all for pennies. It's ubiquitous, cheap, and global. "It's like water in a thirsty desert," says

Internet consultant Aileen Ichikawa. "It was never there, then one day, bam, it is! And flowers spring up overnight and the desert comes alive and the landscape is transformed." In ways that no one yet fully knows.

How Wintel's Dominance Threatens the Infosphere

Pioneer species prepare the ground for more resilient species to follow. Sometimes the pioneer continues to thrive in new, more narrowly drawn niches. Other times, the pioneer is so inflexible that after dominating its niche for a time, it finally collapses, once the superior capacities of its successors overwhelm it.

The Intel x86 is the pioneer microprocessor architecture in personal computing. By tying itself to this architecture, Windows has become the dominant operating system. But just as the earth's first *anaerobic* life support system could not support more advanced forms of life that required oxygen, the Wintel platform will not be able to support—and may deter—the healthy development of the Infosphere.

Perhaps ten or twenty more factor leaps in computing productivity will be needed for the Infosphere to fully emerge. Advanced platforms provide factor leaps by enabling software developers to concentrate on the architecture of innovative features and human interface design rather than on routine tasks like drawing windows and managing text. This reduces the chasm between human interaction, machine readable code, and productive output and makes it possible to achieve breakthroughs in application capabilities and performance with minimal coding.

Among the most important computing breakthroughs are operating systems that rely on *modular design*. A modern operating system includes a core operating system that schedules tasks for processing and manages hardware resources, one or more application development environments with interfaces that provide reusable code for software development, and one or more human interfaces. In a modular operating system each of these major layers includes a number of distinct modules. With modular design, software developers can easily add or replace modules with superior or special purpose components without hidden code dependencies interfering with the rest of the system.

A related breakthrough is *object oriented programming*. Object oriented application environments provide developers with reusable software "objects" that replace millions of lines of code that would otherwise would have to be written for each individual application, in many cases offering a Factor Ten gain or better. By combining these information-packed "objects" in various ways, even casual users can create custom applications with advanced features, first creating the application interface and then linking its interface elements to existing "objects" that do almost all of the work. That could democratize programming, making it accessible to many more people than ever, much as the printing press democratized reading and writing.

Another important breakthrough is microprocessors that rely on *reduced instruction set computing* (RISC). RISC microprocessors have fewer instructions than complex instruction set (CISC) counterparts like the Pentium IV. This enables microprocessor designers to use less complicated logic and makes for a more efficient overall design. RISC already offers at least Factor Four improvements in processing power, price, and energy efficiency, with more to come.

Like the rainforest, modular design, object oriented programming, and RISC processing do more with less. These innovations closely imitate the elegant design of living organisms, in which nature uses the dynamic organization of a relatively small number of kinds of cells to create its vast diversity of complex life forms from scarce resources. This elegant design is a key to making the power of the Infosphere available to the many rather than the few.

In a competitive market, these innovations would likely have penetrated deeply by now. But the dominance of the Wintel, and its power to thwart competition, makes it virtually impossible for even superior competitors to gain a foothold. Although these innovations have already been proven in isolated niches, they remain endangered by the Wintel monoculture.

NeXTSTEP, introduced in 1988, offered a graphical user interface more elegant and powerful than the acclaimed Macintosh and an object oriented application environment that enabled "drag-and-drop" programming by people with minimal programming expertise. It allowed individuals and small teams to rapidly develop sophisticated applications with advanced capabilities. Its successor, the multiplatform OpenStep, ran on a variety of different micro-processor architectures. Of greater importance, the OpenStep application environment was a distinct module than also ran on other operating systems, bypassing many of their most limiting features. Applications written for OpenStep were thus able to run on those systems, offering developers the crucial "write once, run anywhere" capability popularized years later by Java.

The Be operating system, introduced in 1996, was developed from its foundations as a cross-platform operating system. It specializes in a different set of digital age capabilities. It enables software developers to break large tasks into smaller tasks and precisely orchestrate the way the microprocessor carries them out. This delivers unparalleled performance for advanced video and audio production, virtual reality, and other next generation digital media applications. It also offers the speed and responsiveness to take full advantage of next-generation optical fiber networks and realize advanced peer-to-peer computing.

OpenStep and Be embraced modular design and open interfaces, allowing developers and even individual users to rapidly integrate new media standards, file systems, or other features and enable applications written by different developers to communicate and share services. This enables component-by-component evolution of these platforms and, like the rainforest, allows superior small components to find a niche. It also makes it easy to combine the best technologies from multiple sources.

Workstations from Sun and IBM have used RISC processing for over a decade, but its real potential is providing PC users with supercomputing power at low cost and energy use so they can run demanding Infosphere applications.

These technologies offer the promise of making custom Infosphere applications like television quality desktop webcasting, personal software agents, three dimensional videoconferencing, and simultaneous language translation available to everyone, instead of just large institutions, vastly enriching the worldwide conversation that today's web has begun.

But Wintel rejected modular design, object oriented programming, and RISC. Why? For the same reasons AT&T stayed with circuit-switching. Just as AT&T's capital, knowledge, and culture was trapped in the old system, Microsoft and Intel have huge investments in these old architectures. And Wintel is not switching now, because moving to a new architecture would make it easy for users to move to a platform other than Wintel. That would open up a market where its share is now over 90 percent, a forest in which they are already the dominant species. So Wintel continues to worship at the altar of backward compatibility. Every new generation of Wintel remains constrained by obsolete predecessors, forcing the world to adapt.

In 1991, Apple, IBM and Motorola formed an alliance to produce the Power PC, a RISC processor for the desktop. In 1994 this alliance announced the Common Hardware Reference Platform (CHRP), an open platform specification, as a broadside against the Wintel platform, promising twice the performance of Intel processors at half the price. Motorola and IBM invested billions. Combining the existing market share of Apple's Macintosh plus IBM's new OS/2 would have given CHRP 25 percent of the operating system market, enhanced competition, and provided a habitat for multiple operating systems like OpenStep and Be. This would have made it easy for people to switch from one to another *without buying a whole new computer.*

Microsoft initially supported CHRP, porting Windows NT over to the new platform. But when it realized the ease of switching to other operating systems would threaten the Wintel monopoly, it decided to kill CHRP by withdrawing support at a critical moment. Without Windows, CHRP was less attractive as a common platform. Hardware developers and critical customers lost confidence in its viability, and the promise of effective competition in the personal computer market faded.

Then Wintel received a surprise assist from an unexpected source—Apple. After Steve Jobs and his allies regained control of the company in 1997, Jobs announced a "normalization" of relations with Microsoft. Microsoft dropped its recurring threat to cancel Office for Macintosh, and promised a version with Macintosh only features. Within weeks, OpenStep products that competed with Windows were removed from Apple's price list. Then Jobs reversed Apple's commitment to clones. He abruptly abrogated the company's licensing agreements, including those with PowerPC partners IBM and Motorola, which had already begun producing CHRP computers. That eliminated the threat to both Windows and the Pentium.

The demise of CHRP deprived Be of its habitat and forced it to switch to Intel based computers. Then Microsoft used exclusionary licensing rules to threaten the Windows licenses of several computer makers who had agreed to bundle Be as a second operating system. That placed the most advanced operating system in the market on the endangered species list. In August 2001, the Be technology was sold to Palm, which announced it has no plans to continue development of the operating system. The $11 million fire sale price was equal to about one day of Microsoft's profits.

Many people look to the open source Linux operating system as the answer to the Microsoft threat. CHRP would also have provided Linux an opportunity to effectively compete against Windows, unlike on Intel based computers where Microsoft's exclusionary licensing rules have effectively locked Linux out. Not only would CHRP aid the progress of Linux, Linux would have induced more hardware makers to produce CHRP computers. The combination might also have encouraged efforts to develop a richer application environment and user friendly interface to make Linux more attractive as a desktop operating system.

Without the market share that would be enabled by Apple clones and CHRP, Motorola and IBM couldn't generate the sales volume needed to continue major investments in the PowerPC. Meanwhile, Intel protected its monopoly by hiring away PowerPC engineers to graft RISC-like features onto to the archaic Pentium architecture.

This illustrates the dilemma facing those who want to accelerate migration to the Infosphere. Overinvestment of monopoly profits in continuous improvement of an obsolete design can outperform underinvestment in a new breakthrough design and delay, perhaps for years, its day of reckoning with innovation.

But that day of reckoning must come. Even some executives at Microsoft recognize this is ultimately inevitable. They recognize that the strategy of protecting the Windows franchise through endless interlocking of components imposes a "strategy tax" that thwarts innovation. They have pressed the company to drop the ties to Windows and Office and start fresh with a less encumbered approach to Internet software. Several such projects have been initiated in recent years. Indeed, there have been internal proposals to break Microsoft into as many as six separate companies.

But in the end Microsoft has pulled the plug on these initiatives in order to protect the Windows franchise. Microsoft's announced strategy for next generation Internet software leaves no doubt that protection and extension of its monopoly power is its highest priority.

Microsoft's partner in the de facto Wintel alliance is slowly coming around. Intel has been struggling to break away from its x86 CISC architecture and create new processors with a fresh design. But even its successors have been repeatedly delayed and their performance burdened by Microsoft's insistence that Intel build x86 compatibility into new microprocessors. So Intel continues to invest in the Pentium architecture, well beyond the point of diminishing returns, achieving higher clock speeds that maintain the illusion of Wintel superiority only by sacrificing overall performance.

What market conditions will be needed to protect modern platform technologies, encourage development of more advanced technologies, and realize the Infosphere's potential? According to Drexel Sprecher and Michael Vlahos, the crucial condition is simple. *Competition must be a la carte, no less fine grained than the process of innovation.* Everything must be able to run on everything. Developers must be free to remove, replace and combine components, and compete on the merits of each component. This will ensure robust competition, with many innovators competing to improve every type of component and many vendors competing to assemble them in different combinations.

There will be little competition or dynamism in the market for platform software if neither innovators nor users can replace anything without having to replace everything. Sprecher points out that no company or alliance can replace Wintel and its third party products at once. Even if it could, computer users have large investments in software and in the files they have created. Just as a family moving to a larger and better home expects to move most of its existing furniture and to add new furniture, users need the freedom to choose new products without having to abandon their investment in the products they already own. Sprecher identifies "Four Freedoms" necessary for a competitive market in computing platforms. The first is the freedom to switch to new applications without abandoning data. The second is the freedom to switch to a new operating system without abandoning applications. The third is the freedom to switch to a new processor architecture without abandoning operating systems. The fourth is the freedom to replace modules with superior or special purpose components.

In a competitive market this would occur naturally. Everyone would want their software to run on every other platform, and software from others to run on their platform. Competitors would have incentives to cooperate to establish standards and publish interfaces to ensure interoperability. Cross platform software would proliferate. Operating systems with multiple application environments would be common. Developers would be able to write for the application environments with the best capabilities for their specific application. Most operating systems would run on more than one processor architecture.

A competitive market would provide companies real incentives to pursue breakthrough innovations. Small producers with an idea for one great application or one great component would have a chance to bring it to market.

Reversing the current drift to monolithic platforms will require that the rules of information age competition align profit and innovation. This can be accomplished with new rules that mandate modular components, open interfaces that define all the ways a component communicates with the rest of the system, published file formats, and mandatory licensing of components. These rules would give developers the freedom to innovate and users the freedom to choose.

All of this can be accomplished without infringing on intellectual property rights. As long as there are distinct modules for distinct functions, all the code within the modules can still be proprietary, providing abundant incentives for competition.

Cross-platform competition would counter the abuse of network effects by Wintel. Just making the Windows application environment a distinct module that runs on other operating systems would make the installed base of existing Windows applications available to new competitors. That would go a long way toward breaking the "applications barrier to entry" and leveling the playing field enough to open the market to modern platforms. Making Microsoft applications and components modular and portable to other operating systems would prevent the company from using these products to extend its monopoly to cyberspace. Making Windows run on other microprocessors would restore competition and innovation in computer hardware.

Reforming the rules of competition would not deprive Wintel of any incentives for genuine competition. Microsoft could profitably sell implementations of the Windows application environment to potential competitors, who would buy it so their customers could run both legacy Windows applications and the digital age applications that can only run on more advanced systems. Microsoft could also profitably sell versions its operating system that run on other microprocessors and versions of Office and Explorer that run on other operating systems. Intel could embrace new technologies that work with all operating systems. And both would have incentives to innovate.

But why would Microsoft or Intel want to, given their current market dominance? It is much more profitable to exclude competitors and protect the monopoly. Without a competitive marketplace that allows new computing platforms to enter the market, it is likely that Wintel will continue on the path of least resistance, extending its monopoly, and it could be many years before sufficient factor leaps make a robust Infosphere a reality.

Wintel's dominance won't last forever, however. Today's Pentium runs instructions through such a complex, overconnected architecture that "Intel Inside" laptops often need fans to keep from overheating. The tens of millions of lines of commingled Windows code will be increasingly vulnerable to viruses. Leaders, citizens and courts may see the need for information age market rules to promote free and open competition. Ultimately, Wintel will lose the dominance of its niche.

But ultimately can be a long time. The persistence of an obsolete architecture vests power in the large institutions that can bear the cost of its inefficiencies, and slows the democratization of the web and the emergence of the Infosphere. The longer the computing forest remains a Wintel monoculture, the hotter its chips will grow, the more deadwood will accumulate, and the more incendiary the transition to a more diverse forest will become.

CHAPTER SIX

Diversity

LESSON SIX:
DIVERSITY = CHOICE = RESILIENCE

IN THE RAINFOREST, *diversity brings choice, and choice brings resilience and sustainability. Each diverse species is designed to excel in a particular niche—to carry out its functions there more efficiently or effectively than any other.*

IN BUSINESS *too, diversity gives a company a greater choice of tools and capacities—just what it needs to grow more efficient and more effective, to get more from less.*

I n our jump from the airplane, we each had only one kind of technology at our disposal. If this technology didn't work, we would have been out of luck.

But what if we could have chosen from any number of technologies: a parachute, a hang glider, an airplane, or even learning to fly?

IN THE RAINFOREST

DIVERSITY = CHOICE, CHOICE = RESILIENCE

Diversity promotes sustainability simply because *diversity is choice.* The more diverse the organisms in an ecosystem, the more types of resources are available to deal with any challenge and the greater the likelihood of success.

W. Ross Ashby articulated that view back in 1958, when he studied gene pools and biological adaptability and composed his **Law of Requisite Variety.** Ashby's law states that "the survival of a system depends on its ability to generate at least as much variety within its boundaries as exists in the form of threatening disturbances from its environment." In other words, the survival of any system—organism, person, company, or community—depends on its ability to adapt to challenges. If the number of challenges that it faces is even one greater than the variety it can overcome, then when faced with that challenge, it cannot survive. But while diversity is fundamental in the long term, it can involve conflict in the short run, especially when diverse elements are first thrown together in the same niche and before they have been integrated to create new wholes.

Between our trips through Corcovado and Tortuguero, we spent an afternoon in San José, the capital of Costa Rica. There we stopped at the Costa Rica Marriott, an exclusive hotel property on the outskirts of the city. The Marriott, with its formulaic are-we-in-Phoenix-or-Florida design, is one of those hotels people go to if they want to travel without going anywhere different.

To fence out diversity, seemingly in all forms, the Marriott has removed all traces of the forest that once thrived at its site and replaced much of it with a blanket of lawn, manicured so precisely that visitors could play a few rounds of Palm Springs-style golf there. Grass lawns are monocultures, pioneer species that require huge amounts of water and energy to grow and volumes of pesticides and fungicides to protect them from the species of plants and animals that in nature they are designed to attract.

Along the outer edge of the lawn, and stretching to the front gates of the hotel, is another barrier, a guarded fence and a buffer zone of undeveloped land that separates the hotel from people in the local communities. This buffer exists because San José, while one of the most affluent of central American cities, is not a uniformly safe town.

The fortress Marriott is not a classic example of a verge. It epitomizes a form of economic development that replaces one system with another, walling it off behind a border rather than integrating the two. In this way, it places cultural uniformity above diversity and may thus fail to make the investment in cultural integration vital to creativity and innovation, in nature and in business.

Verges, places where two cultures overlap, can be difficult and uncomfortable places, threatening to the stability of established interests. But it is through these cultural combinations, where the essence of one culture overlaps and ultimately integrates with another, that innovations emerge, bringing qualities to parts of life that enrich the whole.

IS DIVERSITY A HANDICAP?

Not all ecologists agree on the value of diversity. Some suggest that rather than being an asset, diversity may be a handicap. Here is one theory. Say you have a forest populated by ten major species of trees. A pest enters the forest and virtually destroys the population of one of those ten species. In most real-world cases scientists have studied, the devastated species will not fully rebound to its former population, if it rebounds at all.

Compare that to a simpler forest, one dominated by a single species of tree. If pests virtually destroy that species, it is much more likely to rebound the next season than the species in the first example. Does this fact mean that the simple forest is more resilient than the complex one?

Biologist Daniel Goodman of Montana State University suggests that this might be the case. Numerous studies support his view. Where food webs are simple—that is, made up of just a few species—populations of a reduced species will often rebound. But where food webs are complex, a reduced species may never recover. Others quickly move in to take its place. Goodman's explanation is mechanistic: "The more complex a machine," he writes, "the more things can go wrong."

Other ecologists suggest the opposite: Complex ecosystems are probably more resilient. Biologists Joseph Connell and Wayne Sousa, for example, propose a theory called *persistence within bounds*. They say that after a disturbance reduces or increases population to extreme levels, at least some members of the species will survive (*persistence . . .*), and their population will tend to rebound to a point within a broad range (*. . . within bounds*). Overall ecosystem biomass—its volume of living things—will remain essentially stable. For example, if oak and maple are common in a particular temperate forest and pestilence destroys the oak, then maple may move in to take the place of the oak and increase their own numbers. The oak will rebound, but perhaps to a much lower population than they had before.

A third set of ecologists offers another perspective. They base their belief on information theory. A species is, in essence, a form of information. Its DNA is an embedded code that defines a particular set of capabilities different from any other. The more species in an ecosystem, the more information it contains and thus the more tools it has to deal with different types of challenges. In a simple ecosystem, a fallen species may rebound simply because no others are standing in line to take its place. But in a complex ecosystem, many species may fit reasonably within a variety of niches. The first species may decline or disappear simply because its place has been taken by others or because in the new environmental conditions, its information set is of less value. The diversity of the ecosystem as a whole makes it more resilient even in the face of this loss. "When climatic variations harm some species, unharmed competitors increase. Such compensatory increases stabilize total community biomass, but cause species abundances to be more variable," writes David Tilman. The results reconcile the diversity-stability debate, he says, "thus helping to reconcile a long-standing dispute."

From our adventures in the rainforest, we tend toward the latter two views. In Costa Rica, species from both the North and South American continents have been forced together at the verge. Their meeting invariably brings conflict at first. Two species cannot long occupy exactly the same niche. Sometimes they adapt, other times they die. But, in fact, in Costa Rica, *all the species, from both continents, were changed.* All became intermingled so that ultimately there were no species of north versus south, only species of Costa Rica. As the species came together, most adapted, radiating outward from their origins to create a greater diversity of life than had arrived there, from north and south combined.

In economic terms, the increase in diversity means an increase in efficiency, *and often* in effectiveness, too. Species take on physical characteristics that align them more precisely to the conditions of their environment. They undergo continuous improvement; they are *better.* But because each new capacity that fosters their survival also broadens their capacities in other ways, they may also add something *new and different* to the environment, a fundamental breakthrough. Because of this, diversity serves to advance both of these types of value-by-design at once: more tools more precisely matched to the job at hand. And fundamentally better tools. Therefore, because diversity serves both, it is fundamental to sustainability.

IN BUSINESS

DIVERSITY DRIVES EFFICIENCY AND INNOVATION—IT IS THE FOUNDATION OF SUSTAINABILITY: ECONOMIC, CULTURAL, AND ENVIRONMENTAL

DIVERSITY AS A MARKETING IMPERATIVE: THE NEW COCA-COLA COMPANY

Back in the 1970s, Coca Cola launched an advertising campaign in which young, idealistic singers on a hill declared their desire to "buy the world a Coke" and live in peace and harmony. Coke in those years was a symbol of western culture and an emblem of globalization, a single brand pushing a single product with single-minded determination.

Lately, however, Coca-Cola has changed strategies. Before, it aimed to convince consumers everywhere that their favorite soft drink was Coca-Cola. Now, instead of just *persuading* consumers, the company is determined to *mirror* them—to give them the beverages *they* want, not just the ones Coke initially wants to sell. That means, rather than putting all its resources behind its flagship flavor, it is spreading them across 170 brands and encouraging its bottlers to listen to their local markets and cultures, and to introduce more brands.

That's not all. Coke has revamped its corporate mission. Now, Coke declares its mission to be "to benefit everyone touched by our business." Its CEO says Coca-Cola is determined "to be a model corporate citizen." To prove it, he tied his salary not to sales but to workplace diversity.

Furthermore, he has called for an end to marketing that simply imposes the Coca-Cola flagship on consumers in emerging markets. *Cultural* diversity is also a core value at Coca-Cola, he says. "We have to maintain our special place in local cultures, recognizing the differences between countries and regions."

The architect of the change is the company's global Chairman and CEO, Doug Daft, the first CEO to come from outside the Americas. Head of the Australian unit for more than a decade, in 1999 he took charge of the Coca-Cola Company worldwide and began to change the company from a Georgian transplant to a diverse worldwide firm.

Why would the world's most ubiquitous brand name—a company

that had profited from uniform global mass markets and tastes—suddenly devote itself to diversity?

Coca-Cola's new focus reflects the personal commitment of people like Daft and his team. But there is a lot more going on here. Coca-Cola has solid business reasons to want to "benefit everyone the company touches" and "ensur[e] integrity in everything we do." Their market is demanding these things.

When he took the CEO job in December 1999, Daft's charge was to take a century-old conservative company managed to maximize performance in the old industrial economy and "transform it into something nimble, agile, creative, responsive, and dynamic," he says—into a sustainable company that could excel not just in the old economy but in the new one as well.

His first lesson came as an entry-level employee, when Coke single-mindedly marketed its flagship brand everywhere. That produced fast growth for a while, but ultimately the company found it to be a nonsustainable course. By the time Daft headed Coke's operations in Australia, the one-brand-fits-all strategy had been largely spent. "We found we could not sustain this company with the old western, top-down management strategy or impose a top-down marketing strategy to blanket the world with a single, western soft drink. Instead, we had to completely reverse our management and marketing strategy. Instead of top-down, it had to be bottom-up: We had to be responsive to local markets. We had to learn."

So Daft began to listen to his communities, to establish links with an array of stakeholders. In response to what he heard, he introduced new brands, new flavors, made in local facilities often locally owned and operated by local managers and employees, serving locally defined desires. "Coca-Cola remained our flagship as the world's most popular, recognized brand. But we leveraged our product development, marketing, and distribution systems to bring an array of locally defined beverages to the market."

In every market under Daft's charge, the pursuit of diversity bolstered Coke's markets. It enabled them to create and deliver more value to their customers and shareholders. To achieve this, Coke had to discard the machine style of management that had helped the company expand, "where we just duplicated the products, facilities, and distribution systems we had developed in the west." They had to awaken the company as a dynamic, responsive, learning organization. To use the terminology of Shell visionary Arie de Geus, they had to make Coca-Cola a *living company*.

This change created waves back in Atlanta. The idea of dramatically broadening Coca-Cola's products and services ran counter to company tradition. Daft remembers struggling repeatedly with the parent company over the concern that introducing new soft drinks in every market would water down the Coca-Cola brand. But his strategy proved itself in the marketplace.

Why? Coca-Cola's most valuable asset is not its plants, bottlers, truck fleets, or even products. Its most valuable asset is its brand name, Coca-Cola. Yet in a way, it doesn't even own that brand anymore. Coke is "magic" because its stakeholders make it so. "Our company doesn't own the magic; it's not an ingredient in the secret formula. It's something that emerges from the imagination of everyone who is touched by Coca-Cola," says the company's 2000 annual report. That's an unusual way for a company to describe its equity: *It emerges from the imagination of everyone touched by Coca-Cola. It's owned not by the company, but by the stakeholders.*

No wonder Coca-Cola now wants to hear *from* its market. By mirroring more precisely the subtle tastes and preferences of its stakeholders, Coca-Cola can more fully convert its brand equity into earnings. That changes the direction of its marketing drive. Rather than buying the world with advertising, Coke is beginning to let the world buy it, so the company reflects the diverse people and markets it serves.

Coke learned its lesson the hard way. In the early 1980s, archcompetitor Pepsi began to win over young consumers with the claim that Pepsi tasted better. Market share shifted toward Pepsi. By September 1984, Coke thought it had an answer to the Pepsi Challenge: a new formula that beat both Pepsi and old Coke in blind taste tests. If a Coke is just a cola, then a "better tasting" Coke should be a hands-down winner. So, on April 23, 1985, New Coke was released to a great deal of fanfare. But by the middle of June, people were saying "No" to New Coke. Cokeaholics began stockpiling Old Coke in their homes. One fan likened the new formula to "chiseling Teddy Roosevelt off the side of Mount Rushmore."

In a country where "new and improved" is an almost sure bet in marketing, Coke drinkers rebelled *en masse*. The rebellion made one thing clear: To both the company and its consumers, Coke was *not* just a cola. It was a tradition, owned not by the company but by the whole community. Within weeks, the parent company was forced to bring Coca-Cola Classic back to the market. It was rewarded by gains in market share that none of its recent *intentional* marketing campaigns had matched.

Daft built on that experience. He recognized that the future of the company wasn't in making the single best-tasting soft drink in the world. Coca-Cola's success lay in its social license, the trust and esteem with which people held the company, a contract more binding than anything written on paper.

To build sales, Coke didn't have to invent the perfect cola and press everyone to buy it. Their real opportunity lay in providing people with a greater variety of products, all within the terms of Coke's social contract with them—the qualities they found intrinsic to the brand. Thus Daft has two paramount responsibilities: first, to protect the integrity of the Coca-Cola brand and live up to the terms of the company's social contract; second, to expand the variety of products offered under that contract. Like a simple pioneer forest that prepares the ground for differentiation into a richer, more diverse ecosystem, Coca-Cola is increasing the diversity of its products, without ever watering down the inner qualities of the brand.

Why? The first responsibility—securing the integrity of the Coke brand—protects Coke's current market. The second responsibility—diversifying brands—enables the company to serve a greater array of tastes and create more value for its customers, stakeholders, and shareholders. In nature and in business, diversity means choice, and choice creates value. The more diverse the species in an ecosystem, the greater its capacity to respond to any change in climate or conditions. Similarly, says Daft, "the more diverse the people in a business, the greater its capacity to respond to any change in the market. The more diverse the marketplace, the more niches can be filled in ways to provide unique services and sources of value. The more diverse cultures in the global economy, the greater our human resources as a global community."

One major test of the company's citizenship is environmental, and Daft knows it. He wants Coke to be a model of corporate sustainability, to measure and continuously drive down its environmental costs and boost its resource productivity. "We want to know how much energy, packaging, and water we use for every beverage we deliver," he says.

Coke's ideal is to drive pollution, consumption, and waste continuously toward zero. "We know that achieving absolute zero in plant injuries, product defects, or pollution and waste is not possible. But we know that we have the ability to drive them continuously toward that ideal."

Why the focus on corporate environmental leadership? Again, it's a convergence of personal commitment and corporate imperative. Anything that threatens the brand threatens everything. Coca-Cola can't afford to be a second-class act on environmental or social issues. It can't afford to be lax.

Daft's strategy is bold, risky, and essential. He must simultaneously protect the company's core asset while taking a chance on new ideas and products. There is no guarantee that his strategy will bear its full fruit during his tenure. The whole organization, not just the CEO, will need to undergo a cultural shift.

Remember Ashby's Law of Requisite Variety: "The survival of a system depends on its ability to generate at least as much variety within its boundaries as exists in the form of threatening disturbances from its environment." To succeed long term in a global market, Coke must mirror internally Coke's external potential market not just in race, ethnicity, and nationality but across a vast range of human qualities.

The key is, in some measure, to let the company go and to allow it to be managed by the community that defines it, to allow it to evolve into what they desire it to be. From the collective actions of its executives, employees, customers, and other stakeholders, something new will emerge. The company will be a product of their mutual creation.

This process could change, in fundamental ways, what a company is. Like it or not, the corporate system that dominated industry in the 20th century, the company whose mission was nothing more than to maximize return to shareholders, may need to evolve into a form more representative of and responsive to all its stakeholders.

CHAPTER SEVEN

Succession

**LESSON SEVEN:
LEARN THE FOUR PHASES OF SUCCESSION—
INNOVATION, GROWTH, IMPROVEMENT,
AND RELEASE**

IN THE RAINFOREST, *to create all kinds of value successfully, nature follows a simple management strategy.
Through the process of succession, every complex system
cycles through four phases: innovation, growth, improvement, and release.*

BUSINESS *also cycles through these phases and in the process
creates the same types of value. Breakthroughs begin the
innovation phase. That leads to growth by replication,
which, at its limit, triggers continuous improvement. And
that creates the surplus needed to support new breakthroughs, renewing the cycle.*

The act of skydiving is, in a way, a high-speed metaphor for the
phases of a person's life. Stepping from the plane, for example,
is like birth: One is "thrown" out there, into the air, into life.
The free fall is a bit like childhood and adolescence—a time of freedom
to explore in comparative safety, while you're far from the ground.
Preparing and opening the chute is adulthood—assuming responsibility and thinking and planning, in increasing detail, for the speed, path,
and manner of your descent. Now—to avoid the sudden onset of the
fourth phase—your competence really does matter.

IN THE RAINFOREST

EVERYTHING CYCLES THROUGH FOUR PHASES—INNOVATION, GROWTH, IMPROVEMENT, AND RELEASE

Ecosystems of all types tend to cycle through four distinct phases, or "seasons": innovation, growth, improvement, and release, followed by a renewed phase of innovation. Ecologists know these as the four classic phases of forest **succession.** Ecologist C. S. Holling and steel industry executive David Hurst use an infinity loop to diagram the phases.

The first phase—**innovation**—is driven by processes of integration, as dissociated parts come together into unique wholes, special arrangements yielding a synergetic quality. This breakthrough innovation is the first way nature creates value by design.

The second phase—**growth**—is driven by replication, as a successful design is repeated over and over without significant change. Growth multiplies the value first created through innovation and spreads it widely. This process of replication is the second way nature creates value by design.

The third phase—**improvement**—is driven by differentiation, as a once-successful design faces constraints and adapts to them. Once-uniform populations of identical individuals may become more diversified. Individuals and groups adapt to specific local conditions to become more efficient. This continuous improvement is the third way nature creates value by design.

The fourth phase—**release**—is a consequence of disintegration, as a once-functional system grows obsolete and breaks down, liberating its physical components to be taken up in new forms of integration, as the cycle begins again.

The four phases go by other names as well, which call attention to their different qualities. For example, *innovation* phases are sometimes called seasons of creation or renewal. *Growth* phases are also called exploitation, expansion, or pioneer phases. *Improvement* is also known as efficiency, conservation, continuous improvement, development, authority, or bureaucracy. *Release* can be called decline, disintegration, death, release, creative destruction, or reorganization. And there are still other names. Scholars debate and argue about which names are "right."

Whatever we call them, we can all relate to the four phases. They happen not just in the forest but in many types of systems. For example, innovation phases are times of birth. Growth phases are times of physical expansion, the realm of the r-strategists. Improvement phases happen as physical growth reaches a limit, and the system develops inwardly, increasing its efficiency, diversity, and complexity—the K-strategies. This is the phase of Darwinian variation and of Deming's continuous improvement. Release happens when one system reaches a limit it cannot transcend, and it dies, releasing its resources to fuel a renewal phase. Or, it happens when the system changes in some fundamental way and through breakthrough innovation, end-runs its demise and begins the cycle anew.

The Four Phases of Succession

Phase 1	*Phase 2*	*Phase 3*	*Phase 4*
The Effect of the Phases			
Innovation	Growth	Improvement	Release
What Drives the Phases			
Integration	Replication	Differentiation	Disintegration
Phases of Life			
Birth	Growth	Adulthood	Death
Phases of the Year			
Spring	Summer	Fall	Winter

Understanding the four phases would be interesting but not too useful if it did not offer two distinct advantages, which we describe in more detail in the next chapter. First, the four correspond to four distinctively different sets of management principles—you master success in each phase quite differently. And second, if you manage the phases well, you create new kinds of value in three ways: through breakthrough innovations, through their replication, and through continuous improvements of successful designs. In so doing, you begin to tap the potentials of sustainability that nature has mastered so well. You increase business profits and performance, sustainably. And you truly maximize profit, for the whole.

All living systems pass repeatedly through these phases. Although all systems are nested within other systems, the phases of different nested systems are seldom in alignment. A man finds that with the birth of a new child—creation—his family is growing, while he himself is facing challenges and improving, working at a business whose product line is in decline. The nesting and overlapping of systems in various phases of development—some innovating, others growing, improving, and dying all at once—are like the complex web of species in the canopy of a forest. They help provide the ecosystem as a whole with a healthy mix of qualities and conditions that increases its resilience. Breakthrough innovation, replication, and continuous improvements happen all at the same time.

SUCCESSION AND SUSTAINABILITY

The essence of sustainability, in nature and in business, is learning to master not just one phase but all phases—innovation, growth, improvement, and release. We do this not just for the sake of surviving, but because by prospering through those phases we walk an evolutionary path that leads toward overall development, advancing not just our own needs *but the needs of the systems in which we are nested.*

It is easy to observe the four phases in the forest, especially the temperate forests of the north. In the California Sierra Nevada, for example, in a field burned clear of vegetation by fire, a tiny stand of trees will begin to grow. Among the tiny seedlings might be pine, birch, poplar, oak, tulip, maple, and sequoia redwood, their seeds carried in by wind, water, and wildlife.

All the young plants appear healthy in this phase of *innovation* for the forest. But within a few months most are gone, unable to withstand

SUCCESSION AND SUSTAINABILITY

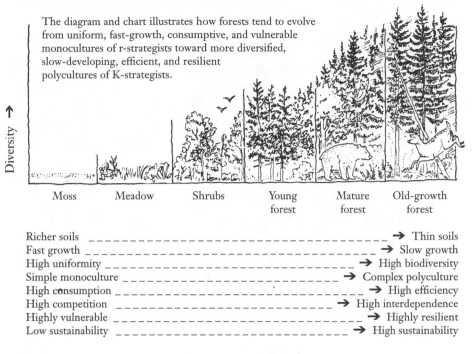

The diagram and chart illustrates how forests tend to evolve from uniform, fast-growth, consumptive, and vulnerable monocultures of r-strategists toward more diversified, slow-developing, efficient, and resilient polycultures of K-strategists.

Diversity ↑

| Moss | Meadow | Shrubs | Young forest | Mature forest | Old-growth forest |

Richer soils _____ →	Thin soils
Fast growth _____ →	Slow growth
High uniformity _____ →	High biodiversity
Simple monoculture _____ →	Complex polyculture
High consumption _____ →	High efficiency
High competition _____ →	High interdependence
Highly vulnerable _____ →	Highly resilient
Low sustainability _____ →	High sustainability

the torrid heat of the valley sun. One species remains to dominate, however. The pine quickly establishes itself, consuming the abundant resources that surround it. That marks the start of a new season, the season of *growth*. Soon the field is covered with a dense stand of young, healthy pines.

Shaded by the dense bristles of the dominant pines, the tender leaves of red oak seedlings now gain protection from the searing heat and so gain a foothold where they previously could not. Nursed by the more sun-tolerant pines, the oaks soon overtake them in height. Within a few years, the oaks grow so abundant that they crowd out the pines that gave them their chance at life. Casting the forest in deeper shade, they deny the seedlings of pine the sun they require to grow and so force their forebears into more narrowly drawn niches where sunlight and water are sufficient to feed their appetites. The succession of pines by oaks marks the beginning of the third phase of forest succession, the season of *improvement*, where a variety of new niches begin to be formed, each seemingly tailor-made for another species.

But gradually, as the forest grows even denser with oak, the sunlight their seedlings require is blocked off. The oak alters the very climate that sustained it. Now, in the shade of the forest floor, it is time for the giant sequoia redwoods to rise. Thousands of redwood seeds, previously held in check by the scorching heat, emerge from the earth, spread roots, and grow.

More intricately designed than any of its predecessors, better able to conserve energy, recycle water, withstand fire, and protect its young, the sequoias draw much less from their environment than the pioneers that preceded them, and they deliver much more. In and around them throughout the forest, myriad new microniches emerge, each providing a home for additional species of plants and animals, as the forest grows richer in diversity and complexity.

But so thick does the forest grow, and so circuitous become its linkages, that deadwood builds up on its floor, fire returns, and a fourth phase of the forest begins, *release*. In the face of fire, the land and nutrients previously held by the mature forest are released, available to nourish seeds of a new phase.

The lengths of the different phases can vary dramatically. In temperate regions like the Sierras, the climatic seasons of the year may be close to the same length, so we assign them official durations of about three months each. But in the tropics, and in business, this is not generally the case. Often phases of growth are relatively quick; phases of improvement and differentiation may last a very, very long time; phases of release can happen with lightning speed; and phases of innovation may be short or long in duration.

In Corcovado and Tortuguero, for example, for the forest as a whole two seasons dominate the year. The wet period lasts from about May to November, the dry one from December to April. In the wet period, water is abundant, and vegetation may grow prolifically as a consequence. In the dry period, rainfall is very limited, and both animals and plants must have the capacity to make do with less or tap sources where past surpluses have been stored. This has interesting implications for sustainability, both in nature and business. The repeating cycles of wet and dry in Costa Rica's forests make for a long phase of differentiation and improvement. This may be one reason the rainforest offers such extraordinary variations on themes. Species are kept constantly on edge, constantly challenged to refine their form to deal with relative shortages of water and resources or to take advantage of slightly different conditions in a neighboring niche. Seldom are the challenges great enough to cause the death of a whole forest. True periods of destruction are generally localized, so long as volcanoes and chainsaws remain dormant or distant. An ancient tree may topple over and fall to the ground, creating an open path for the sun to penetrate the forest canopy and reach the ground directly. These small, frequent openings are vital to perhaps three-quarters of the tree species of the rainforest. The major dose of energy in the form of sunlight fosters growth, and a new season begins there. Their seeds long latent, pioneer grasses, shrubs, and trees quickly emerge, capturing the water and sun, holding the soil in place, and creating niches for fast-growth plants and animals.

So as the dominoes of evolution complete their fall, a new cycle begins, but at a new starting point. The relentless processes of evolution—the natural selection of beneficial variations, the spontaneous emergence of evolutionary leaps—draw the ecosystem along a staircase of development, as complexity-on-complexity compound slowly to create new starting points, new species, and whole new systems.

STAGES AND PHASES

If rainforests merely cycled endlessly between the four phases of succession, how would advanced forms of life evolve? If every living system merely followed a cycle that began with birth and ended with death, how would whole new species advance? If all change is incremental, and temporary, how can breakthrough innovations occur?

One hint may lie in the relationship between phases and stages. Phases are recurring, like the phases of the moon, the seasons of the year, the stages of succession. At the end of each cycle, you find yourself back at the start.

Stages, by contrast, move forward or back, or up and down. Think of the steps in a staircase. As you step up, you get further from your starting point. You can never return to it without stepping down.

Drexel Sprecher suggests that there is a natural rhythm of development that allows evolution to occur within a context of stability. All living systems progress to more advanced stages of development through the four phases of renewal. The interaction between stages and phases allows for both breakthroughs and gradual change.

The stages of development are directional. Just as a person steps up or down a staircase, natural systems move up toward more complex order, or down toward chaos. A natural system that returns to its original condition is regressing rather than developing.

The four phases of succession are, in contrast, recurring. Every time a system repeats a cycle of development, it returns to the starting point. Phases of renewal can enable a system to progress from simple toward higher, more complex stages of development.

Businesses and economies also evolve to higher stages of development through the four phases of succession. Each succeeding economic system is born, grows, develops, and declines. Yet each leaves a legacy in the form of acquired knowledge, skills, and wisdom—a step in a staircase. The physical form of a business may die. But the inner qualities are often retained. In fact, they *must* be retained to move to the next step. They form the foundation that supports the economy in its next stage of development. If an intermediary step in a staircase disintegrate, the whole structure collapses. So too with businesses and economies.

The relentless processes of evolution—the natural selection of beneficial variations, the spontaneous emergence of evolutionary leaps—draw ecosystems from one stage of development to the next, each time creating a richer and more diverse legacy of innovations that support the stage to come.

Sustainability can only be achieved through the both restoration of the old and the emergence of the new. A culture that systematically rejects the old destroys its own foundation. We in the industrial world sometimes imagine that economic progress requires that prior economic systems be replaced by today's. But we are the beneficiaries of centuries during which prior economies have been laying down foundations of knowledge, skill, and belief. These cultural resources are our support and sustenance. What do they teach us about how to support ourselves now, and how to take our next steps?

IN BUSINESS

BY NAVIGATING THE FOUR PHASES, INNOVATIVE COMPANIES TRIGGER GROWTH, IMPROVEMENT, AND MORE INNOVATION

FROM AUTOMOBILES TO THE INTERNET— THE FOUR PHASES OF INDUSTRIALIZATION

Look carefully at the evolution of any individual, community, or business—any living system, even human society itself—and you will see that each passes repeatedly through the phases of succession. As we have said, excelling throughout these phases, as they draw you from one stage to the next is the essence of sustainability.

Why would that be so? Because the four phases encompass a process by which living things not only serve their own interests but also interact with their environment to serve broader interests as well. In business, for example, Adam Smith's invisible hand is handicapped when a company seeks only to grow and never to improve or innovate in response to external needs. The invisible hand works best when businesses are open to feedback in all its forms and adapt so they tend to "do well by doing good"—whether they consciously choose to or not.

Consider how these phases have shaped the birth, growth, and development of centuries of industrialization, as well as its gradual succession by a new kind of economy, now emerging to take its place.

Phase One: Innovation. Industrialization's *innovation* season began with the first scientific revolution and the ideas of the great thinkers of the era: Copernicus, Galileo, Descartes, Newton, and later Adam Smith and Charles Darwin. They planted the conceptual seeds from which grew the industrial economy; its chief source of value, the machine; and its preeminent technology, the automobile.

Nicholas Copernicus began the rush toward a mechanistic universe, and Galileo's theories of mechanics described celestial dynamics. Descartes extended mechanistic thinking to the biological world, asserting that plant and animal behavior too could be reduced to mere mechanism. And Isaac Newton argued that these machines, living and nonliving, were made entirely of solid, impenetrable particles, "even so very hard, as to never wear or break in pieces; no ordinary power being able to divide what God himself made one in the first creation."

By explaining the dynamics of nature's machines, Newton and his contemporaries gave humanity the foundational theories needed to build its own machines. But theory is not practice. To move industrialization from its innovative to its growth phase, a forcing function was required—a compelling need that would cause the theories to be applied, to take root and spread.

Phase Two: Growth. The forcing function turned out to be the European timber famine, an energy crisis caused by deforestation. Forced to dig deeper mines for coal, Europeans found that their mines filled with water, creating a shortage of coal as well. Here the ideas of the Enlightenment began to take material form, the then-emerging economy to take direction. Newcomen developed his steam engine to pump water out of the mines. James Smith then radically improved on Newcomen's design with his compressor and rotative engine. That led to affordable steamships and locomotives and the steam-powered horseless carriage.

Within a century, the seeds had taken root, the industrial economy was firmly established and growing rapidly. That gave rise to an economy that, like the mechanisms it employed and the science it applied, was "a great machine" consisting of deterministic chains of causes and effects, according to Adam Smith. In this machine, three factors of production were vital: land, labor, and capital. By apportioning these three factors in the right combinations, the economy could be left alone to grow and develop like clockwork, as if guided by an invisible hand. Little or no external thought, planning, or regulation was required.

That growth accelerated when Henry Ford put into place his assembly line and multiplied the efficiency of manufacturing. As do grass seeds in an open field, the products of industry were replicated quickly and in great abundance and spread rapidly toward the outer bounds of the environment open to them.

Ford's machine-style management became a model not just for business but for the economy and culture that nested it. If wealth was a function of resource consumption, and machines were the agent to extract and use them, then the bigger the machines and the faster they operated, the more wealth could be drawn from the earth, made into products, and delivered to people.

The process of industrial assimilation led to what some systems scientists call **reverse causation**: From the convergence of small systems, a larger one emerges, which then effectively reaches down and regulates the behavior of the subsystems that constitute it. In this case, the subsystems were people. The cost of the industrial system was a reduction in the freedom experienced by people.

But the benefits of the tradeoff were extraordinary. The growth phase of the industrial economy led to great gains in social welfare, from a material perspective and more. So long as the industrial machine was fed a continuous supply of the energy, materials, and supplies it needed to keep running as designed, business and workers pros-

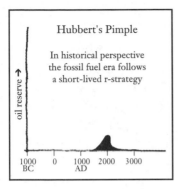

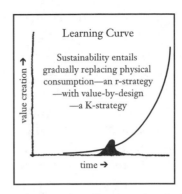

As limits are imposed, feedback causes learning and adaptation. Consumptive designs are gradually replaced by smarter designs, and r-strategies give way to K-strategies shown in the Learning Curve.

pered. But no system that consumes its own capital can grow forever. In the 1950s, petroleum geologist M. K. Hubbert issued his famous "Hubbert Pimple", which illustrated that no matter how much oil, coal, and natural gas we could extract from the ground, the fossil fuel era would be a short-lived one from an historical perspective. By the end of the 1960s, an increasing number of indicators suggested we might soon be approaching a wall.

Phase Three: Improvement. In 1974, we hit one. That year the Arab oil embargo sent price-increase shock waves streaming through the economy. The feedback was direct and painful. All the industrial economies were wounded. The rigid machine-like economies of the Soviet bloc never recovered.

The shortage of oil forced a transition from industrialization's growth phase to an era of improvement, when emphasis on size and quantity declined and value emerged instead from quality, efficiency, and variety. Soon a few companies began to learn that the machine model was not nature's ultimate creator of value—that in the face of change, the resilience of adaptive living systems gives them the edge.

Efficiency turned out to be cheaper than waste. But machines could not make themselves more efficient. That required creative people. As energy prices increased, people were reawakened and intervened in the machine economy, employing thousands of technical innovations and system changes and product refinements that reduced demand for the resource that was being most constrained—oil. The rigid, unthinking machine of industrialization's growth phase began to transform into the learning organization of its improvement phase. Quality, efficiency, variety, agility, flexibility—these became the qualities business needed in their organizations, people, and even their machines.

A family of technologies—semiconductors, microprocessors, computers, faxes, modems, and the Internet—emerged, and soon, from the painful feedback of the energy crisis, information surpassed fossil fuels as the primary catalyst for economic growth.

In the generation that followed, efficiency—not consumption—became the largest "source" of energy and materials in the industrial world. Between 1972 and 1990, what we call *immaterials* grew to supply nearly a third of the materials consumed by the U.S. economy; *negawatts* supplied a third of our energy needs.

The effect on the information industry was massive. Rising energy prices slowed the whole economy at first, but soon the information sector exploded, driven in part by unprecedented demand for technologies that would enable people to do more with less. The tools they developed fomented a productivity revolution that persisted through the end of the century.

Phase Four and One: A Nesting of Systems—Industrialization Begins Its Decline as the Cyber Economy Is Born. As we have said, systems are nested in systems. One gives rise to another from within it, which then changes the environment within which the first one prospered. Just as agriculture gave rise to industry, the industrial society gave rise to the cyber economy. Now, after first improving the efficiency and performance of industry, the cyber economy is undermining its foundations, and hastening its decline and release. The child begins to supplant the parent.

In nature, it's not always the fittest that survive but the one in the right place at the right time, the one that captures the network and corners the benefits of Metcalfe's Law. In 1975, as IBM comfortably grew its mainframe computer business, Bill Gates and Paul Allen happened on a *Popular Mechanics* article, took a simple and readily available programming language at the time to create the first product of Microsoft, and helped birth the microcomputer, threatening IBM's dominance. Then IBM made a strategic miscalculation that gave control of its DOS operating system to Microsoft, which turned MS-DOS into a PC stan-

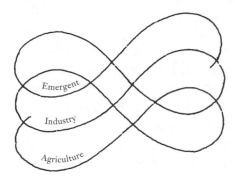

dard. That was the beginning of Wintel. Wintel became the pioneer growth species of the new economy, not as its cause, but as its effect. IBM and Apple had better seeds, but no interest in filling the niche. While Gates's drive was a factor, it was his capture of network effects that made the success extraordinary.

Paradoxically, the worldview that led Microsoft to translate a little luck and a lot of persistence into a dominant software empire may combine with the Internet to produce a counterrevolution of sorts. The PC revolution undermined the giant mainframe computers that IBM used to dominate the market. Now, as Microsoft edges toward its next generation Internet strategy in which applications are accessed over the Internet, we could in effect recreate the mainframe in the form of "servers" a billion times more powerful than their predecessors.

But contrary to popular belief, the information age did not itself signify a revolution. Most of the changes caused by computers simply refined what remained a predominantly industrial economy. Computers advanced the improvement phase of industrialization, making it operate faster, cleaner, and more efficiently, with greater quality and variety. But they did not change industrialization at its roots. That process of transformation has only begun.

FORCING FUNCTIONS:
THE END OF THE INDUSTRIAL ERA

But in the end, only the outer forms of the old economy need fall. Its inner qualities must be retained for the new economy to flourish.

No economy or technology, no matter how advanced, can merely replace its predecessors. Each is supported by the ones that came before. And in a healthy system, each reaches back to restore the health and vitality of its predecessors. Each generation of technology transcends, and then transforms, the one that came before, notes Drexel Sprecher. Industrial machines transformed agriculture, expanding its productive capacity. Computers are transforming industry, and transforming the way industry transforms agriculture. New technology does not vanquish the old—it renews it. Over time, the more subtle technologies tend to advance and the grosser tend to decline. The more efficient succeed the more wasteful. K-strategists squeeze out r-strategists. Complex rainforests replace simple mangrove swamps. This is the way information overthrows the dominance of matter.

Every stage of economy has a seed phase, a growth phase, an improvement phase, and a decline phase. As a new economy is born and grows, it overlaps a predecessor that is already highly developed. Just as today's ten-year-olds are more tech-savvy than their parents, the new stage may be more advanced, but it is also less mature. Similarly, an industrial economy may be more advanced but less mature than the agricultural or hunting economies it may supplant.

Thus the advocates of new economies, or new technologies, often claim to have swept aside the need for all that came before, just as each generation of teenagers claims to have the answers to all the world's problems. In reality, it takes time for every new generation to mature. In time it learns to open itself to input from its elders, the generations that came before.

Western industrialization is a young and vibrant culture. Like an r-strategist, it is eager to spread quickly, dominate the globe, and prove that its way of living is the greatest on earth. But while it is more tech-savvy than its predecessors, it is not always wiser. While it may have the answers, it doesn't know all the questions. To learn them, it must begin to listen.

What are the implications for business leaders? They must recognize that the information and industrial cultures are at a more advanced technological *stage*, but a less mature *phase*, more technologically advanced but less mature than many traditional cultures.

This fact gives rise to conflict. Globalization brings the conflict to a head. Just as adolescents rebel against their parents as they approach maturity, advocates of the information and industrial economies rebel against more mature cultures. Divergent living standards, cultural ignorance, and ecological limits make it more explosive. The longer business leaders resist the feedback from their communities near and far, the more incendiary will the conditions of the global rainforest grow.

Leaders must transcend the limits of the r-phase of industry. We must move beyond the management, marketing, and strategic imperatives of the past, and become more responsive to feedback from cultures we may have once regarded as backward. We must become K-strategists, highly adaptive to the environmental and cultural conditions into which we are injecting our products, processes, and companies.

Agriculture nested, nurtured, and gave rise to industrial technologies. Now, the industrial is giving rise to the cyber economy. The infusion of industrial technologies into more traditional economies is disrupting the nest within which they sit, even as information technologies disrupt the industrial economy. The first species to fall were the most rigid industrial machines—the machine economies of the Soviet Union, the entrenched corporate bureaucracies of the U.S., Europe, and Asia. But that may be just the beginning. Remember the mangrove, the pine, the oak. As global conditions change, the species that succeed will not be the strongest and most consumptive. They will be the most responsive and adaptive.

At the level of industrial economies, business and political leaders must recognize that fundamental economic transformations are extremely disruptive. Each prior transition has resulted in at least one major depression, and all have been followed by explosive expansions in economic and social capacities. Industrial leaders want developing economies to avoid patterns of denial, and acknowledge that their systems must change. But industrial leaders too must avoid denial, and recognize the impending end of the fossil fuel era. Classic free market thinking, with national and cultural borders totally open to the inflow of industrial technologies and capital, before cultural feedback can influence it, could be counterproductive in this context. Proceeding in simple-minded ways, without understanding the importance of global diversity and adaptability, could lead to painful consequences.

At the level of their individual businesses, leaders must be able to attune to the rhythm of development and work with the forces of change, according to Sprecher. They must synthesize views of the market, technological advances elsewhere, and their own situation into a comprehensive view of technology and product development. They must monitor new trends and innovations with the potential to disrupt or destroy their market niches, and be prepared to make the larger shift to different niches with new technologies—even while most of their company concentrates on the next generation of existing products. Working with, rather than against, the forces of change is the test of corporate sustainability.

Business leaders who want their companies to succeed must master the principles of succession, and apply them in the form of practical systems of management.

PART TWO

How to Use the Principles:
Strategy, Management, Tactics,
and Tools for the Living Business

CHAPTER EIGHT

Management

LESSON EIGHT:
MAXIMIZE TOTAL PERFORMANCE—
MASTER THE FOUR PHASES OF MANAGEMENT

IN THE RAINFOREST, *nature creates diversity and abundance over the course of the four seasons of succession.*

IN BUSINESS, *companies can maximize profits sustainably by mastering the four seasons of management.*

If, at the initial failure of Bill's parachute, we had focused on a comprehensive redesign of the technology, so that such events did not recur, it is unlikely that we would have been able to complete the necessary modifications, and have them installed, in the 60 or so seconds remaining before Bill hit the ground.

When managing, you must know what phase you are in, and which quality will be of greatest immediate value during that phase: the intuitive innovation of the creation phase, the exuberance of growth, the meticulousness of improvement, or the focused attention induced by the prospect of imminent disintegration.

Know the four seasons in the cycle of succession, master at least one, and excel in them all. This offers two distinct advantages. First, these four phases teach you how to develop and achieve the objectives you desire and to discover possibilities and potentials that you may never have known you had. Second, they will bring you greater mastery of business and life and the increased success and fulfillment that can come along with it—continuous improvement, as you hone your intrinsic capacities, and personal breakthroughs, as you discover the richness within you.

In Bill's case, falling through the air with a malfunctioning parachute, we faced a challenge, one that could either develop into a solution or degenerate into a disaster. If we acted with calm intelligence, we were likely to emerge whole and a little smarter. So that is where we focused our energy.

IN THE RAINFOREST

ABUNDANCE AND RESILIENCE FLOWS FROM THE FOUR SEASONS

In an open field of possibilities, the seeds of fast-growing pioneers take root and grow. Mangroves at the water's edge in the rainforest, pine in the forests of the Sierras, weeds in the cracks between sections of sidewalk—each is selected because the plan inscribed in their seeds match the conditions of their local environment.

Thus begins the innovative phase in the life of an ecosystem, and in the growth phase that follows, the pioneers replicate to cover the territory available to them. As we have learned, they lay down a blanket of support for myriad other species that find homes more to their liking in the niches created by the pioneers. These more resilient species, using resources more sparingly, filling their niches in more focused, specialized ways, foster a rich and varied forest ecosystem. That ecosystem evolves into a crosshatch of thousands of species and subsystems in all phases of the cycle.

Businesses also evolve through the four phases or seasons. As they do, they have the opportunity to grow more productive, efficient, and specialized, and then either to die, or to renew themselves in potentially more resilient and profitable forms.

To grow bigger or more efficient requires just one form of management. But to be truly resilient—to have the capacity to excel through the whole business life cycle, and emerge from change more profitable—requires that the business master all four seasons.

IN BUSINESS

PROFITS ARE MAXIMIZED BY MASTERING THE FOUR SEASONS OF BUSINESS

LEARN TO MANAGE ON THE VERGE

There is a secret to managing a business like a living system, a secret every gardener knows: You cannot manage the business the same way at all times. Instead, you must manage it in four different ways—a different way for every season. And you must learn to manage *between* the seasons, to prepare for the transition from one to the next.

In the past three centuries of industrialism, we have learned to excel in one of those seasons: the season of physical growth, when material resources are abundant and capital accumulated over geological ages can be consumed *en masse.*

When resources are vast, that makes ecological sense. But it can carry us only so far. Sustainability, in nature and in business, requires learning to prosper in all seasons.

That may sound complicated, but it's much less so than today's approach. Every year, as do the annuals that come and go with every spring, a new crop of consultants converges on corporate America and Japan, offering a new theory of business management, each with its own ideology and guru.

The theories all sound dramatically new and different. But if you look at them very closely, you begin to notice that they all recycle four basic theories of management, one for each phase of business.

First there is scientific management, the ideas of Frederick Taylor that helped shape pioneer mass manufacturing enterprises such as Ford Motor Company at the start of the 20th century. Business is a machine. It is to be run as a hierarchy, with every worker a machine part that carries out functions very precisely, according to central directions.

That works fine when a business is in its *growth* phase, quickly expanding its physical size, adding new machine parts—more workers, factories, resources. But because machines are not flexible, it fails when a business has to change.

To meet this need, there is the second theory, quality management, the ideas of people such as Edwards Deming, Kaoru Ishikawa, and

Joseph Juran, which provided the foundation for Japan's leap to global economic power through the 1980s. They say the business is a learning community, where people work together to continuously improve efficiency and quality.

This approach works fine when the business is in its *improvement* phase, when a company is gradually refining its products and processes, a phase in which Japan has excelled. But it fails when the business must change suddenly, seemingly overnight.

For that, there is the third theory, most recently cast as reengineering, the ideas of Michael Hammer and James Champy. They say that a business is like a garden: It must be radically pruned in the fall or winter, so that it can avoid static maturity and grow abundantly in the spring.

That works fine once or twice. But it fails if the business must be pruned every year, because people always feel they are the ones about to be pruned. The business loses their trust, confidence, and loyalty, and often with it their initiative and creativity.

To protect the company and its people at the same time, there is the fourth theory representing the ideas of Jim Collins and Jerry Porras as described in their book *Built to Last*. They say a business often can't sustain major change unless it has a deeply planted sense of enduring purpose. This allows it to revisit its purpose in light of changing times, and find new goals and a new path of development even when its main products become obsolete.

That works fine when a company is searching for direction, either at its inception or in highly disruptive times, but it can be counterproductive if the company fails to isolate that process from the ongoing need for most employees to focus on growth and improvement.

All these theories work sometimes and fail other times. What is needed is a way to integrate them so that businesses can excel in every phase.

The four-season management system explains how to do this. The basic idea is simple and revolutionary. Every business is a living organism. It is born, it grows, it matures, and it dies. Each phase is different, and each demands a different management strategy.

First, *innovation*. In the economy, the first phase happens when Steve Wozniak tinkers with a MOS microprocessor and learns how to multiply its functional power, creating an Apple II. Or when Bob

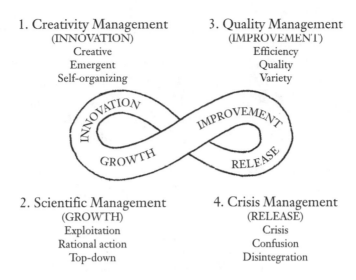

1. Creativity Management
(INNOVATION)
Creative
Emergent
Self-organizing

3. Quality Management
(IMPROVEMENT)
Efficiency
Quality
Variety

2. Scientific Management
(GROWTH)
Exploitation
Rational action
Top-down

4. Crisis Management
(RELEASE)
Crisis
Confusion
Disintegration

Taylor brings together a creative band of engineers at Xerox PARC, and they hatch technologies that eventually populate the Internet. *In the first phase, also called the creation phase, you have to plant many seeds— many ideas and fundamental innovations—then nurture them in an environment protected from normal business controls, and see which ones grow.*

Second, *growth*. In the economy, this happens when Steve Jobs takes Wozniak's idea, realizes he has a successful seed, and gathers together the people, money, and resources to grow lots of them. *In the second phase, often called the pioneer, expansion, or exploitation phase, you must grow and replicate en masse to fill the available niche.*

Third, *improvement*, also called the phase of *quality, efficiency, variety, or development*. In the economy, improvement happens when the Apple II runs out of new market to penetrate but realizes (if it ever does) that it has created a whole new economic rainforest, with niches for new varieties of computers, software, and peripherals. *In the third phase, the business must improve efficiency, variety, and quality.*

Fourth, *release*, also called *disintegration, decline*, or *death*. The fourth phase happens when competitors chip away at Apple's market, stealing it one niche at a time, and Apple is forced to reinvent itself or decline toward death. This phase is a time of deterioration, but it also sets the stage for reorganization or rebirth. *In the fourth phase, the business must dig beneath its products to find its enduring purpose, and use that purpose as a guide to focus its resources.*

The four-phase cycle, operating at many levels, helps provide the rich combination of creation and destruction that keeps the economy healthy and vital. The qualities of each phase combine to provide a healthy mix of innovation, growth, improvement, and decline. Economist Joseph Schumpeter coined the term *creative destruction* to describe this capacity of free enterprise. He called creative destruction "the essential fact about capitalism." Competition was important because it helped drive prices down and quality up. But far more significant was the capacity of free enterprise to eliminate and disband obsolete industries. By setting small fires that keep the business rainforest free of technological and bureaucratic deadwood, said Schumpeter, it fosters "[i]ndustrial mutation—if I may use that biological term—that incessantly revolutionizes the economic structure *from within*, incessantly destroying the old one, incessantly creating a new one."

The four-season management system acknowledges that, for a business to be successful in a fast changing economy, it must often apply all four management disciplines simultaneously. But this system presents the phases in a logical, integrated framework. It tells you which methods to focus on, and when. The phases also provide the framework within which systems gradually evolve into new and more elaborate forms, creating new types of value along the way.

In addition to sustaining *themselves*, businesses that master the four phases of management can operate in ways that are more culturally and environmentally sustainable. They grow more responsive and adaptive to their total stakeholder marketplace, the economic as well as the social and environmental.

To earn your 30-minute MBA, consider this: The four phases of succession in nature enable us to incorporate much of the history of management consulting, all in one. Understand natural succession, and you will know in broad terms how to navigate a business through all times of opportunity, adversity, and change.

We learned the management value of the four phases from David Hurst, who learned them from ecologist C. S. (Buzz) Holling of the University of Florida. In the 1980s, Hurst was the number two executive at Russelsteel, a Canadian steel company, when it was thrust into the middle of a crisis caused by a leveraged buy-out gone bad and had to reinvent itself.

Facing the prospect of bankruptcy, Hurst and the company's new president gathered a group of respected employees, explained the gory details of the crisis, and asked for ideas, drawing the company together as a community behind a central mission. Hurst and the president shared an office "so we could hear what the other was doing in real time." Almost immediately, the company began to restructure itself naturally. The old bureaucracy was ignored. Staff solved problems as they emerged, and made radical changes easily. Spontaneous networks enabled people to get things done quickly and invisibly. Costs were cut, and tax liability slashed. Within four years, the company was so successful it could be recapitalized and sold.

Hurst was struck by the dramatic differences in operating styles between the company's growth, improvement, and release phases. Over time, he drew on Holling's work to develop a four-stage system of management.

Because most of us can relate to the four seasons, they provide a superb framework for illustrating dynamically how businesses can prosper from the principles of nature. They help us explain confounding management paradoxes that may have left us baffled before—why tactics that work one year fail the next, why a superb manager succeeds for a time, then seems hopelessly incapable, why benchmarking against the best sometimes improves performance and other times worsens it.

Do the four seasons offer solutions for *small* businesses? In many ways, they can be more vital to small than large businesses. For example, they help explain why entrepreneurs often get stalled for years in periods of creation, never able to focus on one promising idea and turn it into a profit driver. And, they show why successful start-ups often explode through years of fast growth and high profits, then overextend themselves and crash when competitors emerge or their easy market is filled.

For the world as a whole, the four phases may show us how to grow more sustainable businesses and economies, where economic, social, and environmental imperatives are positively correlated.

However, using the four phases is not as simple as just managing for a single phase. Just as the four phases combine to foment creative destruction in economies as a whole, they coexist within businesses. Break a business down into its parts, and you will find that it is operating in many phases at once. One product may be in the innovation phase and another may be in the improvement phase. One unit may be in growth while the company as a whole is facing bankruptcy.

More important, however, is this: Because change happens so fast, you can't manage just for the *current* season. You have to prepare for the *next* phase as well. You have to learn to manage on the verge.

MANAGING ON THE VERGE: THE KEY TO CORPORATE SUCCESS

To "succeed" literally means *to follow in order*, to move from one phase to the next. Business success therefore means not just excelling in one phase but making the leap to the next phase, and the next.

The way to succeed in today's fast-changing economy is to manage on the verge. In nature, verges are among the most dynamic and creative places. As we learned earlier, a verge is a rich mixture of ecosystems that happens where two distinct systems overlap and begin to intermix. Verges in nature are the points of greatest diversity, and they provide the conditions for the explosive combinations that lead to striking innovations.

Creativity in human organizations also happens on the verge. In music, jazz appeared on the verge between African polyrhythms and European popular songs, the place where two distinctive cultures find a form that transcends their differences and draws them into one.

In culture, Daniel Boorstin sees verges as the catalyst to much of America's creativity: "America was a land of verges—all sorts of verges, between kinds of landscapes or seascapes, between stages of civilization, between ways of thought and ways of life . . . The creativity—the hope—of the nation was in its verges, in its new mixtures and new confusions."

In the economy, the Internet is on the verge between the industrial economy and its successor, a place where old-style commerce is exploding and where new forms of human connection are coming into being.

Verges are not monocultures, places where two or more forms meet in combat and only the "most fit" survives. Verges are a locus of creativity. They bring complementary opposites together, make parts into wholes, bring thesis and antithesis together to form a new synthesis. They are the places where new value is generated, and, perhaps, where the potential for sustainability arises.

How can a company manage effectively on the verge? By mastering the principles of the current season and taking the actions that will facilitate a transition to the next. The examples and summaries that follow show how.

Managing on the Verge: Nike

Nike provides a good case study of the challenges of managing on the verge. Back in 1972, Nike was a small start-up with an ambitious goal: to beat the market leader, Adidas. They were 48 people. Adidas was 3,000.

Nike chose its seed well. It found a niche in high-quality athletic shoes, applying European designs made less expensively in Asian factories. By delivering a high-demand product at an affordable price, Nike saw its sales explode. For the 12 years beginning in 1972, Nike grew a thousand-fold, from $1 million to $1 billion in sales by 1983.

"Then things changed," says one Nike executive. "The business got so large and so complex that it was impossible for [cofounder and CEO] Phil [Knight], or any of us, to play the same role." Growth and profits reached record levels. The company looked healthy. But it was becoming machinelike, blind to changes in the market. It totally missed the growth of the aerobics market.

But Reebok didn't. Between 1981 and 1987, Reebok's sales grew nearly a thousand-fold, mostly at Nike's expense. Nike responded by applying the principles of a Deming-style learning organization. It decentralized authority, increased diversity, and differentiated its product line. The shift in management strategy worked. Within 18 months, the company stabilized, and sales began to grow. Between 1993 and 1997, they exploded a second time, this time from $2 billion to $9 billion.

Then the company was surprised again, this time by media and activists who claimed it was using child labor to make its products. That began to tarnish its most valuable asset, its brand, but taught it a powerful lesson: It must monitor more than its customers *as customers.* It needed to be responsive to their total needs, as stake-holders.

Nike responded with an aggressive campaign to improve working conditions and set and verify standards throughout the global network of independent suppliers who make Nike products. To its critics, Nike may always remain a poster child for activist causes in the apparel industry, ripe for attack as a symbol for all of globalization. That is what every brand leader must expect in the age of Internet activism. But the company's ability to adapt to the feedback it received was critical to its regaining its momentum in the marketplace, and retaining its leadership position.

Nike's long-term resilience now depends on its ability to maintain the trust, loyalty, and support of its full array of stakeholders. With those, it can grow, develop, and even redefine its product line at the moment it needs to. It can excel on the verge.

BRIEF ON EVERY PHASE

MANAGING FOR INNOVATION

In the season of innovation, business is like a laboratory. Power is up for grabs by anyone with a promising idea and the vision and drive to transform it into a product, process, or service. Leaders are therefore self-defined and selected.

The most valuable form of capital in the innovation phase is creativity. Achievement is motivated by one's vision or ability to devote oneself to the vision of another. Status comes from understanding and dedicating oneself to the vision, or carrying the vision to successful application.

Creative organizations often become locked into cycles of dead-end creativity, where too many ideas and too many visions compete with one another, none given the time or focus to succeed. That leaves the organization spinning without direction and ultimately undermines its effectiveness.

For that reason, the quality needed to foster transition to the growth phase is the ability to *choose the right seeds—ideas* with the capacity to succeed—and to focus attention on them. Often this discipline must be imposed from the outside, by investors or directors who have their eyes on the future bottom line.

MANAGEMENT PRINCIPLES
IN THE SEASON OF INNOVATION

Indicators	*Typical Management Focus*
• Free experimentation	• Reward creativity
• Emergent leadership	• Reward initiative
• Self-forming teams	• Teach and reward individuality and teamwork; discourage individualism
• Meet social needs	• Apply core values to meet social needs
• Few winners	• Distribute rewards broadly; select and grow innovations with market potential

---

MANAGING FOR GROWTH

In seasons of growth, the workplace tends to be highly regimented. Planning and "brain work" is often done centrally, at the top of a tall hierarchy. Power tends to be held by designated authorities who enforce rules. The most valuable form of capital in the growth phase is generally physical capital: facilities, equipment, inventories. Labor is relatively interchangeable, so individual workers lack leverage unless they engage together, as through collective bargaining.

Achievement in a machinelike organization is motivated by goals and compensation, and status corresponds to money, power, and possessions. Personal success is closely linked to conformity, self-reliance, and hard work, since these are the qualities that help advance the smooth functioning of the machine.

Product development in the growth phase often focuses on making more, bigger, and faster or more powerful versions of the same basic line. Houses may get bigger, cars bigger and faster. Factories may become huge and uniform.

MANAGEMENT PRINCIPLES
IN THE SEASON OF GROWTH

Indicators	*Typical Management Focus*
• Fast growth	• Aggressive production
• Mass production	• Focus on one thing
• Standardization	• Establish rigid procedures
• Conformity	• Reward individual performance
• Machinelike organization	• Top-down hierarchy
• Opportunity is more profitable than efficiency	• Invest in physical capital for mass replication

---

MANAGING FOR IMPROVEMENT

In seasons of continuous improvement, the workplace is often more like a learning community, a campus where people are motivated by the ability to apply their own intelligence and skill. Power is decentralized. People work together in teams and networks. Hierarchies are relatively flat. Leadership is held by those able to facilitate functional relationships between formal and informal teams of specialists.

The most valuable form of capital is information. Workers create and apply it to continuously refine and improve products and processes. Achievement comes from recognition from one's colleagues. Status is based on how well a person's specialty contributes to team success.

Product and process development in the learning organization focuses on variety and quality. Few dramatically new products are introduced; instead, seemingly endless variations are developed. Marketing may diverge from mass to niche markets. The key competitive drives are to differentiate one's own products and services, lock in a secure customer base, and drive down costs per unit.

Personal success is a function not of conformity and self-reliance but of distinctiveness and interdependence. The principal unit is the group, not the individual. In the group, people become whole. Over time, however, learning organizations often ossify into bureaucracies.

To stave off decay, a learning organization must embrace its underlying mission and core values, its sense of enduring purpose, for direction in times of fundamental change.

MANAGEMENT PRINCIPLES
IN THE SEASON OF IMPROVEMENT

Indicators

- Resources become scarce
- Markets diversify and products differentiate
- Customers differentiate

- People individuate (they become less alike)
- Interdependence increases
- Continuous reorganizations —no revolutions

Typical Management Focus

- Reward efficiency
- Introduce product and service variations
- Improve customization and service
- Reward individuality and unique skills and attributes
- Reward teamwork
- Make continuous improvement

MANAGING THE SEASON OF RELEASE

In the release or decay phase, a business is like a burning forest or a burning platform. Structure begins to disintegrate. Power is diffuse and liberated. Leadership moves from designated authorities or facilitators to charismatic individuals, people who from within the chaos convey a sense of purpose, clarity, and certainty.

Achievement is motivated by a desire to survive or accumulate power. Status and personal success are related to one's adaptive skills, comfort with change, and ability to convey a sense of direction to others.

The most valuable forms of capital are a company's core values and sense of mission and purpose. These provide the structure that holds the company and its people together in crisis.

Product and process development focuses on beginning with the company's mission and purpose, and exploring out-of-the-box ideas that may reflect and advance them. Marketing focuses on holding on to the remnants of declining markets, through broad restructuring to cut costs and free up capital, and paradoxically, spending freely to identify new opportunities for growth.

Successfully navigating a company from release to a new cycle of innovation and growth requires total commitment to the company's mission and purpose, as well as leaders who gain the trust of employees devastated by the effects of the fire ablaze around them.

MANAGEMENT PRINCIPLES
IN THE SEASON OF RELEASE

Indicators	*Typical Management Focus*
• Old structure disintegrates	• Identify mission, purpose, and values
• Diversity declines and uniformity increases	• Set common vision
• Old products and processes no longer serve; new ones must be developed	• Reward creative thinking
• Power is liberated	• Reward spontaneous leaders and natural work groups
• Accelerated entropy and stranded capital occur	• Redirect capital

---

MANAGING ON THE VERGE

Managing on the verge means mastering the overlap *between* two phases, which requires that you manage for *both* the current phase and the next one and, at just the right moment, make the leap between phases.

To make the leap from innovation to growth, you must have the ability to choose winners from the innovative options on your menu, as well as the requisite discipline to focus your attention on them.

To make the leap from growth to improvement you must develop the ability to generate different and better variations of your core products or services, as well as the requisite variety of people and skills to launch them as needed.

To make the leap from improvement, to release, and finally to a new cycle of innovation, you must know the underlying mission and enduring purpose that gives life to your company, and have the requisite vision to express that mission in ways that follow the plans and serve the role your stakeholders expect of you.

One helpful way to advance all these steps is to enhance your responsiveness to changes in your total marketplace. Metrics can help. Metrics are to a business what the five senses are to humans—systems of feedback that improve our capacity to adapt and excel over the long run. In the industrial age, companies focused mostly on metrics like sales, market share, and profits—metrics for the growth phase. In today's more dynamic economy, a more comprehensive set of metrics may be needed, such as the one described in the table below.

CORPORATE PERFORMANCE REPORTING: KEY ELEMENTS OF A COMPREHENSIVE APPROACH

INNOVATION	Corporate mission and social needs targeted Number of prototypes or product launches Success rate
GROWTH	Production Sales Market share Profits Labor productivity Return on capital
IMPROVEMENT	Eco-efficiency Resource productivity Quality/defect rate Customer satisfaction Employee retention Employee satisfaction Benchmark all above with competitors
RELEASE	Core values Core mission and enduring purpose Social needs served by core mission Stakeholder satisfaction

HOW 3M MASTERS THE FOUR SEASONS

IT DOESN'T JUST CREATE SEEDS, IT SELECTS
THE BEST ONES—THE ONES WITH KILLER APPS

Innovation doesn't just mean creating new seeds. To bear fruit, the seeds must be planted and nourished. Not just any seeds—the right seeds. 3M has a knack for selecting the right seeds, growing them, and continually refining and improving them to extract their full value. It sets aside time for its people to explore interesting ideas, then supports them in finding the "killer ap" for promising ones, to borrow a term from software designers. Perhaps as a result, a third of the company's profits consistently come from products invented in the previous three or four years. If any major company in the world understands corporate sustainability—the capacity to master all four phases of a living business at once and to sense and serve the economic, social, and environmental interests of its full community in the process—it may be 3M.

3M is a 100-year-old, $15 billion, 70,000-employee corporate behemoth that can act like a start-up, a growth machine, a learning organization, and a too-big bureaucracy, all at once. It is more a network of semi-autonomous branches than either a formal hierarchy or learning organization. Units of 3M are dynamically interactive, cooperating and competing, "hiring" and "firing" people from project to project. Coordination isn't imposed; it emerges from the swarm.

3M's DNA comprises the company's mission and its 30 core technologies, 30 designs that 3M scientists and engineers continuously rearrange to create new products with new qualities, at the rate of more than one a day.

It is part of 3M's philosophy to take responsibility for the effects of everything it does, not just the internal effects but the social and environmental ones as well. It discovered early on that the company has no reason to exist if it is not to serve society—solve problems and create opportunities. Rather than shifting costs to society, 3M aims to take them for its own. The first plank of 3M's environmental policy, for example, is that 3M "solve(s) its own environmental problems." It lives that value. 3M pioneered the global Pollution Prevention movement.

3M creates new seeds through innovations founded on its core values. 3M makes things stick. Its core competence is the development of coatings and adhesives for almost any use. 3M's product-development efforts are guided by its four core values: "Respecting our social and physical environment. Satisfying our customers with superior quality and value. Providing investors with an attractive return through sustained, high-quality growth. Being a company that employees are proud to be a part of."

Stories tell of deeper values. Many companies have an historic figure who brought vision to the company and serves as a continuing source of inspiration. 3M has one—William L. McKnight, chairman from 1949 to 1966, who decentralized authority long before it was fashionable and rewarded innovators and risk takers even when they challenged internal priorities. He even encouraged 3M's employees to develop innovations that might cannibalize 3M's own products: Better to be cannibalized by your own than by another tribe, he figured. McKnight's management theories remain guiding principles for 3M.

But 3M is a community of people and, throughout the company, credit is spread to hundreds of people inside and outside 3M's formal boundaries. Their stories emphasize the personal qualities that 3M encourages: ingenuity, resourcefulness, the courage to question and even thwart authority, devotion to society and the environment.

Crisis is often the force that fashions a company's core values and embeds them in its people, processes, and products. That is the case with 3M.

To select seeds with growth potential, 3M looks for killer apps. 3M has long been making profits by accident and listening carefully to its customers. By finding out what they were doing with 3M's products, the company found it could continuously refine its products to fill new niches. Among the products for which 3M's customers found the purpose are waterproof sandpaper, the Thermo-Fax™, adhesive tapes of all kinds, audio and video tapes, carbonless papers, overhead projection systems, and an array of medical and dental products. Each new product seemed to create niches for yet more products, creating a developmental path that 3M simply had to follow.

Over time, that path led to a *de facto* "3M system" that has since been developed, improved, and documented as a model of corporate *intrapreneurship* by Gifford and Libba Pinchot, who pioneered the intrapreneurship concept and used 3M as one of their corporate models.

The first part of the 3M system is the individual. In 1949,

McKnight declared that 3M was a company that encouraged productive disobedience. His policy was to advance people to executive positions only once they had demonstrated the courage to defy authority in the name of something they believed in, according to the Pinchots. "If management is intolerant and destructively critical when mistakes are made [we] think it kills initiative, and it is essential that we have many with initiative if we are to continue to grow," McKnight said.

To formalize that philosophy, 3M established the "15 percent rule": Employees can spend 15 percent of their time checking out ideas they think may be useful, without having to justify their decisions or gain approval from superiors. That latitude is a big departure from the conformity often imposed to maximize machine-style growth. It provides opportunity for the process of specialization and differentiation essential to the improvement season.

The second part of 3M's innovation transfer formula is the team. McKnight's philosophy led to the idea that new products should be advanced by self-forming teams that include three experts: one technical, one marketing, and one manufacturing. Intrapreneurs with a good idea must recruit at least two additional co-conspirators—one from each of these three categories—to move the idea toward launch. By bringing these three areas together, 3M accomplishes what other companies often fail to do: It selects and develops seeds with the capacity to grow.

That's the theory. In practice, interdisciplinary teams, or business development units (BDUs) have often been used to advance new-product ideas, but the practice is far from universal. Products are invented and developed in all kinds of ways by the company's 45 divisions. It is certainly true that new product will have to involve marketing and manufacturing at some stage, but the process differs among products, inventors or development teams, and divisions. It can sometimes take years for even the most promising 3M ideas to germinate and grow, and require the dedication of internal advocates and change agents to make it happen.

The best-known example is the Post-it note. Dr. Spence Silver developed the repositionable adhesive used on Post-it notes—not surprisingly, by accident. In 1968, while looking for ways to improve the adhesion of 3M's acrylics, he stumbled on a way to *reduce* their adhesion.

But what could be done with it? For the next five years, Silver gave seminars and buttonholed individual 3Mers. A few products followed, but nothing revolutionary. Then Art Fry, a new product researcher, attended Silver's in-house lecture and hit on an idea that would become the killer app for Silver's adhesive.

Fry faced internal opposition from operations people who thought Post-its would be technically difficult to make, and executives who thought it would never sell. The technicians were right, but when executives made cold calls to try to sell the product, demand was so strong that the technical challenges were quickly overcome. In 1981, one year after their introduction, Post-it® Notes were named the company's Outstanding New Product. Fry was named a 3M corporate scientist in 1986.

In its seasons of improvement, 3M seeks to drive waste toward zero. One of 3M's most powerful improvement-phase business tools is what they call 3P, for *Pollution Prevention Pays.* Joe Ling, known worldwide as "Mr. Pollution Prevention," is legendary for creating the program in 1975. The idea was to recognize employees who eliminated pollution at a savings. In its first year, Ling reported that 19 projects had eliminated 1.5 million pounds of pollution with first year savings of $11 million.

The success of 3P was an inspiration, not just at 3M but globally. Twenty-five years later, 4,650 employee projects have prevented the generation of 1.6 billion pounds of pollution. Savings are conservatively estimated at $810 million (3M tracks only first-year savings from 3P).

Over time, Ling expanded 3P to encompass sustainable development. Sustainability "is the mechanism by which we strive for a desirable quality of life, not only for ourselves, but also for all future generations," he says. To promote sustainability, 3M became one of the first companies to embrace life cycle management (LCM), a process they increasingly apply in new product development to drive down environmental impacts from design and manufacturing to customer use and disposal. In the mid-1990s, LCM was introduced to the company's divisions as a voluntary method. In 2001, it became 3M policy for LCM to be a part of new-product development and for divisions to develop a prioritized plan for applying LCM to their existing products.

By closing the loop on waste, since 1990 3M has found ways to cut manufacturing releases to water 82 percent, volatile organic air emissions 88 percent, solid waste 24 percent, and rates of waste generation 35 percent.

3M keeps its core products from becoming commodities by continually creating new core products. After a company creates a new product, imitators often follow it into the marketplace. Over time, experience will streamline manufacturing, and competition will drive down prices, eventually turning high-margin innovations into low-margin commodities. 3M constantly avoids the chase of commodification by creating new products and product varieties. Its 15 percent rule, and the systems that drive innovations past the line into growth vehicles, have kept 3M young and vital for a century.

In many ways, 3M isn't really an industrial corporation in the traditional sense, and hasn't been for most of its 100 years. It is a web, a network, an industrial ecosystem evolving gradually away from its roots as a consumptive industrial enterprise toward one that boosts performance while driving down consumption, pollution, and waste.

ON THE VERGE BETWEEN ORDER AND CHAOS: VISA

Can a company be structured to excel on the verge? VISA is one such organization. VISA International isn't a traditional corporation. Its founding CEO, Dee Hock, used the synergetic qualities in biological systems as his model for a business that he believed would grow almost by itself—if he could just get the design right.

His strategy worked. By structuring VISA to grow the way natural systems do, he created a business whose success is powered by the relationships among its member companies. VISA has changed significantly since Hock moved on, but it remains a model for growing a business by emulating principles of nature.

Hock was 20 years old when he took a job at a small, floundering consumer finance company in 1951. Within months, the manager was gone and his job fell to Hock. Not knowing any better, he and his barely-twenty-something colleagues "trashed the company manual, ignored commandments, and did things as common sense, conditions, and ingenuity combined to suggest."

Within two years, business tripled and the office was leading the company in growth. Naturally, headquarters decided to buckle down, and institute controls on the youthful renegades.

After repeated battles with bureaucracy over the years, Hock was recruited by the National Bank of Commerce, and later tapped by its president, Maxwell Carlson, to lead an accelerated 90-day campaign to launch a joint credit card venture with Bank of America. That soon expanded to encompass a regional committee of banks, all of whom needed an interbank card system that would be financially secure and easy for consumers to use. "Suddenly, like a diamond in the dirt, there it lay," says Hock. "The need for a new concept of organization and a precarious toehold from which to make the attempt."

Hock set about to invent the interbank credit card industry. Since neither he nor anyone could do such a thing alone, he looked for a successful business model to emulate. He found his model in biology. "The trick for a biological organism in a changing environment is . . . for each part of the organism to assume a form useful to the evolving whole. It is no different for organizations," he decided.

That inspired Hock to rethink his committee's plan. Instead of arguing about the terms of their joint venture, they began to think of its genetic code—its core design. If they could get the design right, Hock was convinced the organization would grow itself.

That led Hock to devise his concept for **chaordic organizations**. *Chaordic* is a term Hock coined to describe organizations always on the border between order and chaos. They share the order of the tightly structured growth machine, the continuous improvement of the developing company, and the free-wheeling chaos of the creative organization. Healthy ecosystems are always chaordic, in Hock's view. So are healthy businesses.

Hock's working group focused on devising the purpose of their enterprise, and its founding principles. For example, it would be jointly owned by all participants. Each participant would have equitable rights and obligations. Power would be distributed as broadly as possible. The enterprise should induce change, not compel it. And it should be infinitely malleable yet extremely durable.

By coming together, the smaller banks Hock represented had negotiating leverage greater than Bank of America, which owned the BankAmericard franchise. B of A, which at first balked at the business structure, finally gave in. In 1970, VISA International was born, with Dee Hock its founding CEO.

Today, three-quarters of a billion people use VISA to make 14 billion transactions producing annual volume of $1.25 trillion—the largest single block of consumer purchasing power in the world.

What made VISA succeed? Hock emphasizes that the first step is to get the design right—the purpose, the principles, the concept. His team devised a purpose and principles that attracted a wide following of banks and financial institutions. That gave them the combined leverage to overcome opposition from the big bank in town, Bank of America, and win the market on their terms.

Then, they got the structure right: a highly decentralized organization with authority and responsibility broadly distributed among its parts. Members weren't coerced into cooperation; instead, incentives were structured so that each part served its own interest by serving that of the whole.

As a result, no one was really in charge at VISA. No one needed to be. VISA self-organized from the uncontrolled actions of all its members, who self-regulated their activities to serve both themselves and the whole organization.

THE CHAORD—A CORPORATE MODEL THAT PROFITS THROUGH SYNERGY

After years of building VISA, Hock began to consider at a deeper level the systems-based principles that made VISA succeed. He wondered how they might be applied to advance a revolution in business that would topple the machine form.

Hock was convinced that in a fast-changing economy, traditional business structures were neither economically nor environmentally sustainable. "Our current forms of organization are almost universally based on compelling behavior . . . The organization of the future will be an embodiment of *community* based on *shared purpose* calling to the *higher aspirations of people*."

Hock's model for an organization that profits by creating net gain is what he calls a *chaord*. A chaord is "any self-organizing, self-governing, adaptive, nonlinear, complex organism, organization, community or system, whether physical, biological or social, the behavior of which harmoniously blends characteristics of both chaos and order." Its behavior is "not governed or explained by the rules that govern or explain its constituent parts."

The old approach to designing a business is to start with the product and work backward: Define the Practice—what the company will make or do—then the Structure—how the company will be controlled and managed. Then the People and Principles—who will be hired, and what beliefs and principles will they be expected to follow. In this model, the Purpose of the company is an afterthought at best.

Chaordic organizational design takes traditional wisdom and turns it upside-down. It begins with corporate Purpose—something of compelling importance that will motivate people to join and believe in the company. From there, it proceeds to Principles, People, and Concept, and finally Structure and Practice.

In many ways, Hock's chaordic organization develops the way nature's own living systems develop, following patterns of succession.

SIX STEPS TO A CHAORDIC COMPANY

Purpose: A clear, simple statement of intent, a worthy pursuit that identifies and binds the community together. It can't be the standard, "we'll make good products and give our shareholders a healthy return," Hock suggests. It should speak to people so powerfully that they can say—and believe—that "if *we* could achieve that, *my* life would have meaning."

Principles: The behavioral values and aspirations of the community—how the whole and all the parts intend to conduct themselves in pursuit of the purpose. These include principles of structure, such as "all partners will have equal ownership," and principles of practice, such as "we will respect the diversity of the communities we serve." The principles don't talk means, only ends. They aren't prescriptive—they are the what, not the how.

People and Organizations: The number and variety of people and organizations to be involved in governance, ownership, rewards, rights, and obligations. Here the company needs the requisite variety to fully mirror the demands of its environment, and meet any challenge it might face.

Concept: The "animal"—the organizational relationships among the parts that would lead to the most effective whole. This is where many efforts fail, Hock says. Why? People fall back on old, familiar, prescriptive business models that contradict the purpose and principles they previously set forth.

Structure: Once a group has conceived its purpose, principles, people and concept, nothing will stop them from attempting to build the business. Now they will have the insight and inspiration to develop its structure—a detailed description of the concept, in a written form that can form the basis of legal contracts. The structure includes details of eligibility, ownership, voting, bodies, and methods of governance.

Practice: Everything up to this point is what the business *is*. The practice is what the business *does*. It is the actions of all the participants functioning within the structure, in pursuit of their common purpose, in accord with their principles, enabled and motivated by incentives that advance the needs of the parts as they advance the whole.

Six steps, not always sequential, often overlapping, always chaotic, but with underlying order. The key is to get the purpose and principles right. Once that core design is right, it will inevitably attract the people and resources it requires. If it can then fully mirror its market, if it has the requisite variety to reflect internally the needs it must fill and challenges it must meet externally, then "profit becomes a barking dog begging to be let in," says Hock.

MANAGEMENT PRINCIPLES AND PRACTICES OF THE FOUR SEASONS OF BUSINESS

Strategy	Phase 1 Innovation	Phase 2 Growth	Phase 3 Improvement	Phase 4 Release
Business is like	A Laboratory	A Machine	A Campus	A Burning Forest
Profit comes from	Innovation	Replication	Differentiation: efficiency, variety, quality	Underlying identity: a mission and sense of enduring purpose
Power is	Up for grabs	Centralized in a tall hierarchy	Decentralized flat network/hierarchy	Liberated

MANAGEMENT PRINCIPLES
AND PRACTICES OF THE FOUR SEASONS
OF BUSINESS *(continued)*

Strategy	*Phase 1* *Innovation*	*Phase 2* *Growth*	*Phase 3* *Improvement*	*Phase 4* *Release*
Leaders are	Self-defined	Designated authorities who enforce rules	Facilitators who can manage people in teams	Charismatics
The most valuable form of capital is	Design	Physical	The design you apply to refine the old physical capital	The mission and core values that provide a path from chaos to order
Achievement is motivated by	Vision	Goals and compensation	Recognition and appreciation	Desire to survive
Status comes from	The success of my innovations	What I have— my money and power	What I do— my specialty and how it benefits the team	Ability to convey comfort and certainty to the confused
R&D focus is	Create brand new products and processes	How to make more, bigger, faster	Refine, improve, and differentiate existing products and processes	Mission and values to guide a new creative phase
Product development strategy is	New stuff	More stuff	Different, better stuff	Be open to new stuff that reflects your values
Personal survival strategy is	Entrepreneurship	Conformity, self-reliance, hard work	Specialties, teamwork, smart work	Adaptability, leadership
Marketing focus is	Try things, see what takes off	Single-focus, mass market	Multiple focus, niche markets	Refocus, new market
Succeeding on the verge: *What quality is essential to make the transition to the next phase?*	Ability to choose winners and focus on them: *The requisite discipline*	Ability to create different and better variations when the market demands it: *The requisite diversity*	Ability to invent a whole new business from the old one *An organizational mission and values*	Ability to excel amid chaos and tap the power liberated by change *A sense of identity— enduring mission and purpose*

CHAPTER NINE

New Tools and New Values

LESSON NINE:
GATHER THE TOOLS TO CARRY OUT BOTH PLANS—
THE ONE INSIDE AND THE ONE OUTSIDE.

IN THE RAINFOREST, *life flourishes when it has the tools to follow its inner plan— the one in the seed of every living thing—AND adapt to the outer plan—the one defined by its environment.*

IN THE ECONOMY, *too, a business needs tools to follow its inner plans, AND adapt to its total environment.*

When Bill's parachute failed to open, we began to ponder the nature of planning, and the curious ways that, in the face of new circumstances, our plans often change. For example, Bill's free-fall path through the sky was not the result of one plan, but the convergence of two very different plans. First, Bill's plan, which was to slow his fall to the point that he could land gently and join Tachi and our colleagues to explore the rainforest. Second, nature's plan, which seemed to involve propelling Bill with great force *into* the rainforest, in a manner that would have compelled further changes in our plans.

To carry out Bill's current plan, rather than nature's, we needed tools. Our parachutes. Our emergency chutes. The hands and arms we would use to release them. And especially, the wisdom to use them in ways that would harness nature, align her plans with our own, and carry us safely home.

IN THE RAINFOREST

THE FIRST PLAN IS INSIDE THE SEED, THE SECOND IS IN THE ENVIRONMENT

The Monstera is one of the reasons the rainforest looks like a jungle. A lanky vine that stretches its way through the rainforest, it springs out of the ground, then seemingly looks around and takes off running, straight for the biggest tree in its locale. Then, once it reaches its target, it suddenly changes direction and shoots up the tree, using the tree trunk for support, until it bursts through the canopy at the top of the forest and begins to take in the direct light of the sun. After that, it ceases to go anywhere in particular and seems satisfied to just get fat on the bounty it discovered in its youth.

Why does the Monstera seedling, freshly popped out of the soil and new to the forest, "look" for the biggest tree in its environment? How does it "know," from a great distance, where it will find the biggest tree? Then, how does it figure out when it's time to stop growing toward that tree, change its target, and start climbing toward the sky?

The Monstera's plan is inscribed in its genes. While most plants instinctively grow toward light, the Monstera seedling can't. As a vine, it doesn't have the structural support to just burst skyward. Nor can it simply latch onto any surrounding tree and hope to find sun—the chances of it finding a tree tall enough to reach the sunlight are slim.

So the Monstera is programmed to take a different strategy. First, it follows Internal Plan A, "grow toward darkness"—specifically, toward the darkest places in the rainforest, the bases of the largest trees. Then, once it finds its big tree, Internal Plan B kicks in: "Grow as fast as you can, up the tree, toward the light." Its behavior shifts, and off it goes.

In the rainforest and in life, however, nothing ever goes exactly as our initial internal plan would have it. The internal plan must be siphoned through a second plan, the external plan imposed by the conditions of the environment. In the Monstera's case, that plan consists of the nutrients in and around the seedling, the conditions where it pops through the topsoil, the location and distance from there to the darkest spot, the height of the tree in that spot, the effects of thousands of animals and plants that will also vie for space and resources, and many other factors.

So, the Monstera is also encoded with some capacity for a change in plans. Only if it has the requisite variety of tools and tactics to adapt to every obstacle it reaches does it survive.

Why plan at all, given that these external factors will invariably force a change of direction? Because without a plan, Monstera would never be able to adapt to change and weave its way to the sun. To reach its destiny, Monstera must follow its plan, not in disregard of its environment but in full responsiveness to it.

IN BUSINESS

NEW TOOLS AND NEW VALUES

In the old industrial economy, businesses and consumers used machines that accelerated production and spread affluence, consuming enormous volumes of the earth's resources in the process. It seemed that every economic gain meant another tree chopped down, another barrel of oil extracted from the earth, another ton of carbon polluting the air. Many of us came to believe that economic well being requires that resources be consumed beyond sustainable levels.

That's not surprising. Every pioneer species grows principally by consuming without restraint the resources that surround it. But the reign of the pioneers, like that of all species types, is a temporary one. The global bank account of ecological capital can't be consumed forever. Eventually, value must be created to replenish it. Without that, it isn't just plants and animals that are at risk. People and businesses are endangered species too.

In the emerging economy, businesses are learning a few simple ideas. All pollution and all wastes are lost profit. All value and all profit are created by design. Business can consume profit the old way—by taking just the *physical* resources from nature and incrementally destroying nature in the process. Or it can create profit the new way—by mimicking the patterns, principles, and ideas of nature, by learning how nature creates value sustainably.

In 1994, we took a walk through the rainforests of Borneo. There we began to learn the principles that nature uses to create value sustainably. In December,1995, we brought together 60 corporate leaders in Aspen, Colorado, and formed the Future 500.

The Future 500 is a global network of leadership companies whose mission is to apply principles of nature to improve the performance and sustainability of business. Our goal is to cultivate businesses and an economy where economic, social, and environmental performance are positively correlated, where every gain in profit yielded an environmental and social gain as well. Using the rainforest as our business model, we aim to apply these principles through tools that any company can use to become both more profitable and sustainable.

Rather than the old business-as-machine model, we see the business as a living ecosystem. We diagram the business ecosystem as a set of five nested systems, represented by concentric circles each of which signifies one of the spheres of the ecosystem. The core circle represents the company's enduring purpose, and the leaders responsible for serving it. This core is nested in the company's workplace, community, marketplace, and environment. Each sphere is interdependent, both transcending and including the spheres within it. To thrive, a company must serve not just its core but each tier of its nest. Feedback helps to gradually align self-interests and broader interests.

The Business Ecosystem: Companies are living ecosystems, nested within a series of other living systems, each more complex and encompassing than the one before. Picture this as five concentric circles: one each for Corporate, Workplace, Community, Marketplace, and Environment. The core circle, *Corporate*, is the genetic code of the company—its mission, values, and shareholder priorities. *Workplace* includes its employees and labor policies and practices. *Community* includes the physical communities within which its facilities operate. *Marketplace* is the broader set of communities, physical and otherwise, into which it stretches—its supply chain and dealer chain, as well as the political and stakeholder communities it touches. *Environment* includes the physical resources and living systems from which it draws physical resources and to which it deposits products and wastes. Together these five tiers form a nest that supports the company, so long as the company supports the nest.

Traditionally, tools of management, accounting, and communications have been designed to reflect the machine model of business. To apply them to this new model of business, we recruited specialists who were expert in both traditional and emerging business models. Many had already begun to redesign established management, accounting, and communications tools to more effectively apply principles of living systems.

For example, applying principles of feedback, Deloitte & Touche provided accounting tools that could track costs throughout the five spheres of the business ecosystem. Applying principles of succession, Visa founder Dee Hock and corporate renewal specialist David Hurst provided management tools designed to maximize performance through all four phases of the business life cycle. To create value-by-design, naturalist Janine Benyus showed us how nature evolves toward processes and products that yield value not with hazardous materials but by elegant and life-friendly design. To wire together the whole business ecosystem, Manning Selvage & Lee provided communication tools that help assure that each level of the business ecosystem supports every other.

We brought together two broad types of companies to develop and test practical tools. The first group comprised the leadership companies that joined the Future 500 in order to use these tools, such as Coca-Cola, Coors, Ford, Mitsubishi, Nike, and Weyerhaeuser. The second group comprised companies that concentrated on developing the tools. They included consulting and technology companies such as Deloitte & Touche, Hewlett-Packard, Manning Selvage & Lee, Pitney Bowes, ERM, Det Norski Veritas, WSP, and Ecostream. This group came to be known as the Future 500 Corporate Accountability Practice, or CAP.

FUTURE 500 TOOL PROVIDERS (PARTIAL LIST)

Deloitte & Touche	*Accounting and Assurance*
Det Norski Veritas	*Certification and Verification*
Ecospring	*New Media*
ERM	*Environmental Management*
Global Futures	*Conflict Management and Stakeholder Partnership*

Hewlett-Packard	*E-Services, World E-Inclusion*
Manning Selvage & Lee	*Communication*
Pitney Bowes	*Document Management*
WSP	*Engineering; Environmental Management*

So that companies would have tools to improve their performance, we developed a "tool kit": accounting and assurance tools by companies like Deloitte & Touche; communication tools by Manning Selvage & Lee and Ecostream; efficiency tools by H-P and Pitney Bowes; planning tools by Global Futures, E-Square, ERM, WSP, and others. Through workshops, manuals, consultation, our annual conferences, and even trips to the rainforest, we began to disseminate these tools to our member companies. Examples from the tool kit are in the accompanying table. Additional tools are in the Appendix, the Future 500 website (*www.future500.org*) and in various business manuals for Future 500 members.

Some of these tools could be applied generally, to almost any unit of any company. Others were designed to meet specialized needs. For example, the CAP Audit gave a comprehensive snapshot of a company's impacts throughout all five tiers, from corporate to workplace to environment, and provided a menu of things-to-do to increase value and cut costs across all of these. The CAP Scan inventoried specific problems or opportunities and generated a menu of possible solutions. The CAP Plan detailed step by step how to implement the findings of the CAP Audit or Scan. And the Future 500 CAP Workshop Series, *What We Learned in the Rainforest*, taught the principles, management methods, and tools that companies can use to profit sustainably.

Future 500 companies use these and other tools to create value four different ways, each corresponding to a different phase or season of the business. The first is through breakthrough innovation, the phase of creation. In the springtime, the forest sprouts thousands of seeds. Each seed is like an idea, waiting for the perfect environmental conditions to grow. In business, phases of innovation can be stimulated using tools like *biomimicry*, which companies such as British Telecom used to create innovative ways to help people communicate. Or through 3M's 15-percent rule, which motivates employees to create a continuous stream of prospective new products, some of which turn out to have significant market potential.

FUTURE 500 CAP TOOL KIT

Topic	Expert
Overviews:	
What We Learned in the Rainforest	Tachi Kiuchi and Bill Shireman
Industrial Ecology	The Future 500
Building Core Capacities:	
Accounting and Measurement	Deloitte & Touche
Management	David Hurst
Chaordic Management	Dee Hock
Strategic Planning	Cate Gable
Engineering	WSP
Communications	Manning Selvage & Lee
Solution Sets and Specialized Disciplines:	
Biomimicry	Janine Benyus
E-Solution Technologies	Hewlett-Packard
Document Management	Pitney Bowes
Certification and Verification	Det Norski Veritas
Organizational Development	ERM
Power Cause Coalitions	Manning Selvage & Lee
Leadership	American Renaissance
Green Technology	Joel Makower
Business Activism	Doug Ivey, Anita Burke
Market-Based Law and Regulation	Global Futures and WSP
Conflict Resolution	Global Futures
Planning and Assessment Tools:	
CAP Audit (comprehensive)	CAP companies
CAP Scan (targeted)	CAP companies
CAP Plan	CAP companies

The second way nature creates value is in the season of growth. Through growth, nature *replicates* the seeds that best meet its immediate needs. It takes a valuable design, inscribed in the chemical or genetic code of its creations, and reproduces it over and over, multiplying this embedded value. Companies like H-P, Intel, and Mitsubishi Electric do the same thing with microchips and software. Instead of taking a scarce resource like oil and using it up, they take an abundant resource like sand and inscribe the value right into it.

Following their example, numerous Future 500 companies use the CAP Scan to highlight valuable product and process designs and create strategies to replicate them throughout their companies or communities. For example, a major soft drink company used an early CAP Scan tool to identify possible breakthrough systems for delivering beverages to people, using a fraction of the resources required today. Procter & Gamble used a CAP Scan to identify a public policy that would create positive incentives to reduce packaging demand and costs and successfully replicated the policy in communities throughout California.

The third way nature creates value is through continuous improvement. In times when sunlight, water, and minerals are in short supply, the forest responds by adaptation. Species refine and improve their design, to match environmental conditions more perfectly. They grow more specialized and efficient, and, as they do, the connections that draw every species to every other grow to form a more complex web.

Coca-Cola, Coors, Mitsubishi Electric, and Nike have all worked to put this principle to work. Using CAP Scans to identify untapped profit opportunities, they have developed menus of options through which they can measure their triple bottom line performance, cut costs, save materials and energy, reduce packaging, and become more responsive to their stakeholders. The Future 500 and Asian Productivity Organization are co-publishing a comprehensive menu of measurement tools drawn from their experiences and others.

The fourth way nature creates value is by decay and release, which clears away space for innovation, through destructive tearing-apart processes. In the forest, fire burns away deadwood, liberates resources, and enables sunlight to reach seedlings long in the shadow of once-dominant species.

The CAP Audit is a comprehensive learning tool that Future 500 companies use to clear away their own deadwood, so their stakeholders in the marketplace don't do it for them. The audit is designed to provide feedback through 108 data points from across the full spectrum of a company's stakeholders: corporate, workplace, community, marketplace, and environment. It highlights business opportunities and red-flags risks that may impose costs through litigation, regulation, or stakeholder conflict. It identifies capital trapped in outdated or costly practices, and enables companies to redeploy to more profitable endeavors. Rather than creating a new framework for measuring and reporting corporate accountability, it integrates elements of existing frameworks, such as the Dow Jones Sustainability Index, Domini Social Index, and Global Reporting Initiative.

Today, the machine-based industrial economy is entering its season of winter. The companies that dominated the Fortune 500 in the past have two choices. They can adapt, create value sustainably, and learn to excel in the future. Or they can decline and be taken out by the fires of change that open the economy to innovation and growth. We believe that without applying principles of nature to bring their companies alive, the Fortune 500 won't have a future. By working together, we can all have one.

BEYOND TOOLS: VALUES

No physical system can grow forever. Like it or not, the industrial era and its exponential growth in resource extraction and dissipation will end. With it will likely end the dominance of the machine model for business.

Yet many fear this will be too little too late. They believe we have violated the limits of nature so severely that difficult, even draconian, change is inevitable.

That could turn out to be true. When small fires are repressed in the forest, big fires tend to follow. When small changes are repressed in a company or an economy, pressure may build, and thresholds may be surpassed. When feedback about ecological or social impacts is inhibited, painful change may be imposed on us by force.

How long will it take for feedback to compel adaptation? Many believe that industrialization is so powerful a force, and so resistant to change, that it will decimate the global cultural rainforest long before it is influenced by ecological or social feedback. They fear that cultural diversity will be replaced with a western materialistic monoculture, leaving the earth without the requisite cultural variety to sustain us for the long term.

That could also turn out to be true. If industrialization proceeds across the globe without adjusting for cultural feedback, it may suffer a backlash from cultural forces that feel threatened by its spread.

But a different outcome is also possible. If we learn to apply the principles of nature in business—if we use tools to adapt more readily to feedback—we can begun a transition to a model with an even greater capacity to support, sustain, and nourish us: business as living system, the economy as rainforest.

The tools above can help smooth the transition. But are these simple tools powerful enough to bring a machinelike company or economy to life? Many doubt it. They believe the transition to the next economy will require a wholesale transformation in values.

Market analyst and sociologist Paul Ray has identified a cultural group that generally takes this view. In 1996, Ray published a study contending that a whole new culture was emerging in our midst, bringing with it a new set of values. He called the group the "Cultural Creatives" because, he said, they were actively creating a new culture. The discovery of a new consumer segment made news in marketing circles. "Values are the best single predictor of real behavior," says Ray. This means that when peoples' values change, their buying practices follow, and new business opportunities may develop.

Ray's study, which measures people's changing values and lifestyles, suggests that there are three major cultures in America. Ray believes that Western Europe and much of the rest of the industrial world is also divided among these three groups.

Traditionals, about 29% of the adult American population, are what Ray calls the "heartlanders." They are drawn to images of small towns and small churches and believe in the old-fashioned American dream. They generally call themselves religious and tend to be conservative.

Moderns, about 47% of the adult American population, are the dominant American culture. They see the world "through the same filters as Time Magazine," says Ray. They tend to value personal success, consumerism, materialism, rationality, and technology. They often call themselves secular and tend to be liberal or libertarian.

Cultural Creatives, about 24% of the adult American population, are intrigued by diverse cultures, ideas, and beliefs, and often choose travel and experience over consumerism. They are socially and environmentally concerned, express a deep longing for meaning and human connection. They often call themselves spiritual rather than religious or secular and tend to be liberal.

"Despite their numbers, Cultural Creatives tend to believe that few people share their values," says Ray. This is partly because their views are a departure from the mainstream that arose with industrial expansion through the 1960s, when less than 4% of the U.S. population was a Cultural Creative.

With the advent of the Internet, the Cultural Creatives are finding each other, and building their community in cyberspace, according to Ray. "The Cultural Creatives have grown in numbers to a quarter of the population *without any mutual awareness of one another*. Most Cultural Creatives tend to think they are pretty much alone. If Cultural Creatives become aware of themselves—as an alternative to the mainstream modernist culture, and also as 44 million people, a quarter of Americans—then a big result follows: Any device that lets them communicate to one another will accelerate the change in society. Use of online services could be such a communication device. Wonderful changes are possible once the synergies become obvious, and we start co-creating a viable and positive image of the future, and even more so if we stop acting like an audience, and start acting like a community."

Are any of these three value systems "right" or "best?" As the industrial era gives way to the information economy, will one triumph over the others? Not exactly. Experts say that is not the way values evolve.

Values reflect society's needs. A society's values reflect its beliefs about what qualities serve to sustain it. Every economic structure comes with its own value system. Japanese economic scholar Taiichi Sakaiya says that all peoples have what he calls an "empathetic impulse" through which they value what is most plentiful in their culture.

Thus, in agricultural economies, Sakaiya believes, where land and labor are plentiful, values shift toward the accumulation of land and labor. Status may go to those who have large properties and a large number of servants. In industrial economies, where machines create an abundance of material things, people naturally become materialistic.

Status goes to those with the biggest accumulation of things. In information economies, where knowledge is most plentiful, people come to appreciate the intrinsic value of knowledge. Status goes to the educated and experienced, he suggests.

But more is not always better. Over time, cultures become saturated with the benefits of what is most plentiful. The incremental value of getting more declines. They begin to sense when "enough is enough." The satisfaction they derived from their first acre of land, first set of material goods, or first field of expertise, is not as great with their second or tenth or hundredth.

Driven by a desire to live better lives, people respond in two ways to what economists call declining marginal return. They may intensify their efforts, seeking to draw in more and more of what they once valued most, hoping that increasing quantity will overcome declining incremental gains. Or, they may begin to value something different. Thus, saturated with material goods, people may paradoxically pursue even more, at a faster rate than ever. Or, they may decide that the cost of this strategy is too great for the marginal benefits it offers, and begin to pursue something different. These two strategies—more versus different—show how a culture may seem to be going in two directions at once, with some people deepening their commitment to old values, while others begin to develop a whole new set.

In Sakaiya's view, the industrial world is on the verge of what he calls a "Knowledge-Value revolution." Our system of values, once focused on material acquisition, is shifting. As prosperity grows and the rewards of additional consumption for the already affluent decline toward zero, we are beginning to reduce our attachment to these sources of wealth. As information grows in abundance, we are shifting our values toward the accumulation of knowledge and, perhaps, to the development of wisdom.

But these "Knowledge Values" will not supersede prior value systems. If they emerge in healthy forms, they will *transcend and include* the others.

As cultures respond to the feedback triggered by changing conditions, their value systems grow more complex. Just as a simple forest grows more diverse as successive waves of plants and animals define new niches, cultures grow richer and more diverse as they adapt to successive waves of change.

Can a society maintain several distinct systems of values at a time? This is inherent in the process of cultural development. Cultures are formed by the emergence of value systems in response to life conditions, according to Don Edward Beck, founder of the Institute for Values and Culture. Cultures should not be seen as rigid types, having permanent traits, says Beck. Instead, they ebb and flow, progress and regress, and have the capacity to lay on new levels of complexity when challenges or opportunities arise. Much like an onion, they form layers on layers on layers. Although more advanced cultures have more layers, there is no final state, no ultimate destination, no utopian paradise in which the best value system triumphs. Each stage is a prelude to the next, then the next, then the next. Successive value systems never completely replace their predecessors. As the distinguished philosopher Ken Wilber says, each new cultural stage "transcends and includes" all of those which have come before.

Beck has developed a more comprehensive model of values and culture. He has identified at least eight distinct systems of human values. Cultures tend to evolve through these in stages, one after the other. In healthy development, these value systems are not in destructive competition with one another. In fact, each time a culture makes a healthy transition, its new stage transcends and includes the stage that came before. However, if a new stage fails to include the prior stages, the emergence of the more complex value systems may destabilize the entire culture.

This need to both transcend and include prior cultural stages is essential to peaceful transitions and cultural sustainability. If a society seeks to impose new values *in place* of old ones, it may inadvertently weaken its foundations, foster conflict, and create the conditions for collapse. But if it augments traditional values by adding new values to a foundation of traditional ones, it can cultivate a more complex and enduring culture.

In the first of Beck's eight values stages, people value only what ensures their immediate *survival*. The mode of thinking is instinctual. Identity is exclusively physical. Social organization is limited to small groups that wander together.

In the second stage, people value ritual. The mode of thinking is superstitious. People fear the mysterious forces of nature. Identity is primarily tribal. Social organization is clans or tribes based on family ties.

In the third stage, people value strength and dominance. As some clans become stronger, they use force to unify other clans into ethnic groups. The mode of thinking is impulsive. People believe might makes right. Identity is primarily ethnic. Social organization is directed toward building ethnic empires controlled by the strongest. Stability is attained only after the identity and cohesiveness of the ethnic group is secure.

In the fourth stage, people value order and security. As the brutality and chaos of these aggressive empires becomes intolerable, the great world religions emerge. The mode of thinking is moral. People make absolute judgments about right and wrong. They believe that injustice in this life will be corrected in an afterlife. Identity is primarily religious. Social organization is directed toward building religious states based on common codes of conduct. This is the stage that dominated Europe in the Middle Ages. It is the predecessor to Ray's Traditionals.

In the fifth stage, people value individual success. As the rigidity of religious states becomes burdensome, people break free of socially imposed codes of conduct. They begin to emerge as distinct individuals. This is the stage of individual freedoms and universal rights. The mode of thinking is rational and strategic. People learn analytical thinking and science and seek to use the laws of nature. Competition promotes excellence and rewards the exceptional individual with material wealth. Identity is primarily individual and national. Social organization is directed toward building corporate states. This is the stage that dominated the Enlightenment and industrial era. It corresponds to Ray's Moderns.

In the sixth stage, people value subjective experience. Once people gain a degree of material satisfaction, most begin to sense that something is missing. They begin to search for meaning and develop increased sensitivity to others. In the healthy version of this stage, the mode of thinking is sensitive and relational. Identity is primarily individual and global. Social organization is values-based networks that seek to influence existing institutions and create the seeds for new ones. This stage corresponds to Ray's Cultural Creatives. Activists at this stage are sometimes called "greens."

But the good intentions of the greens almost invariably fall short because their initial approach is reactive, suggests Beck. Frustrated by their slow progress at social change, many greens become reactively and virulently anti-materialistic and anti-hierarchical. Instead of building the new and improving the old, the focus is often on destroying existing religious and corporate structures, and the values that support them. In attempting to transcend without including, the greens fail to transcend and may create the conditions for regression.

Each value system has both positive and negative aspects. Each adds to human capacities, yet each is missing something—something that is partially filled in by the other value systems. This is seldom acknowledged by advocates of specific value systems. They tend to become too wrapped up in their immediate values, and often lose sight of important values from prior stages. This creates an us-versus-them mentality, and a military mindset that focuses on the identification and destruction of enemies.

In the seventh stage, a small number of people—less than three percent of Americans to date—recognize this and make a leap to what Beck calls a "second-tier" value system. At this stage, the ability to accept and work with multiple value systems first emerges. Each of the prior value stages is represented. The mode of thinking is *systemic*, focused on the relationships of individuals, cultures, and nature. Identity expands to include the progress of humanity through all the stages of development. When this mode of thinking becomes more influential, Beck suggests, social organization will begin to integrate the structures from various stages.

In the eighth stage, an even smaller number—less than half a percent of Americans—make another leap to a still more integrated value system. At this stage, the ability to work with multiple value systems is enhanced. Each of the prior value stages is more fully and compatibly represented. The mode of thinking is *holistic*, focused on still more complex sets of relationships. Identity continues to expand. When this stage becomes influential, social organization will begin to more fully mesh the structures from the previous stages.

What Makes a Culture "Sustainable?"

Don Edward Beck suggests an "S-Culture Index" to measure various societies and cultures on these dimensions. He proposes that Sustainable Cultures:

• Develop, propagate and update a compelling vision, a sense of transcendent purpose, and a series of superordinate goals to create common cause for a complex culture.

- Focus on systemic health and well-being rather than on one-time initiatives or any magical "quick-fix."
- Embrace the evolutionary dynamic and recognize that the center of gravity for the culture will shift as conditions of existence change in the milieu, either progressive or regressive.
- Accept that dynamic tension is part of life itself and have learned how to differentiate between destructive and constructive conflict.
- Disseminate self-reliance and responsible decision-making at every level, in every function, and on every issue.
- Mesh four bottom-lines - purpose, profit, people, and planet - and realize that to sustain any one of the four they must also experience success in the other three.
- Develop a sense of collective individuality in that the two are seen as cyclical blends and ratios rather than extremes or poles.
- Respect the past-present-future timeline and think of each as an element in the seamless flow of nature.
- Deal with causes and symptoms in a simultaneous, interdependent fashion.
- Have the capacity to renew themselves whenever the conditions of existence create greater complexity than available responses can manage.
- Integrate economic, political, social, environmental, spiritual and educational domains in an integral fashion.
- Transmit their cultural codes to the present generation while, at the same time, prepare the youth for different conditions in the near and far future.
- Transcend and include previous ways of being while always anticipating what will be next, thus living in open systems.

To create and sustain an S-Culture with the capacity, resilience, and vision to survive and prosper, Beck points to four necessary actions. First, understand the dynamics that drive change in the culture and all living systems. Second, monitor vital signs. Third, implement integral policies to promote cultural health and sustainability. Fourth, employ skillful means to enhance adaptiveness.

Is it possible a new culture will emerge in response to the new life conditions—environmental and cultural—we have described?

If as Beck suggests, cultures emerge in response to life conditions, the idea that values may change as a result is plausible. But it will not— indeed, cannot—be the sweeping transformation that many greens anticipate. A healthy and sustainable culture cannot reject the old stage in favor of the new, without undermining its own foundations.

How do cultures evolve from one set of values to the next? Drexel Sprecher has developed a pioneering approach to leadership and the dynamics of renewal and development. He suggests that no culture can replace its values all at once. There is a natural rhythm of development that balances cultural progress and stability. Cultures, like all living systems, progress to more advanced stages of development through the four phases of renewal. Effective leaders need to recognize the distinction between stages of development and phases of renewal in order to accelerate the diffusion of new values.

As we have suggested, cultures evolve through stages. Stages are progressive and directional like steps on a staircase. New stages represent distinct milestones on a path of development, each richer and more encompassing than its predecessor. With every stage come new aspirations, new perspectives, new moral ideals, new promises and new perils. Every new stage of cultural development appears initially to represent the highest human ends. Paradoxically, when it reaches its highest level of realization, it becomes a step on the path to still higher ends.

The four phases of renewal represent the process by which new values diffuse through a culture, gradually replacing more and more of the old. Phases are cyclical and recurring, like phases of the moon or seasons of the year. These four phases are the means through which individuals and cultures progress through the stages.

In the first phase, *awakening*, which has many of the characteristics of the emergence of new species in nature and breakthrough innovation in technology, a small number of individuals in a few cultural niches awaken to new aspirations and begin to adopt new values. Some awaken to these aspirations as they recognize the intrinsic benefit of new possibilities. Others awaken as they sense that existing aspirations offer decreasing marginal benefits at increasing marginal cost.

In the second phase, *growth*, the new values from the awakening grow and spread rapidly, like r-strategists in an open field. Advocates of the new values often expect them to quickly overthrow and replace prior value systems. Yet invariably they find that the new values come into conflict with their predecessors. Individuals at the new stage see its new freedoms and expanded identity as a moral advance. Those at the older stages see its rejection of established norms as moral decline. The newer values may establish niches that take territory away from the old. Then a backlash occurs. Defenders of the old protect their territory and call for restoration of the old values. This is a time when a culture can appear to be moving in two directions at once.

This conflict shatters the existing cultural consensus on values. The accumulating cost of the conflict depletes resources, reduces cultural trust, and erodes established institutions. Eventually an institutional crisis demands a new consensus.

In the third phase, *restructuring*, which has many of the characteristics of continuous improvement, a new consensus crystallizes and provides the organizing principles for restructuring of major institutions. Since only a portion of the population truly embraces the new values as their own, the consensus invariably reflects an imperfect accommodation between those who hold the new values and those who hold the old values.

As new institutions are built, the new consensus begins to transform the older values. Aspects of the new values work their way through the culture, gradually transforming the ways people live. People who hold the old values begin to interpret and internalize the new values within the limits of their existing stage of development.

In the fourth phase, *decline*, a culture enjoys the benefits of the new values and institutions. Many of the aspirations that initiated the awakening are fulfilled. The marginal value of more diminishes, and the costs increase. Although the new institutions appear stable, some people are already beginning to question the legitimacy of the values that created them. This is another time when a culture can appear to be moving in two directions at once.

Eventually the values consensus begins to erode. A crisis of legitimacy occurs. The stage is set for a new awakening.

Through the four phases of renewal, individuals and cultures lay down a foundation for future stages of development, which then proceed through the same four phases from a higher starting point. Sprecher calls this recurring process the *cultural long wave*. Every stage of values emerges and grows to dominance in a series of these waves.

With every wave, newer values are woven deeper into the fabric of the culture.

As a long wave rolls across a culture it initiates transformations in many individuals. Some advance to the next stage. Others gain insights from the new stage and remain at their present stage. A few who are deeply threatened may regress to a previous stage. The number of individuals at newer stages grows and the number at older stages declines. Yesterday's innovators become today's progressives, and today's progressives become tomorrow's reactionaries.

With every cultural wave, the newer values take more and more cultural and institutional niches away from older values before encountering territory they cannot take. By the time a new stage achieves dominance, the leading edge of a still more advanced stage is already beginning to emerge. This gradual infusion of new values ensures a dynamic stability that tends to be self-correcting. Although adverse events may cause a culture to revert for a time, the direction of development over the long term remains clear. The center of gravity of the culture shifts from more fundamental values like security to more significant ones like the pursuit of happiness.

Throughout history, a wave carrying new cultural values has initiated each of the major waves of civilization—agricultural, industrial, and information. It took several millennia and countless cultural waves for religious values and agricultural civilization to become dominant. It has taken over five centuries and at least five major cultural waves for secular values and industrial civilization to become dominant. Now we are experiencing the first wave carrying the values of a new stage. It will take a series of waves for this stage to become dominant.

Why is the distinction between stages and phases so important? As a wave sweeps through a culture, it carries the qualities of higher stages, first as an invading pioneer, then as a mature dominator. It is tempting to conclude that the older values are immature r-strategists and the newer values are mature K-strategists. For example, business leaders often assume that values in a market economy are necessarily more advanced than those in an agricultural or hunting culture. This confuses stages of development with phases of renewal. There are r-strategists and K-strategists at every stage of development. A new stage of values is more advanced though less mature than the dominant stage. Leaders who miss this distinction will miss opportunities to accelerate the diffusion of new values.

As individuals and cultures progress to higher stages of development, they gradually transcend the idea that the cultural forms and rules inherited from their ethnic and religious communities are necessary for morality and goodness. As they become free from these concrete forms, they tend to gain an appreciation and caring for others outside their own communities. The aspiration for greater personal freedoms and an expanded sense of responsibility begin to develop in concert.

At the highest stages of development, beyond the traditionals, moderns, and greens, a small number of individuals transcend their attachment to the values of particular stages of development as well as particular cultural and institutional forms. These individuals gain a great appreciation for the experience and perspectives of people at all stages. They also gain the ability to distinguish cultural and institutional forms from the value stages that generate them. Their new perspective enables them to see more deeply into their own culture and other cultures.

Sprecher suggests that leaders with these rare capacities have the potential to orchestrate cultural conflicts in ways that lead to better institutions and greater cultural harmony. Although many cultural conflicts appear to be conflicts between cultural forms, they are almost always conflicts between stages of values. Leaders who appreciate the experience and perspectives of different stages are better prepared to create a genuine synthesis of conflicting values. These leaders can assist people in finding common contexts that encompass the values of different stages and in bridging the differences between conflicting cultural and institutional forms.

Today's leaders have their best opportunity to shape the conflict between new and old values in the growth phase. The consensus and organizing principles that result from that conflict are crucial to the quality of the new institutions that ultimately result from the awakening. If that consensus reflects a genuine synthesis of the newer and older values, maximizing the benefit of the new while minimizing the threat to the old, then common institutions will tend to work well. If events force a consensus before a synthesis is achieved, the result may be little more than a fragile truce, with cultural and institutional niches divided between the old and the new based on the power of different interests rather than the good of the whole. Leaders who can discover common contexts and sustain creative tension between conflicting values will improve the prospects for a synthesis.

Even after a social consensus has crystallized and organizing principles are defined, leaders still have opportunities to shape the way institutions develop in the restructuring phase. New institutions must assimilate and accommodate people who have not had the same inner transformation. Leaders who appreciate and embrace the experience of people at older stages will be more able to share insights from the new in ways the old can appreciate. This approach will assist those who hold older values in adapting to the new and even open them to the possibility of transformation. Leaders will then be able to manage the tension between new and old values in ways that accelerate the diffusion of the new and achieve a better integration of the new with the old.

What are the implications for global leadership? Sprecher says that leaders must be able to attune to the rhythm of development and work with the forces of change. They must resonate with the experience of people at all stages of development, synthesize multiple views into a comprehensive view of world development, and articulate overarching goals in terms people at all stages can appreciate. Working with, rather than against, the forces of change is the test of leadership.

Advocates of green values, such as the Cultural Creatives, have not yet met this test of leadership, Sprecher says. Many misapprehend the process by which new values diffuse and are integrated. They imagine that a massive cultural transformation will roll across the globe, awakening all the world to the limits of materialism, and bringing everyone to *their stage* of development at once. A recognition of the dynamics of developmental stages reveals that this will not occur. New values take hold not by vanquishing the old, but by extending and building on them. Efforts to force global community by imposing a global set of values are doomed to fail.

As a new value stage emerges, advocates of different value stages often become polarized. Those who outgrow one set of values tend to become advocates of another set, forgetting that each developmental stage is the foundation that supports that next stage.

The first wave of green activists has adopted a reactive rather than transformational approach to their social goals. Many equate the idea of a developmental hierarchy of values with oppressive power hierarchies. Rightly sensing that industrialization has surpassed long-term limits, they have declared political war. Rather than transcend and include the prior stages of values, their moral stance and political strategies seek to demonize, deconstruct and discard them to clear the cultural landscape so that it can be populated with their own species of truth. In opposing one form of global monoculture, many impulsively advocate tearing it down and replacing it with another. Yet this slash-and-burn approach mirrors the tactics of the r-strategist religious fundamentalists and market fundamentalists they criticize

The image of global cultural transformation and the denial of developmental stages often combine to energize a relentless opposition to globalization. Many green activists resist any and all forms of globalization because they believe it will establish centralized control of the global marketplace by a small number of corporations or nations and impose a uniform world culture modeled on western industrialization.

But globalization need not take this highly centralized form. The sweeping opposition to globalization has consequences. It often blinds activists to the very real developmental needs of the three billion people in the developing world, slows the development of more ecological paths to globalization, and undermines their opportunity to have a positive influence on the course of development.

It is tempting, especially from our comfortable vantage point in the industrial world, to point to the harm caused by materialism and the rapid depletion of physical resources, and to reject these values as fundamentally harmful. Yet paradoxically, these values must be embraced, and transcended, to achieve the cultural and ecological goals of the green worldview.

In the developing world, many nations lack basic material comforts. Without stable supplies of food, water, and housing, and without modern transportation and communications, they cannot even imagine focusing on the trans-acquisitional aspirations that are beginning to emerge in the industrial world. Quality of life and universal human rights are distant abstractions to a family struggling just to survive.

The people in the developing world demand and deserve the same level of physical comfort the industrial world enjoys. Until they achieve it, sustainability will be impossible. Yet if they seek to achieve it as today's industrial world has—through vast material acquisition—they will also fail. The drive of six billion people to live today's version of affluence will overrun the earth's capacity to sustain the population.

All systems grow until they reach limits, and one of the classes of limits is ecological limits. The exhaustion of resources from hunting and gathering was one of the limits that drove the innovation of agriculture. The exhaustion of resources from agricultural civilization was one of the limits that drove the innovation of industrialization. In celebrating the values of hunting and gathering or agricultural civilizations, the green worldview sometimes elevates them to higher moral standing than the industrial.

This can easily degenerate into wholesale rejection of all that industrialization brings, the good and the bad. Elevating these cultures and opposing what could transform them deprives them of their opportunity to develop and their right to participate fully in the world community. Seeking to transcend the industrial stage while leaving behind its legacy of valuable knowledge, skills, and market institutions could deprive billions of their opportunity to achieve material comfort and develop and participate fully in the world community.

Another consequence of the polarized worldview of many greens is a blindness to other global issues. Immersed in the conflict between secular capitalism and environmentalism, green activists have failed to recognize that in most parts of the world the underlying conflict of our times is capitalism versus tribal, ethnic and religious fundamentalism. Battling on the leading edge of development, greens may confuse the cause of these fundamentalists on the trailing edge of development as their own.

That creates a potential danger. It is tempting for fundamentalists from one culture to align themselves with fundamentalists from another. The leading-edge pioneers may share with trailing-edge reactionaries their opposition to the dominant value system. In forming a broad anti-industrial coalition in an effort to destroy their common enemy, they may suppress their own even more fundamental differences. And if their coalition succeeds in its aim, they may find they have destroyed the very foundation required for the preservation or advance of their own cultural values. There is no way to leap from patriarchal values to feminism and multiculturalism without material values. The chasm between green values and those of the fundamentalists is too vast.

Building a coalition of pre- and post-industrialists against the industrial stage leaves the world vulnerable to fundamentalists—ethnic or religious or otherwise. If we undermine the capacity of any people to gain the benefits of material well-being, we will have to live with more fundamentalism longer, and that means we necessarily will live without global ecological thinking—or action—a lot longer.

The seriousness of this oversight was vividly illustrated on September 11, 2001 when terrorists destroyed the World Trade Center and much of the Pentagon in the most devastating foreign attack on American soil in history. Their sponsors—rigid fundamentalists who believed their rule-bound system of values was under siege—debased the ancient religion of Islam by using it as a rationale to commit extraordinary evil. The target of their attack was freedom and materialism. Ironically, their tools were technologies that were a product of the very values they condemned.

This was possible because technology expands power faster than wisdom, shrinking the physical distance between cultures faster than the worldviews of most people can expand to embrace them. Religious fundamentalists use television and the Internet to promote their values. Ethnic fundamentalists use military technology to impose theirs. While connecting the world technologically will enable information to be shared, this cannot ensure that values are shared, let alone create a world culture.

Throughout the developing world, a small number of people on the leading edge of development recognize the need for a more global identity. Many are struggling to expand identity beyond the traditional horizons of their cultures. Yet the kind of identity change that takes place when new values are emerging is deeply threatening, especially in cultures with older ethnic and religious identities. Recall that before the Civil War, America was more a collection of states than a nation. One result of the transition from state to national identity was the bloodiest conflict in our history. The r-strategist abolitionists ended slavery, but made reconstruction of the South after the Civil War almost impossible. The coming transition from national to global identity could be even more wrenching, especially in cultures with ethnic and religious identity.

Will the transition be peaceful? Only if we learn the lessons of development.

Some form of economic globalization is developmentally inevitable, driven by the awakening of economic aspirations combined with advances in global communications technology Sprecher points out. With much of the world aspiring to prosperity, global diffusion of freedom and economic opportunity is necessary before ethnic and religious cultures can release their hold enough for any widespread sense of global identity to develop. Markets are the best way to propagate these ideals into ethnic and religious cultures because introducing market freedoms is less threatening to these cultures than introducing cultural freedoms. The combination of freedom and opportunity with markets also offers concrete benefits that can begin to expand identity. The experience of market exchanges and rising living standards eventually builds ties across ethnic and religious divides, reduces hostility, and promotes tolerance.

So what can be done about the threat of a worldwide industrial monoculture? Sprecher suggests we distinguish between globalization of the values of freedom and economic opportunity, and globalization of particular institutions, corporate cultures, and products. Embracing these values while encouraging a myriad of competing forms will maximize diversity and choice.

Simply blocking the spread of markets will not protect the unique features of pre-industrial cultures. Instead, blocking feedback from a changing world will arrest their development. This could lead to the cultural equivalent of deadwood in the forest, creating the conditions for fiery destruction.

Tragically, the reactive orientation of green activists has often prevented them from making the positive contributions they can make. Proponents of green values have been much less effective at transforming global markets than proponents of market values have been at transforming ethnic and religious cultures.

A transformative approach for green activists would be to work with the forces of change rather than merely struggle against them. Just as information technology is transforming the industrial sector, and even the way that sector is transforming the agricultural sector, green values can transform market values, and even transform the way markets transform ethnic and religious cultures. This will enable globalization to take a more enlightened form that preserves both nature and cultures.

One effective use of green values would be to embrace markets in a more diverse, ecological form, one that promotes green technology, and then assist modernity in embracing and transforming the preindustrial world. It is entirely possible to transform the economy and meet material needs with green technology, without forcing the world to adopt green values.

A rainforest economy, where information and green technology radically reduce the need for physical resources, does not require a global cultural transformation. A rainforest economy based on the principles of nature can bring Factor 10 or better gains in resource productivity—much more value, at much less economic and environmental cost. Such a living economy generates value not just by conformity and consumption, but by diversity and design, first by bringing ideas, things, and people into synergetic combinations that create breakthrough value, then driving continual gains in efficiency, quality, and variety. Its core resource—information—is abundant, so it can be distributed widely. It is synergetic, so it appreciates in value as it is used. It fosters cooperation, since my gain is your gain is my gain. It disaggregates concentrations of power, first decentralizing power, and then more fully distributing it to the individual or local level. And it's virtually impossible to own—it's too porous to be held, and if you're somehow successful, it diminishes in value proportionately to the tightness of your grip. And none of this requires a global culture or a global transformation in values.

Sprecher suggests that, while a global *culture* is not possible in the foreseeable future, a global *civilization* is within our reach. Rather than a common set of values, a global civilization will require a common set of institutions capable of integrating the different value systems that are the inevitable result of human development and cultural renewal. These institutions will need to contain disorder and develop potential. They will need to structure and manage the tensions between global responsibility and local autonomy. And they will need to mediate the conflicts between cultures so they can develop at their own pace without interference and without harming those outside their borders.

A global civilization will also require leadership with the integrative capabilities that emerge in the stage of development beyond the green worldview. Global leaders will need to appreciate the importance of a variety of cultural forms giving diverse expression to each emerging value system as it rolls across the globe. They will need to be gifted at working with the dynamics of the different stages of cultural development and the four phases of cultural renewal. And they will need to be both architects and gardeners, with the vision to design common institutions and the sensitivity to bring them to life by nurturing other leaders at all stages of development.

TOWARD A GLOBAL CIVILIZATION

What is most promising, from our perspective, is how values from different stages of development and a myriad of cultural forms could meet at the verge, and intertwine to create a rich global civilization, as diverse in human terms as the rainforest is diverse in its population of plants and animals.

Many find this meeting-at-the-verge a prescription for a difficult marriage. Environmentalists and business leaders, for example, often see their two value systems in fundamental conflict: one materialistic, the other counter-materialistic; one rational, the other counter-rational. An error both often make is to believe that one must triumph over the other. Yet creation requires the union of opposites. To cause their new values to spread and permeate, pioneers need to include the values of their old adversaries. The integrative qualities of nature suggest that we pursue not materialistic or pre-materialistic values, but trans-materialistic ones. Transcend and include.

The path to a global civilization demands more of business. Today's r-strategist business enterprises must transcend their machine-like, virtually unconscious strategies of growth, and begin to transform themselves into more adaptive, responsive, living enterprises.

To the two of us, business, like life, provides a challenging opportunity to more fully draw forth what is possible within us. Not the old way, by engaging in battle with nature, a battle against our own ship. The new opportunity is to emulate nature, because in so doing, we bring our actions in alignment with our own potential. We begin to get the design right. And as we get the design right, we create pathways through which new capacities, new innovations, new value can flow.

Business, as one of the few globally networked institutions, can help manage rather than worsen value tensions, and align systems of production with the values of local cultures. A living economy, if we can cultivate one, will emerge in part from a marriage of proactive business and environmental leaders who transcend reactive politics. Such collaboration could result in incentives that enable companies to sense the effects of decisions on the global commons, and markets in which the prices of goods and services more completely reflect their social and ecological costs. This in turn could ensure a healthy, diverse biosphere with natural reserves that protect wild intact ecosystems, and prosperous, self-governing human communities in all cultures.

Morley Winograd, former Director of the National Partnership for Reinventing Government and co-author of *Taking Control: Politics in the Information Age*, has studied an emerging constituency, the "Wired Workers," that may form one base of political and economic support for the kinds of institutions needed for a global civilization. Wired Workers work in autonomous teams to produce valuable products and services, which are combined synergistically with the products of other teams. Although strongly ecologically minded, they tend to be more optimistic, more proactive and more integrative than most greens. They have a strong sense of the possible, value market discipline, tend to be socially libertarian, and favor limited government that concentrates on providing the right incentives. Most believe that with ingenuity, technology, and incentives, people will find ways to generate much more value with fewer resources.

The importance of the Wired Workers is that they have discovered ways to organize business enterprises that successfully integrate people with different value systems, and reward them in currencies that are meaningful in their own value systems. Many of their enterprises are global, with teams working across cultures. These enterprises may be prototypes for the kinds of institutions that will embed the qualities needed for economic and cultural sustainability into the fabric of society.

The path to a global civilization also demands more of environmental activists. Today's r-strategist green activists can engage in combat to clear the field, but they must evolve into a more mature stance to advance a sustainable world. Once they have energized activists who share their views, they must change directions, look ahead rather than behind, and grow toward harmony with the culture of enterprise.

This means, at a minimum, outgrowing the military model of activism they have inherited from advocates of religious fundamentalism and market fundamentalism. It means becoming "proactivists" who define themselves by what they are for rather than against. It means adopting a positive agenda founded on principles of ecology, one that seeks not merely to save nature, but to emulate it. It means working toward a synthesis of materialist and ecological values. As consumer advocate James Turner says, "Markets will not ensure human and ecological values, but without markets human and ecological values will fail to develop."

One possible strategy is to target not globalization but economic concentration and coercive monopoly control by corporations, governments, or NGOs, even when well intentioned. For example, activists can target the demands of the World Bank or International Monetary Fund (IMF) that developing nations fully open their markets, without regard to the cultural impacts. They could also challenge the right of a single company to control a sizable share of any national or global market, just as U.S. antitrust rules prevent monopolies here. This would allow developing nations to make their own choices about the tradeoffs between material affluence and protecting longstanding cultural forms.

Another interesting marriage may occur on the verge between the industrial world and the developing world. We learned in Costa Rica that, when two vast continents are gradually drawn together, whole new ecosystems are born. Today, as numerous global cultures meet at the verge, what new forms will emerge?

Materialism has been a powerful catalyst for the emergence of the information-based economy. The growth of material wealth, driven by the productive capacity of machines, has brought extraordinary gains, extending our lives, raising our living standards, enhancing our health, and creating unprecedented opportunities for learning and exploration.

As valuable as materialism has been, however, it suffers from diminishing returns. Each additional unit of material wealth tends to bring a little less well-being than the one before. After awhile, people often sense that what they are lacking in their lives now is no longer material in form. It is something apart from that.

They may find a hint of what is missing in the pre-industrial cultures of the developing world. When we visited the rainforests of Costa Rica, Malaysia, Bali and elsewhere, we realized that there are many forms of poverty in the world. One is material poverty—there are societies with little in the way of material goods, and they sometimes suffer through material hardship, poor health, and lack of education and opportunity. Another form of poverty comes from feeling detached, alienated, from nature, people, companies, and communities.

In the cultures of the north and west, in Europe, industrialized Asia, and North America, material affluence is vast. Yet the loss of connection to a community, and the alienation it brings with it, can erode our own foundations and undermine our culture's capacity to sustain itself, materially and otherwise. In the cultures of the south and east, parts of Latin America, much of Asia, and Africa, we are reminded of the value of human connection. In these regions we find many peoples with a strong sense of connection. Yet many lack the material security that they need.

The loss of connection often observed in industrialized economies is inevitable. Individuals seeking to define themselves must break their inherited ties to community roles and norms in order to make the new connections necessary for pursuit of economic abundance, notes social theorist Lawrence Chickering, author of *Beyond Left and Right*. After economic aspirations are satisfied, people may begin to seek a trans-acquisitional experience of connection and community. Those who choose this path will make new connections and begin to form new communities. The closeness to family, community, and nature may then be rediscovered at a new and higher level of development.

Today these two realms of humanity—industrial and industrializ-ing—are being drawn together, through globalization. What will be the consequence? If globalization is merely a process by which "they" become more like "us," as we replicate McDonald's, Microsoft and Disney across the globe, then we will likely destroy much of the value other cultures have created and, along with it, much of their potential to contribute to us.

On the other hand, if the process of globalization were halted, and developing economies are fully insulated against intrusion from the industrial and post-industrial world, then they will not get the feedback they need to develop and they will fail to gain the capacities required for survival on a planet with six billion people.

But there is a third way. If globalization follows a more integrative, ecological path—if cultures meet and intermix, and in the process evolve into forms that both transcend the parochial value stages that came before and include a diversity of cultural forms, then something new may emerge at the verge. Economic and cultural exchanges among cosmopolitan members of different cultures may lead to them to com-bine forms and create new hybrid cultural niches in which economic activity and human connection thrive.

These niches could be fountains of creativity and innovation, gen-erating new cultural forms, with their creators managing the diffusion of these forms down through the layers of their respective cultures. This will be an important step toward a global civilization that integrates diverse cultures. As the richness of economic and cultural exchange increases, our world may change, unexpectedly, in surprising ways.

A global civilization, if it arises, will be the result of synergy—the tenth domino—the net gain that feeds the whole, the potential that is not yet actual, the capacities we can draw from deep within us, to adapt to the unforeseen and transcend seemingly impossible limits.

The seeds of something new have been planted. Nested in the industrial economy is a new species of human civilization, something we call an information age, but which can be much more. If we find a way to effectively encourage its development, over time it will simmer through the industrial economy, burning away the deadwood and ultimately clearing the way for a new global civilization. If nature's path is an indication, this won't be a uniform industrial culture, but a community of communities richer in diversity, with new qualities and new capacities we cannot yet fully comprehend.

A Journey into the Business Rainforest

In the few seconds after Bill's parachute flew out of its pack and started to flap uselessly in the wind, Bill found himself on the verge between one state and another. The first was fast moving and exhilarating; it consumed his senses completely, leaving almost no room for calm reflection. Not much different, in some ways, from the lives we often live day to day. But life in that situation was not sustainable, and we knew it. We could either ignore the consequences of inaction or make a change.

In the end, the action we took wasn't terribly draconian. Bill simply turned his body to better harness the patterns of the wind, and tugged on the restraint to help guide the air into the failing chute. Within moments, we saw the fabric of the parachute catch the wind and open wide. Bill's fall slowed from 120 miles per hour to ten, and we both glided softly to a safe landing among our friends, ready to begin our journey into the rainforest.

IN THE RAINFOREST

TWO HALVES CREATE A WHOLE

In late 2001, we made one more visit to the rainforest before putting the finishing touches on this book. We visited Bali, an Indonesian island to the south of Borneo and the east of Java. Bali is a world of its own. It gave us an opportunity to focus on a species different from the ones that had previously engaged us. We focused on the people.

Bali's rainforests are hardly untouched by its people. Throughout the more highly populated regions of Bali, the lush hills of the forest have been terraced into a ripple of paddies for rice and other crops that are harvested twice a year by the Balinese and provide more than enough food for most of them.

Even in their agriculture, however, the people of Bali have a relationship with nature that is far closer than the norm in the industrial world. Every morning when we rose, we saw Balinese women passing from tree to tree, using long clipping tools to snip flowers from the upper branches. These would float gently to the ground, where women would retrieve them in mesh baskets filled to the brim with petals. The men and women would then take the flowers and place them everywhere we went—on the statues along every street, at the doors to our hotel, on the headboard behind the beds. Older women and young children would gather and arrange the flowers in a wonderfully woven basket of palm leaves together with incense, nuts, and spices, to form small floral designs. While we were all enjoying breakfast, they would be placing their creations at the entry to every home, on the dashboard of every car, and in other places where people might need protection, as an offering to the gods.

The Balinese are an active people who are always engaged in living. Yet there seems little effort in their work, no resentment at the early hours at which the endeavors often begin, no disputes over rank, role, or compensation. And there is little boredom or loneliness. For every hour an American or Japanese spends sitting in front of the television, living an imaginary drama in an imaginary community, the Balinese engage in ceremonies, an endless stream of festivals and rituals that touch everything they do, to the consternation of western business owners who expect a sharp divide between work and play.

Endeavor for the Balinese is celebration. It is a show of thanks, and an engagement with others in the community, that binds them together as a family.

However, there was something missing in Bali. There seemed to be no anger, resentment, exclusion, or alienation. Never did anyone issue a harsh word to us. Never did we encounter violence, fear, or scorn. If there is a harmful addiction or obsession in Bali, we did not see it. No doubt these qualities exist there—they do everywhere. But their proportions seem less. Always we were met with smiles and greetings of "hello" from a people who seemed delighted to have us there. Faces old and new would open up into delicious smiles whenever we rounded a corner on our bicycles or scooters, or on foot, and encountered a Balinese man, woman, or child going about life. There is something in the Balinese culture, the Bali system, that imbues its people with a sense of belonging, contentment, and fulfillment, a quiet and serene happiness.

The spark that energizes the Balinese is expressed in the belief system of the people, a curious mix called Bali-Hinduism that integrates aspects of Indian Shivaite and Buddhist traditions with ancient indigenous beliefs from the Indonesian archipelago.

The Balinese distinguish between the two halves of reality, the physical world and the underlying reality, with the terms **sekala** and **niskala** which are equivalent to the way we use the Japanese terms *omote* and *ura*. *Sekala* is the world we see—in Bali, the world of ceremony, ritual, dance, drama, and life. *Niskala* is the world we don't see—the codes underlying the rites, the principles that animate nature. To the Balinese *niskala* consists of a tension between two equal forces: the forces of creation, which they call **Brahma**, and the forces of destruction, which they call **Shiva**. The relationship between these two is managed by a third force, **Vishnu**, the preserver. This trinity together constitutes a whole that is beyond human comprehension, which they call **Sang Hyang Widhi Wasa,** the "One Supreme Unknowable God." The Balinese do not typically pray to Sang Hyang Widhi Wasa, which is, after all, unknowable. They pray to the manifestations, the forces of creation, preservation, and destruction that they can relate to in the physical world. (To symbolize the three forces, Balinese temples are often decorated with three thrones—Brahma and Shiva on each side and Vishnu, a bit larger and higher, in the center. Yet oddly, there are no figures sitting in the thrones. To the Balinese, what we call gods are experienced not as characters so much as abstract qualities. The Balinese do not personify their deities in the way westerners often do.)

The compass of the Balinese is contained in the concept of **dharma.** In Bali-Hinduism, the universe is said to consist of a dance between forces of creation and destruction, Brahma and Shiva. Individually, these forces each produce disorder. As a result, writes Fred Eiseman, the Balinese believe that "left to itself, any natural system will tend toward a state of maximum disorder." In this sense, the Balinese parallel the western notion of entropy, the tendency of order to fall to disorder. But "because order does exist, there must be an equivalent organizing force"—something parallel to our concept of synergy. In Bali-Hinduism, this organizing force is *dharma.*

In Bali, the universe is an ordered system in which is nested an array of subsystems, each person, animal, plant, and nonliving component. "Each of these parts stands in a definite and established relationship to every other part—this relationship is *dharma.* A Hindu feels that his actions, his **karma,** must be in harmony with his *dharma*, 'duty' or 'order.' If his *karma* fulfills his *dharma*, he contributes toward order and harmony. If it does not, he contributes toward disorder, chaos, and **adharma.**"

The Balinese seek to live according to *dharma.* When faced with any kind of desire, they try to respond with action, *karma*, that is appropriate to the *dharma.* The key word is "appropriate." "One does not 'do good deeds' as a Hindu, one 'behaves appropriately,'" says Eiseman. "A Hindu cannot look at the world from the point of view of his own interests, without regard for those of his fellow men, his fellow living creatures, and his fellow inanimate objects. His *karma* must be related to them and to his own *dharma.*"

If the actions or *karma* of a Balinese man are not in alignment with nature's organizing principles of *dharma*, then his spiritual fate is at risk. *Karma* that runs counter to *dharma* leads to suffering, either at that moment, in the future, or in another life, when the offending party may return to Bali in a less desirable form. The Balinese believe this cycle of birth, test, death, and rebirth is continued until all actions out of alignment with *dharma* are vanquished, at which point the spirit is freed of all desire and emerges in a new, higher state.

IN BUSINESS

TWO HALVES CREATE A WHOLE

Bali is not a perfect place. The rules of the Hindu caste system, for example, while adhered to flexibly in Bali, limit freedom and can repress individuality. Moreover, in the mountainous region of east Bali, there is true material poverty. Thousands of children live on a diet that consists largely of the local crop, Cassaba, which robs their bodies of the iodine essential to the development of their minds and leaves many of them damaged for life. The East Bali Poverty Project is seeking to provide them with the nutritional foundation and education they need to help themselves.

Another challenge to the serenity of Bali may take the form of globalization. Already, in the Denpasar region and beach communities near the main airport, we and thousands of other tourists are descending on the region, bringing not just the dollars but also the sense of the west, our expectations and beliefs.

Economists can calculate the benefits to Bali of open borders, of an economy that invites in western capital as fast as possible. As in all things industrial, more and faster is always better. The inflow of capital can be good and healthy for Bali. And it can be good for the industrial world. Bali needs a portion of what the industrial world has. And we need a portion of what Bali has.

But the capital must not be blind to *dharma*. The people and businesses that bring capital must do so consciously and conscientiously. If capital were to flow indiscriminately into Bali, leaving nothing but a sequence of pioneer McDonalds, shopping malls, freeways, hotels, and housing developments in its wake, it could have the same effect as an exotic species of wheat entering in overwhelming quantity into the heartland of America. It could destroy the existing crop, the existing economy, the existing culture, and leave the place barren.

Companies built on the old machine model, unconscious companies that seek blindly to maximize their own gain at any expense, are a threat to Bali and to global diversity in all its forms. Living companies, those that are alert to the effects they have and adaptive in their actions, have the capacity to enrich the global ecosystem. In the terms of the Balinese, they can serve Vishnu. By following the principles of nature, living systems, the *dharma*, the Tao, they can create more genuine prosperity for more people and help cultivate a world as ecologically diverse as the rainforests of Costa Rica, Malaysia, Hawaii, and North

America and as culturally varied as the people of Tortuguero, Borneo, British Colombia, and Bali.

Like fires in a forest, two systems of development are spreading fast throughout the global economy. The industrial fire, ignited by the automobile and assembly line methods of the industrial age, thrives on wide-open borders and cultural uniformity. It is an r-strategist that excels in the advance of monoculture. The huge standardized mass markets it fosters yield economies of scale and speed the flow of mass manufactured products and services.

A second source of fire was ignited by computers and the Internet economy. It thrives on individuality and cultural differences. These increase the creation and flow of knowledge, connect people and cultures so they interact in their genuine forms, and foster co-evolution, diversity, and resiliency.

The industrial fire will be quickly spent, geologically speaking. A forcing function will intervene, and we will transition to a new economy. The question is this: How early will we respond? Will we make a smooth transition? Or will we close our minds, our communities, and our companies to the signals and seek a few more decades of industrial-style growth?

As a society, we have barely tapped the potential of the emerging economy. We are still gathering its low-hanging fruit, if not just the fruit on the ground. But we are raising our sights, raising our vision, looking into the trees themselves, finding deeper pockets of value there.

What we learn when we look at a tree is that, in nature, value is not a function of consumption. It is a product of design. As Eric Drexler has written, a tree is high technology. Rockets and microchips aren't. A tree's value comes from its design. It's not just timber, a concentration of cellulose; it's a system whose real essence is its structure.

In a Rembrandt painting, a Beethoven composition, a Balinese dance, we are carried to new heights not by the medium but by the design, the arrangement. It is the pattern of line and line, note and note, step and step that gives music and art its transcendent power.

The same is true in the economy. It is not the elements of hydrogen and carbon that give a gallon of gasoline its power. It is the *arrangement* of the atoms into a complex web of hydrocarbons from which emerges the power to transport us.

We often say there is no waste in nature. But in fact, in nature there are plenty of ecosystems as consumptive and wasteful as the

A Few Business Lessons from the Rainforest

All waste is lost profit.

All value is created by design.

There are three ways to create Value-by-Design:
Breakthrough innovation means making a better product.
Replication means reproducing it over and over.
Continuous improvement means making that product better.

To create value in these three ways, businesses pass through four phases of development.

In the phase of innovation, they develop new seeds—breakthrough innovations.

In the phase of growth, they replicate and grow those seeds aggressively.

In the phase of improvement, they seek to continuously improve efficiency, quality, and variety.

Once they have served their purpose, in the phase of release, they release their resources to be taken up in something new.

To avoid this destructive phase, businesses must be adaptive, able to learn.

The first step is often feedback.

Feedback topples the first domino. It can begin a wave of change that gently awakens the corporate machine, that brings it alive, creating something new that transcends, yet includes, all that came before.

A living system—creative, productive, and resilient.

Topple the first domino, and see what evolves.

human industrial system. Pioneer species enter an open field and grow explosively, devouring every bit of mineral and fuel they can find, until they cover the field from edge to edge, and they reach their limits to growth.

If pioneer species had values like humans do, they would probably be the values that help them survive and excel. Consumption, conformity, competition, domination. If they had problems to solve, these pioneers would wage war to do it.

But nature doesn't stop with the pioneers. The pioneers prepare the ground for those that succeed them—the perennials, the resilient ones. Diverse specialists survive by finding their own niche and fitting it tightly—efficiently, elegantly, with flexibility and resilience. They may be fiercely competitive at the edges of their niche. Yet they find that they depend on their neighbors for the very definition of their niche. If they had values, they might be creativity, diversity, cooperation, and interdependence. If they had problems to solve, they would bring together the diverse skills needed to solve them, for the whole.

Of course, this description is idealistic and oversimplified, in nature and the human economy. Reality is complex, and every system is mixed. Yet, by and large, the industrial economy is at its core a relatively simple, uniform, machine-based, consumptive system. A hunting and gathering system that searches the world for pockets of prefabricated resources, almost ready-to-use.

But industrialization is neither a final triumph nor a tragic mistake. It is simply a stage, and one of potentially enormous value. It prepares the ground for what is to come.

We cannot see what will come, any more than peasants at the close of the Middle Ages could sense the changing role of artisans, or artisans could see the overwhelming transformations that the Enlightenment and industrialization would bring. But if we watch nature, already well along in her own transformations, we can begin to sense the rich mix of values and beliefs of the civilization and culture, the nature of human artistry in our next stage of development, and the vast potentials to profit from sustainability—economic, social, cultural, and ecological.

This suggests one final lesson from nature: The highest mission of business is to help fully develop the human ecosystem, sustainably like the rainforest, in all our diversity and complexity.

What we learned from the rainforest is easy to understand. We can use less and have more. Consume less and be more. It is the only way. The interests of business and the interests of the environment are not incompatible. They are the Japanese *omote* and *ura*, the Chinese *yin* and *yang*, the Balinese *sekala* and *niskala*, product and process, economy and ecology, mind and spirit—two halves.

Only together can we make the world whole.

MANAGEMENT SUMMARY

- Businesses, like forests and all complex systems, tend to evolve through four life phases: innovation, growth, improvement, and creative destruction.

- At any moment, different elements of the business will be in different phases.

- In each phase, *current* performance is maximized through dramatically different and often competing *success factors*.

- In each phase, *future* performance—sustainability of the business—is enhanced by developing the success factors of the *next* phase, even at the cost of the current one.

- The sustainability *imperative* is that, in any one phase, a living system must master the success factors of the *next* phase in order to be sustainable. For example:

INNOVATION-PHASE SUCCESS FACTORS:

- * Manage the business like a laboratory.
- * Make power available to anyone with a promising idea, vision, or drive.
- * Empower self-defined, self-selected leaders.
- * Encourage informal, spontaneous team building.
- * Invest in pure ideas.
- * Sustainability imperative: select and pursue winning ideas from many choices.

GROWTH-PHASE SUCCESS FACTORS:

* Manage the business more like a machine.
* Centralize power, clarify rules, limit flexibility.
* Make jobs more uniform, interchangeable.
* More, bigger, faster products.
* Invest in physical capital: facilities, equipment, inventory.
* Sell to mass markets.
* Fight fires, avoid change.
* Sustainability imperative: develop capacity to quickly improve variety and quality.

IMPROVEMENT-PHASE SUCCESS FACTORS:

* Structure the business like a college campus.
* Decentralize power, clarify objectives, be flexible.
* Encourage specialized, team-based, interdependent jobs.
* Increase variety, improve quality.
* Invest in human capital: education, training, satisfaction.
* Sell to niche markets.
* Manage fires, foster continuous change.
* Sustainability imperative: develop corporate mission and values.

RELEASE-PHASE SUCCESS FACTORS:

* Resources are released as the forest or platform burns.
* Power is diffuse and liberated.
* Past factories, offices, products, and skills may be obsolete.

* People are often frightened and self-protective.
* Leadership is assumed by charismatics who convey order amid chaos.

RENEWAL-PHASE SUCCESS FACTORS:

* Redeploy resources as they are released.
* Reaffirm corporate mission and purpose.
* Embrace change, as a time for vision and opportunity.
* Sustainability imperative: deeply embedded corporate mission and values.

The Future 500

WHAT IS THE FUTURE 500?

The Future 500 is a global network of leadership companies whose mission is to apply principles of nature to improve the performance and sustainability of business.

FRAMEWORK

Rather than the old business-as-machine model, we see the business as a living ecosystem. We diagram the business ecosystem as a set of five concentric circles. Each circle represents one of the living systems that, in a healthy business ecosystem, support and are supported by the business. The core circle represents the company's enduring purpose and its leadership. This core is nested in its workplace, community, marketplace, and environment. Each circle both transcends and includes the circles within it.

METHOD

We develop and apply business tools based on principles of nature. Our member companies take traditional business tools-in management, accounting, and communications, for example-and redesign them so that they more effectively apply principles of living systems. For example, applying principles of feedback, we provide accounting tools that can track costs throughout the five spheres of the business ecosystem. Applying principles of succession, we provide management tools that maximize performance through all four phases of the business life cycle. To create value-by-design, we provide tools in engineering and industrial ecology that substitute resources with information. To wire together the whole business ecosystem, we provide communication tools that help assure that each level of the business ecosystem supports every other. Our tools are developed by leading management and accounting firms that have joined together as Future 500 Partner Members.

MEMBERS

We have three membership categories: Partner Members, Full Members, and Limited Members.

Partner Members both develop and apply the tools. They include companies and experts such as Deloitte & Touche in accounting, Manning Selvage & Lee in communications, Visa founder Dee Hock and David Hurst in management, Hewlett-Packard and Pitney Bowes in technology, WSP in engineering, ERM in organizational development, Det Norski Veritas in certification, American Renaissance in leadership, and Ecostream in new media.

Full Members apply the tools. They include leadership companies such as Agilent, Coca-Cola, Coors, Ford Motor Company, Mitsubishi Electric, Nike, Stanley Electric and numerous others. They work with other Future 500 consultants, members and partners to plan, implement, track, and communicate their efforts to evolve into more high performance, sustainable business ecosystems.

Limited Members gain access to the Future 500 tools and network. They receive a Future 500 tool kit with approximately 100 tools developed by Future 500 members. They also become part of the Future 500 network, listed in our online business directory, and web linked to others in the network. Finally, they participate in conferences, summits, and projects of the Future 500.

Mission: Apply principles of nature to improve the performance and sustainability of business.

Framework: The business ecosystem—a model that nests the business within five interdependent living systems: its core purpose and leadership, workplace, community, marketplace, and environment.

Method: Develop, apply, and disseminate business tools that apply nature's principles.

Members: Partners develop the tools; full members apply the tools; limited members access the tools and network.

FUTURE 500 CONFERENCES AND RAINFOREST EXPEDITIONS

To highlight this living systems approach to business, and stimulate innovative thinking, planning, and spontaneous partnering, we sponsor conferences, workshops, publications, and expeditions to the rainforest.

The Industrial Ecology conference series, held at least every two years, is our largest event, and is open to the general public. We define industrial ecology as *the application of ecological principles to business and industrial practices.* This definition encompasses not merely manufacturing focused waste-as-food systems, or lifecycle analysis, but the full array of business tools that apply principles of nature to every aspect of business.

The Future 500 Japan conference is held annually in Tokyo. Supported by innovative thinkers from fourteen major Japanese corporations, the Future 500 Japan conference draws together hundreds of business leaders that personally embrace the idea that business is an ecosystem, and seek to apply the idea in their companies.

The Future 500 Summit is a periodic working session, open to a hand-selected set of attendees, who work together to plan a specific set of projects.

The Future 500 Rainforest Expedition, held about once per year, provides business leaders the opportunity to explore one of the rainforests of the world, meet the people who make their lives there, and learn first-hand the principles of complex living systems that can help companies grow both more profitable and more sustainable.

FUTURE 500 PROJECTS

The Future 500 also carries out implementation projects, to create working models of business ecosystems. Currently, these include: Computer and Electronics Product Stewardship (to develop model programs to take back and otherwise reduce the life cycle costs of computers and electronics), the Corporate Accountability Practice (to define the partners and practices of the Future 500), and the Eco-Park Project (to site and finance eco-industrial parks, where wastes from one facility are food for others.).

FUTURE 500 WORKSHOPS AND CONSULTING SERVICES

To train companies in the living systems model for business, we provide consulting services and workshops to our member companies. The *What We Learned in the Rainforest* Workshop Series includes a comprehensive introductory workshop, as well as specialized workshops in core business functions, from a living systems perspective: accounting, communications, management, measurement, certification, new media, conflict resolution, document management, environmental management, and technology. The workshops are presented by experts from one or more Future 500 member or partner companies, and from leading authorities in the field.

The *What We Learned in the Rainforest* Series

OVERVIEWS

What We Learned in the Rainforest	Tachi Kiuchi and Bill Shireman
Industrial Ecology	The Future 500

CORE BUSINESS FUNCTIONS,
FROM A LIVING SYSTEMS PERSPECTIVE

Accounting and Measurement	Deloitte & Touche
Management	David Hurst
Chaordic Management	Dee Hock
Corporate Accountability	Charles Altekruse
Strategic Planning	Cate Gable
Engineering	WSP
Communications	Manning Selvage & Lee

SPECIALIZED DISCIPLINES

Biomimicry	Janine Benyus
E-Solution Technologies	Hewlett-Packard
Document Management	Pitney Bowes
Certification and Verification	Det Norski Veritas
Organizational Development	ERM
Power Cause Coalitions	Manning Selvage & Lee
Leadership	American Renaissance
Technology	Joel Makower and Aileen Ichikawa
Business Activism	Ecostream
Market-Based Law and Regulation	Global Futures and WSP
Conflict Resolution	Global Futures

PLANNING AND ASSESSMENT TOOLS:

CAP Audit (comprehensive)	CAP companies
CAP Scan (targeted)	CAP companies
CAP Plan	CAP companies

Limited business members of the Future 500 ($395) receive a Future 500 Tool Kit (a set of publications that detail the tools of living businesses), listing in the on-line Future 500 Directory, invitations to members-only Summits, discounts for all their staff to conferences and events, and periodic publications and updates. Individuals may also join as limited members ($195) but receive no directory listing and only a discount for one to conferences.

Full business members of the Future 500 ($6,000 and up) may direct their dues to a program of their choice, including conference sponsorship, in-house workshops, or consulting services.

Partner members are expected to make a significant annual contribution to develop and promote services that reflect the living systems approach to business.

Future 500
Tool Kit

THE FUTURE 500 TOOL KIT

The Future 500 Tool Kit is provided to members of the Future 500, through manuals and how-to guides. Here, in summary form, are some of the performance tools described in greater depth in the Future 500 Tool Kit.

Many of these tools are the purview of firms such as Deloitte & Touche, Hewlett-Packard, and Manning Selvage & Lee. Bob Jonardi of accounting and assurance firm Deloitte & Touche, for example, works with the Future 500 to provide tools that allow a company's social and environmental performance to be scrutinized alongside its financial track record. Joe Gleason and Charles Banks-Altekruse of Manning Selvage & Lee provide communication services in a corporate accountability framework, utilizing practices such as cause-related marketing.

Hewlett-Packard's E-Solutions unit provides technologies that increase total productivity of energy, resources, and labor, and their *World e-Inclusion* technologies help developing cultures leapfrog consumptive industrial stages of development, through electronic products that enhance social and economic opportunities without uprooting whole cultures and traditions in the process. Pitney Bowes provides document management services that can eliminate the use of the paper and related cost and resource consumption.

Deloitte & Touche conducts assurance and internal controls assessment, so that companies can confirm that financial, management, and other standards are being adhered to both at their own facilities and through their supply chain. It is adapting and applying its attestation procedures for independently examining and certifying the effectiveness of a corporation's internal controls for both environmental and social data collection, analysis, and reporting. ERM applies organizational development techniques and training to ensure that "the right people are doing the right stuff" to meet organizational objectives.

Det Norski Veritas has established systems of certification and verification of a company's technical, financial, social, and environmental performance through its supply chain, on issues such as sustainable forestry, international labor practices, and carbon offsets for industrial activities. WSP provides engineering and environmental management tools, such as market-based and incentive-based tools, public-private partnerships, and the alignment of environmental, legal, regulatory, and economic signals. Ecostream conveys the results of these efforts through "new media" marketing and communication tools, and web-based audio/visual production.

BASIC TOOLS

The CAP Audit, CAP Scan, and CAP Plan are basic tools applied by Future 500 companies. CAP stands for corporate accountability practice. Full members may receive these tools as part of their membership.

The CAP Audit is a comprehensive 108-point inventory of a company's overall performance across five fields of measurement: environmental, community, marketplace, workplace, and corporate. For each one, it inventories and links the asset or liability to one of 18 bottom-line benefits, such as reduced litigation or increased market share. It also scores the company against selected criteria of reporting and performance systems such as the Global Reporting Initiative, Dow Jones Sustainability Index, Domini, Calvert, and Council on Economic Priorities.

The CAP Scan uses a systems-based approach to provide a menu of options or solutions to specific business opportunities and problems. The issue may be a product launch, a marketing opportunity, or a legislative threat.

The CAP Plan is an implementation plan based on the findings of a CAP Audit or CAP Scan.

The CAP Spot, a fourth basic tool now in development, is a one-minute multimedia piece that uses video, audio, graphics, and text to tell an impactful story of a company's environmental efforts and initiatives. It can be placed on corporate websites or in public forums to quickly convey a company's story.

MEASUREMENT TOOLS

Activity Based Costing (ABC) is a system of accounting that measures the cost of an activity, rather than simply the cost of materials or labor.

Benchmarking is measuring a company's performance against a base year, target, or best-in-class, whether that is a competitor, an industry leader, or an experimental maximum.

Business Metabolics is internet-based software developed by Natural Logic, Inc., which calculates and displays resource efficiency and productivity.

CAP Audit is a comprehensive assessment of a company's triple bottom line performance, using a 108-point inventory against selected criteria of groups like Council on Economic Priorities and Global Reporting Initiative (GRI).

Corporate Environmental Report ScoreCard is a self-assessment tool that companies can use to assess their environmental reporting.

Cost of Capital Assessment combines Return on Investment (ROI) with data on the cost of borrowing to help companies decide whether or not to invest in eco-efficiency.

Defect Rate is the ratio of defects per units of a product made or service delivered.

Digital Technology Assessment shows how a company can save money and improve performance through electronic meetings, trainings, videos, webcasts, and other digital communication tools.

Energy Audit is a custom audit of a company or its facilities that includes such elements as an inventory of existing energy use patterns, products, and technologies; an evaluation of existing energy efficiency and energy productivity rates; identification of further savings opportunities; an estimate of the investment and payback; and a prioritized list of To-Do's, in order of Return-On-Investment.

Energy and Resources Opportunities Audit is a combination energy audit, materials audit, and CAP Scan, conducted by the Future 500.

Environmental Audits (energy, materials, toxins) count the amount of energy, materials, and toxins used or generated in an industrial process. In addition to being stand-alone tools, they are also the first stage of a Life Cycle Assessment, the inventory analysis.

Environmental Performance Indices (EPI) aggregate several corporate indicators into s single metric.

Global Reporting Initiative (GRI) is a comprehensive corporate environmental reporting system developed by the Coalition for Environmentally Responsive Economies (CERES) in association with the Tellus Institute.

Impact Assessment is the second stage of the LCA. It seeks normalize environmental impacts according to standard weights, and thereby establish a basis for comparing alternative products and process that contain different mixes of environmental impacts.

Investment Value Added is the enhancement of stock price or growth associated with the implementation of environmental or social programs.

Life Cycle Assessments (LCAs) attempt to assess impacts over at least five product life stages: resource extraction, manufacturing, packaging and shipping, customer use, and disposal, reuse, or recycling.

Mass Balance Analysis follows the flow of materials through a process.

Materials Audit is a custom audit of key materials (such as paper, metals, or hazardous materials) used at a company or its facilities.

MET Analysis—Materials, Energy, Toxins. MET is a combined measure of materials, energy, or toxins associated with a given product, process, or service.

Pareto Diagram is a special bar graph used to display the relative importance of problems or conditions. It is used to: (1) rank issues by importance and frequency, (2) rank solutions by effectiveness, (3) analyze problems from the perspective of different stakeholders, and (4) analyze the before and after impact of changes.

Resource Productivity is the amount of output derived from each unit of input. Outputs may be products, services, or value delivered. Inputs may be materials, energy, labor, information, or a combination of any of these.

Return on Investment is the percentage of dollars returned on every dollar invested.

Social Value Added is the net of the social costs and benefits of a particular product, service, or process.

Social Return on Investment is a method for calculating the social cost savings and benefits of public and philanthropic investments.

Spend-to-Save combines Return on Investment (ROI) with data on the cost of borrowing capital to help companies decide whether or not to invest in eco-efficiency.

Stakeholder Survey is a public opinion survey carried out on a sampling of designated corporate stakeholders.

Stakeholder Valuation analyzes corporate environmental, health and safety, and social performance as they impact shareholder value.

Waste Intensity is the ratio of waste generated per unit of output.

Zero-Based Resource Budgeting is a planning tool that, like zero-based financial budgeting, assumes a zero base for resources at the start of a budget planning cycle.

FEEDBACK TOOLS AND SYSTEMS

Advance Disposal Fees are fees imposed on product manufacturers, distributors, or consumers at the front end to cover the cost of disposing or recycling them at the back end.

Asset Management is the practice of managing the design, distribution and recovery of a company's products to maximize the value derived from them, and minimize life cycle and back-end costs.

Attestation Procedures, typically conducted by major accounting firms, independently examine and certify the effectiveness of a corporation's internal controls for both environmental and social data collection, analysis and reporting.

CAP Scan is a systems-based tool to respond to immediate business opportunities and problems, and sets forth a menu of options.

Cause & Effect Diagram (also called a fishbone diagram because of its appearance and an Ishikawa diagram after the man who popularized it in Japan) is a systems-based tool that attempts to identify the root causes for a problem.

Certification is a process for gaining third party confirmation that a specific environmental or, increasingly, social program or objective is being achieved.

Deposit/Refund systems are a specific type of take-back system, in which a consumer is charged a deposit on receipt of the product, and receives a refund of the deposit when the product is returned to the store or a designated location.

Environmental Product Design Map is a tool developed by WSP that facilitates the product planning and design process by generating a simple and cost-effective life cycle analysis of product content and materials selection.

Forces and Trends Assessment is a tool developed by ERM that reviews the forces and trends most likely to have a significant or short-term impact on the company, builds scenarios, and determines appropriate actions to improve corporate responsiveness.

Greenhouse Gas Validation and Verification Protocols validate complex greenhouse gas emissions reduction projects to ensure effective project design, and help to verify actual emissions reductions for carbon trading markets.

ISO 14000 is a standardized environmental management system that includes written procedures, instructions, forms or records to standardize behaviors and make planning and administration more predictable and controllable, and help to clarify who is responsible for doing what, when, how, when, why and where.

Just in Time Inventory Management (JIT) seeks to minimize the inventory of parts and supplies, by more tightly coordinating members of a company's supply chain.

Processing Fees, similar to ADFs, are fees imposed on product manufacturers or distributors at the front end to cover the cost of recovering, discarding, or recycling them at the back end.

Stakeholder Feedback and Adaptation is a communications process that keeps companies in close touch with its key stakeholders such as employees, customers, communities, media, and activists.

Sustainability Assessment Technique (SAT) is a tool used by WSP to evaluate the expected outcomes of corporate decisions against a range of economic, social and environmental criteria.

Take-Back Systems are systems in which the retailer, distributor, or manufacturer of a product takes the product back after its useful life.

Verification Systems provide for the independent verification of corporate policies, claims, or supplier specifications regarding an increasing array of social and environmental performance standards.

SELECTED TOOLS AND APPLICATIONS

The Tools	*How the Tools Can Be Used*	*Benefits*
Innovation and Product Design		
Biomimicry	Using nature as a model; design cleaner, safer, and better products and processes.	To overhaul its phone network, British Telecom-munications used a biological model based on the behavior of ants, avoiding a 10-year, $46 billion process.
CAP Scan	Provide menu of options for redesign of products or processes, for least-cost end use.	Procter & Gamble was able to design away environmental objections to a new product by selecting options from a CAP Scan.

SELECTED TOOLS AND APPLICATIONS

The Tools	How the Tools Can Be Used	Benefits
Innovation and Product Design (continued)		
SAT	Provides a graphical comparative evaluation of plans/designs/processes/decisions against what is possible across a broad range of economic, social, and environmental issues of importance to the client organization.	Allows the organization to see at a glance where their 'sustainability' performance is strong and weak and to focus on areas where maximum benefit will accrue.
Product Stewardship Initiative	Presents a menu of options to help companies take responsibility for, profit from, and continuously improve the total economic, social, and environmental impacts of the products and services they create.	An alternative to traditional command-and-control strategies, it identifies positive feedback, incentives and organizational learning techniques so a company can continuously drive down costs and increase benefits.
Design For X (DFX)	Designs products for a variety of end-use characteristics: quality, energy efficiency, recyclability, recycling, remanufacturing, durability, etc.	Coors eliminated solvent-based inks to mark cans through a design-for-environment ultraviolet process that improved speed, saved energy, and cut ink consumption up to 90%.

SELECTED TOOLS AND APPLICATIONS

The Tools	How the Tools Can Be Used	Benefits
Sales and Marketing		
CAP Scan	Provides menu of options to maximize sales based on the environmental or social qualities of a product or service.	Increase sales, market share, and brand loyalty.
Market Analysis	Analyzes potential of a product or service in an emerging market category.	Reach the $540 billion global "cultural creatives" market.
Green Marketing Portfolios	Rapidly analyzes environmentally friendly or preferable claims to help insure compliance with U.S., Canadian, and European Union laws regulating green claims and advertising content.	Includes a regulatory overview by practicing U.S. and European environmental attorneys; displays options for advertising and marketing content; flexible application to a product, site, process, or company.
Resource Productivity		
Energy and Resource Opportunity Audit	Provides a menu of options to improve energy and resource productivity, through both efficiency and innovation. Projects the return on investment (ROI) of efficiency options and assesses the marketplace advantages of innovations.	Saves money and improves eco-efficiency. Dow earns a 300% ROI on eco-efficiencies. Procter & Gamble has improved product design and marketing through opportunities assessment.

SELECTED TOOLS AND APPLICATIONS

The Tools	How the Tools Can Be Used	Benefits
Resource Productivity (continued)		
CAP Technology Assessment	Systematically assesses opportunities to save money and improve performance through advanced media technologies. The assessment inventories corporate functions that could be enhanced through these technologies, estimates the performance gain that could result, and provides a prioritized list of To Do's.	Ecostream has an extensive inventory of technologies that can improve internal and external communications, marketing, and education through electronic meetings, trainings, videos, webcasts, and other communication tools.
Document Management	Optimizes the creation, documentation, and use of information for maximum value and minimum cost through an optimal mix of hardware and electronic solutions.	Managing paper can cost 100 times as much as producing it. Union Bank eliminated need for a 200,000-square-foot building by switching to electronic documents.
Energy Management	Optimizes the use of energy for maximum productivity and efficiency and minimum cost.	Proper energy management improves working conditions and product quality. The Reno Post Office improved quality and labor productivity and paid for efficiencies in less than one year.

SELECTED TOOLS AND APPLICATIONS

The Tools	How the Tools Can Be Used	Benefits
Resource Productivity (continued)		
Chemical Management	Manages use of chemicals for minimal cost.	Overused chemicals become pollution and waste. Southern California Edison cut costs, streamlined procurement, and improved safety through chemical management.
Accounting and Financial		
CAP Audit	Scores companies on 108 data points that span all four phases of the business life cycle and all five fields of corporate accountability, and provides "test scores" of business performance according to 12 social, environmental, and financial assessment systems.	Mitsubishi Electric solved a boycott in part by developing a CAP Audit to quantify its environmental and social performance.
Environmental Accounting	Measures the environmental impacts of products or processes, such as through life-cycle analysis (LCA), and report them to meet standards such as the Global Reporting Initiative (GRI).	Lower legal costs, reduced pollution and waste, and better relationships with communities, investors, and regulators.

SELECTED TOOLS AND APPLICATIONS

The Tools	How the Tools Can Be Used	Benefits
Accounting and Financial (continued)		
Management Accounting Improves	management accounting tools, such as through Activity-Based Costing and "spend to save" policies that can reduce total costs, and improve environmental performance.	Target reduced costs throughout its stores by measuring waste intensity through ABC. Compaq improved energy efficiency at a net present savings through a spend-to-save policy.
Social Accounting	Measures and reports on social, labor, health, and other costs using tools such as Social Accountability 8000 (SA 8000) and reporting systems such as SEAARs (social and ethical auditing, accounting, and reporting).	The Body Shop, Dow Chemical, and Royal Dutch Shell report improved performance and reputation owing to their annual social reports.
Procurement and Sourcing		
CAP Audit	Includes assessment of corporate procurement policies and red-flags high-risk and high-benefit options.	Mitsubishi Electric identified paper and wood use reduction strategies with high ROI and environmental benefits.

SELECTED TOOLS AND APPLICATIONS

The Tools	*How the Tools Can Be Used*	*Benefits*

Procurement and Sourcing (continued)

Certification	Certifies that companies or facilities are meeting the management or performance criteria of various assessments (such as ISO 9000 on quality, ISO 14000 on environment, SA 8000 on labor, Forest Stewardship Council (FSC) on sustainable forestry, and others).	Can reduce negative quality, environmental, and social impacts throughout the supply chain. Can enhance corporate reputation among media, investors, and advocates.
Verification	Third-party verification that companies or facilities are operating in accordance with minimum management or performance criteria.	Protects against unexpected controversies initiated anywhere in the supply chain.

Strategic Management

Strategic Management Consulting	Identifies strategic issues that demand top management attention, such as branding, corporate development and restructuring, globalization, mission and values, market strategy, reputation, and technological change.	Using strategic management tools, Canadian forestry giant MacMillan-Bloedel simultaneously solved an environmental conflict and improved its investor value, leading to its purchase by Weyerhaeuser.

SELECTED TOOLS AND APPLICATIONS

The Tools	How the Tools Can Be Used	Benefits
Strategic Management (continued)		
Management Systems Design and Implementation	Provides a framework for engaging the whole organization in the process of addressing significant issues. As a result risks are more effectively managed and opportunities identified and realized throughout the organization.	Reduced operational risks, increased savings, increased market share, improved staff moral and retention-the list goes on, limited only by the design intent of the system.
Organizational Development	Determines who is doing what, who thinks who is doing what, and assess whether an organization's human resources are used most productively to achieve the	organization's goals. Ensuring that people are engaged in areas and on projects where they can be most satisfied and productive can greatly increase the probability of an organization achieving its strategic objectives.
Conflict and Crisis Prevention and Management	Prevents conflicts and crises through advance planning and managing them to reduce their cost and duration.	Johnson & Johnson gained status as a corporate hero through its response to a Tylenol product crisis. Exxon damaged its reputation through poor response to the Valdez oil spill.

SELECTED TOOLS AND APPLICATIONS

The Tools	*How the Tools Can Be Used*	*Benefits*

Strategic Management (continued)

Regulatory Engagement Kit	Sets the frame and foundation for regulatory simplification, consolidation, substitution, and efficiency and helps enhance regulatory partnership through such mechanisms as bubble permits, integrated media regulation, and governmental recognition programs participation.	Applied in 15 U.S. states, three Canadian provinces, and six European Community member states. Incorporates legal issues. Delivered by domestic and international environmental attorneys. Strategic approach based on flexibility, partnership, and simplification opportunities for environmentally exceptional and responsible companies.

Legal and Governmental Affairs

Market-Based Legislation	Uses market-mechanism laws and regulations, rather than punitive measures, to improve environmental and social performance.	Procter & Gamble avoided punitive regulations after it proposed a market-based alternative to California lawmakers.
Conflict Prevention and Management	Prevents litigation and legislative conflicts through advance planning, and managing them to reduce their cost and duration.	Alcoa increased its California market share and promoted recycling through a conflict-management strategy that resulted in favorable state regulations.

SELECTED TOOLS AND APPLICATIONS

The Tools	How the Tools Can Be Used	Benefits
Communicaions and Stakeholder Relations		
CAP Audit	Scores companies on 108 criteria across five fields of corporate accountability. Provides "test scores" as 12 types of stakeholders would rate them.	A major beverage company red-flagged risks to its brand and identified low-cost, high-payback ways to improve its score.
CAP Scan	Provides a menu of options to solve a specific problem or seize a specific opportunity in the field of corporate accountability or sustainability, in partnership with key stakeholders.	A major chemical company identified key government and activist stakeholders with whom to work to rebuild public trust after a chemical disaster.
CAP Spot	A one-minute multimedia piece that uses video, audio, graphics, and text to tell an impactful story of a company's environmental efforts/initiatives. It can be placed on corporate websites or public forums to quickly convey a company's story.	A major distributor of recycled paper uses a CAP Spot to tell a more compelling story than traditional channels allow.

SELECTED TOOLS AND APPLICATIONS

The Tools	*How the Tools Can Be Used*	*Benefits*

Communicaions and Stakeholder Relations (continued)

Cause-Related Marketing	Aligns a company with an important cause, to advance the cause and enhance sales and marketing.	Ronald McDonald House and the Avon Breast Cancer Walk are among "power causes" that improve corporate economic and social performance.
Web-Based Communications Assessment.	Web-based communication tools are themselves an emerging and strategic environmental business practice. This assessment inventories opportunities to use new media tools to enhance economic performance and corporate sustainability.	A Future 500 member company is assessing how it can reduce its ecological footprint by replacing business meetings and international travel with web-based communication technologies.
Public Reports	Any of a variety of corporate reports on environmental and social performance, including so-called SEAAR reports, which account for and audit corporate social and ethical impacts.	Can reduce social and environmental costs and win stakeholder support.

Bibliography

Abe, Joseph M., David A. Bassett, and Patricia E. Dempsey. *Business Ecology: Giving Your Organization the Natural Edge*. Boston:: Butterworth-Heinemann, 1998.

Alden, Edward. *Financial Times*, June 17, 1999.

Ashworth, William. *The Economy of Nature*. New York: Houghton Mifflin, 1995.

Basile, A. *Fodor's. Library Journal*, 123(12), 1998, 34-36.

Beck, Don Edward. *Sustainable Cultures, Sustainable Planet: A Values System Perspective on Constructive Dialogue and Cooperative Action*, Institute for Values & Culture, June 18, 2001.

Beck, Don Edward, and Christopher Cowan. *Spiral Dynamics: Mastering Values, Leadership, and Change*. Osford: Blackwell Publishers, 1996.

Beck, Don Edward, and Graham Linscott. *The Crucible*. Denton, TX: New Paradigm Press, 1991.

Behe, Michael J. *Darwin's Black Box: The Biochemical Challenge to Evolution* New York: Simon & Schuster, 1996.

Benyus, Janine M. *Biomimicry*. New York: Morrow, 1997.

Borsuk, M. *The challenge of information technology to retail property*. Urban Land Institute, 1999. www.uli.org/pubs/UrbLand/infotech/infotech.htm.

Botkin, Daniel B. *Discordant Harmonies*. New York: Oxford University Press, 1990.

Brown, Lester, and Christopher Flavin. "It's Getting Late to Switch to a Viable World Economy," *International Herald Tribune*, Tuesday, January 19, 1999.

FIXBusinessWeek. Industrial Ecology—A Society That Reuses Almost Everything, November 10, 1999.

Caplan, Bryan. *Self-Reliance and Creative Destruction*. Unpublished paper, Department of Economics, George Mason University, 1996.

Capra, Fritjof. *The Web of Life*. New York: Anchor, 1996.

Chandler, Alfred D. *The Visible Hand: The Managerial Revolution in American Business*. Harvard University Press, 1977.

Cohen, Nevin. *Greening the Internet: Ten Ways E-Commerce Could Affect the Environment and What We Can Do*, iMP magazine, October 1999, www.cisp.org/imp.

Connell, J. H., and W. P. Sousa. "On the Evidence Needed to Judge Ecological Stability or Persistence," *The American Naturalist* 121(6), 1983.

Community Environmental Council and Global Futures. *Profiting from Source Reduction: Measuring the Hidden Benefits*, December 1998.

Cringley, Robert X. *Accidental Empires* New York: HarperBusiness, 1996.

De Geus, Arie. *The Living Company*, Harvard Business School Press 1997.

Dobson, Andrew P. *Conservation and Biodiversity*. New York: Scientific American Library, 1996.

Drexler, K. Eric, Chris Peterson, and Gayle Pergamit. *Unbounding the Future*. New York: William Morrow, 1991

Drucker, Peter F. *Post-Capitalist Society*. New York: HarperCollins, 1993.

Dunlap, Albert J. *Mean Business*. New York: Random House, 1996.

Ehrenfeld, John, and Nicholas Gertler. "Industrial Ecology in Practice—The Evolution of Interdependence at Kalundborg," *Journal of Industrial Ecology*, Winter 1997.

Eiseman, Fred B., Jr. *Bali: Sekala & Niskala* (Volume 1). Hong Kong: Periplus Editions, 1990.

"Encyclopedia of the New Economy," *Wired Magazine* website, 1994-1999. http://hotwired.lycos.com/special/ene/index.html?nav=part_two&word=intro_one.

Forsyth, Adrian, and Ken Miyata. *Tropical Nature: Life and Death in the Rain Forests of Central and South America*. New York: Touchstone, 1984.

Gilder, George. *Microcosm*. New York: Simon and Schuster, 1989.

Goodman, D. "The Theory of Diversity-Stability Relationships in Ecology," *The Quarterly Review of Biology* 50(3), 1975.

Hackman, J. Richard, and Ruth Wageman. "Total Quality Management: Empirical, Conceptual, and Practical Issues," *Administrative Science Quarterly*, June 1995.

Hammer, Michael, and James Champy. *Reengineering the Corporation*. New York: HarperBusiness, 1993.

Hawken, Paul. *The Ecology of Commerce*. New York: HarperBusiness, 1993.

Holling, C. S. "The Renewal, Growth, Birth, and Death of Ecological Communities," *Whole Earth Review*, Summer 1998.

"How Will Internet Commerce Change the Retail Scene? *Urban Land*, 56(7), 1997, 70-71.

Hurst, David K. *Crisis and Renewal*. Harvard Business School Press, 1995.

"Internet Pharmacy Begins Operations," *Drug Store News*, 21(2), 4.

Kelly, Kevin. *Out of Control*. Menlo Park, CA: Addison-Wesley, 1994.

Levin, C. „Digital Shutterbugs," *PC Magazine Online*, 1997. www8.zdnet.com./pcmag/news/trends/t970527c.htm.

Lewis, Scott. *The Rainforest Book*. Los Angeles: Living Planet Press, 1990.

Mander, Jerry, and Edward Goldsmith. *The Case Against the Global Economy*. San Francisco: Sierra Club Books, 1996.

Markoff, John. "Intel Hailed for Chip Advance," *The San Francisco Chronicle*, June 11, 2001.

Mathieson, R. *Market of one: Mass customization meets the net*, http://www.hp.com/Ebusiness/june98/.

Miller, James Grier. *Living Systems*. University Press of Colorado, 1995.

Moore, James F. *The Death of Competition: Leadership & Strategy in the Age of Business Ecosystems*. New York: HarperBusiness, 1996.

Moscowitz, Milton. Conference keynote address, *Standards for the New Millenium*.

"MP3 Cutting into Music Sales?" *Wired*, March 24, 1999. http://www.wired.com/news/news/culture/mpthree/story/18693.html.

Narisetti, Raju. *Wall Street Journal*, June 25, 1998.

Neil Gross. *Business Week*, August 24-31, 1998.

Nolan, Richard L., and David C. Croson,.*Creative Destruction*, Harvard Business School Press, 1995.

Peters, Tom. *Lean, Green, and Clean: The Profitable Company of the Year 2000*. Palo Alto, CA: TPG Communications, 1990.

Polis, G. A. "Complex Trophic Interactions in Deserts: An Empirical Critique of Food-Web Theory, *The American Naturalist*, 138(1), 1991.

Postrel, Virginia. *The Future and Its Enemies*. New York: Free Press (Simon & Schuster), 1998.

Prince of Wales Business Leaders Forum website, www.csrforum.com, April 2001.

Romm, Joseph J. *Lean and Clean Management*. New York: Kodansha International, 1994.

Rothschild, Michael. *Bionomics*. New York: Henry Holt, 1990.

Sakaiya, Taichi. *The Knowledge-Value Revolution*. Tokyo: Kodansha International, 1991.

Schafer, S. "Have It Your Way," *Inc.*, November 18, 1997, pp. 56-64.

Schumpeter, Joseph. *Capitalism, Socialism, and Democracy*. New York: Harper Torchbooks, 1984.

Schwartz, M. *The Retailing Revolution: The Impact of Non-Store Retailing on Shopping Centers*. Urban Land Institute. See http://www.uli.org/ [follow "Issues/retail" for information on purchasing this report].

Segaller, Stephen. *Nerds—A Brief History of the Internet*. New York: TV Books, 1998.

Senge, Peter. *The Fifth Discipline*. New York: Currency/Doubleday, 1994.

Shireman, William K. *The Wealth of Notions*. San Francisco: Global Futures, 1995.

Shireman, William K.. *Industrial Ecology and Natural Capitalism*. San Francisco: Global Futures Foundation, 1998.

Sobel, David S. (Ed.). *Ways of Health*. New York: Harcourt Brace Jovanovich, 1979.

Sprecher, Drexel, and Michael Vlahos. *Freedom, Innovation, and Choice: Toward a Competitive Market in Computing Platforms*, white papers prepared for Open Platform Working Group, 1997–2000.

Sprecher, Drexel. American Renaissance lectures and seminars, 1981–2001.

Stein, Sara. *Noah's Garden*. New York: Houghton Mifflin, 1993.

Stein, T., and J. Sweat. "Killer Supply Chains," *Informationweek*, November 9, 1998, pp. 36–46.

Strauss, N. "Free Web Music Spreads from Campus to Office," *New York Times*, April 5, 1999.

Tainter, Joseph A. *The Collapse of Complex Societies*, Cambridge University Press, 1988.

Tapscott, Don. *Creating Value in the Network Economy*, Harvard Business School Press, 1999.

Tibbs, Hardin. "Human Ecostructure," *Whole Earth Review*, Summer 1998.

Tillman, D. "Biodiversity: Population versus Ecosystem Stability," *Ecology* 77(2), 1996.

Turner, R. "Winning Bid," *Money*, 28(3), 1999, 201-203.

United States Environmental Protection Agency. *Sustainable Industry: Phase I Report. Office of Policy Planning and Evaluation*, 1999.

Vlahos, Michael. "Entering the Infosphere," *Journal of International Affairs*, Spring 1998, 497-525.

Wacker, Watts, and Jim Taylor. *The 500 Year Delta*, New York: HarperBusiness, 1997.

Waldrop, M. Mitchell. *Complexity*. New York: Simon & Schuster, 1992.

Walker, B. "Which Way to Bill Your Customers: By Mail or Electronic Delivery, or Both?" *Direct Marketing*, 61(10), 1999, 44-47.

Walker, Jesse. "Jacobean Tragedy," *Reason*, July 1998, p 50.

Watanabe, Chihiro. "The Feedback Loop Between Technology and Economic Development: An Examination of Japanese Industry," *Technological Forecasting & Social Change*, June 1995.

Wheatley, Margaret, and Myron Kellner-Rogers. "Questions That Could Revitalize Measurement," *Journal of Strategic Performance Measurement*, January 1999.

Whyte, David. *The Heart Aroused—Poetry and the Preservation of the Soul in Corporate America* New York: Currency/Doubleday, 1994.

Wilber, Ken, *Sex, Ecology, Spirituality: The Spirit of Evolution*, Boston: Shambhala Publications, 1995

Winograd, Morley and Dudley Buffa. *Taking Control: Politics in the Information Age*, New York: Henry Holt, 1996.

Winograd, Morley, and Dudley Buffa. "Wired Workers," Institute for the New California, 1996.

Womack, James P., Daniel T. Jones, and Daniel D. Roos. *The Machine That Changed the World*. New York: Rawson, 1990.

Yoshikawa, Hiroyuki. "Manufacturing and the 21st Century," *Technological Forecasting & Social Change*, June 1995.

Zell, Deone. *Changing by Design—Organizational Innovation at Hewlett-Packard*. Ithaca, NY: Cornell University Press, 1997.

Index

About the Authors

One a corporate CEO and maverick executive, the other an environmental CEO and entrepreneur. One from Japan, the other from the United States. The authors come from opposite sides of the same world.

Tachi Kiuchi is one of Japan's most iconoclastic corporate executives. As Chairman and CEO of Mitsubishi Electric America, he built the Mitsubishi Electric brand in the United States and managed the company's transition from the old to the new economy. As Managing Director of Mitsubishi Electric Corporation, he broke with Japanese corporate norms to champion a "living systems" approach to business that included rapid adaptation, financial transparency, openness, cultural diversity, executive positions for women, and environmental sustainability. He even forged a bold agreement with Rainforest Action Network (RAN) to promote corporate sustainability. Today he continues to press for profitable *and* sustainable business practices at Mitsubishi and through the Future 500 and E-Square, Inc., based in Tokyo.

Bill Shireman is called a "master of environmental entrepreneurism." One of America's most effective "new environmentalists," he develops *profitable* business strategies and laws that drive pollution down and profits up. As CEO of the largest recycling lobby in the country, Shireman wrote California's bottle bill recycling law. At Global Futures, he brokered deals between some of the world's largest corporations and most impassioned activists—from Coca-Cola, Coors, Nike, Mitsubishi, and Weyerhaeuser, to Greenpeace, Rainforest Action Network, and the Sierra Club—to recycle more than 100 billion beverage containers, help save four million acres of forest, and har-

ness corporate buying power to drive down consumption of nonsustainable resources. Today he serves as President of the Future 500, is
CEO of Global Futures, and is developing the Future 500 Corporate
Accountability Practice (CAP), in partnership with leading management, accounting, engineering, environmental, and communications
firms.

In his spare time, Kiuchi runs marathons, climbs Mount Fuji, rides
his bicycle to Mitsubishi Electric headquarters in downtown Tokyo,
and does 1,200 push-ups a day.

In his spare time, Shireman is somewhat less active than Kiuchi. He
often enjoys a brisk walk.

To join the Future 500, arrange for a workshop at your company, sign on for our next conference, or take our next business expedition to the rainforest, please visit our web site, www.future500.org or www.globalfutures.org. Or select a membership category from the description in the Appendix, and email, fax, or mail to the Future 500, 415 Jackson Street, San Francisco, California 94111, fax (415) 693-9163, email nikole–globalfutures.org.

Berrett-Koehler Publishers

BERRETT-KOEHLER is an independent publisher of books, periodicals, and other publications at the leading edge of new thinking and innovative practice on work, business, management, leadership, stewardship, career development, human resources, entrepreneurship, and global sustainability.

Since the company's founding in 1992, we have been committed to supporting the movement toward a more enlightened world of work by publishing books, periodicals, and other publications that help us to integrate our values with our work and work lives, and to create more humane and effective organizations.

We have chosen to focus on the areas of work, business, and organizations, because these are central elements in many people's lives today. Furthermore, the work world is going through tumultuous changes, from the decline of job security to the rise of new structures for organizing people and work. We believe that change is needed at all levels—individual, organizational, community, and global—and our publications address each of these levels.

We seek to create new lenses for understanding organizations, to legitimize topics that people care deeply about but that current business orthodoxy censors or considers secondary to bottom-line concerns, and to uncover new meaning, means, and ends for our work and work lives.

See next pages for other publications from Berrett-Koehler

Lean and Green

Pamela J. Gordon

No longer will managers think they have to choose between doing the right thing for the planet and doing well in business. This book gives hundreds of examples—at well known organizations including Sony, IBM, Intel, Apple Computer, and Louisiana-Pacific—in which a lean and successful operation comes from making green decisions.

Paperback, 250 pages • ISBN 1-57675-170-8
Item #51708-391 $24.95

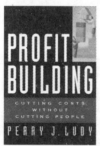

Profit Building
Cutting Costs Without Cutting People

Perry J. Ludy

Cultivating a loyal, productive workforce is crucial to business success. In *Profit Building,* Perry Ludy—who has worked for top companies in every major field from manufacturing to retail—introduces a five-step process called the PBP (Profit Building Process), which offers specific techniques for improving profitability by stimulating creative thinking and motivating teams to work together more effectively.

Hardcover, 200 pages • ISBN 1-57675-108-2 • Item #51082-391 $27.95

The Knowledge Engine
How to Create Fast Cycles of Knowledge-to-Performance and Performance-to-Knowledge

Lloyd Baird and John C. Henderson

The Knowledge Engine shows that in the new economy, knowledge must be captured from performance as it is happening and used to improve the next round of performance, integrating learning and performance into a continuous cycle. The authors show how to produce knowledge as part of the work process and quickly apply that learning back to performance to create a "knowledge engine" that drives ongoing performance improvement and adds value in every area of your organization.

Hardcover, 200 pages • ISBN 1-57675-104-X • Item #5104X-391 $27.95

Berrett-Koehler Publishers
PO Box 565, Williston, VT 05495-9900
Call toll-free! **800-929-2929** 7 am-12 midnight

Or fax your order to 802-864-7627
For fastest service order online: **www.bkconnection.com**

Affluenza
The All-Consuming Epidemic

John de Graaf, David Wann, and
Thomas H. Naylor

Based on two highly acclaimed PBS documen-
taries, *Affluenza* uses the metaphor of a disease to
tackle a very serious subject: the damage done—
to our health, our families, our communities, and
our environment—by the obsessive quest for
material gain that has been the core principle of the American Dream.
The authors explore the origins of affluenza detail the symptoms of the
disease, and describe a number of treatments options that offer hope for
recovery.

Hardcover, 275 pages • ISBN 1-57675-151-1 • Item #51511-391 $24.95

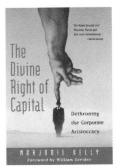

The Divine Right of Capital
Dethroning the Corporate Aristocracy

Marjorie Kelly

In *The Divine Right of Capital*, Marjorie Kelly argues
that focusing on the interests of stockholders to the
exclusion of everyone else's interests is a form of
discrimination based on property or wealth. She
shows how this bias is held by our institutional
structures, much as they once held biases against
blacks and women. *The Divine Right of Capital*
shows how to design more equitable alternatives—new property rights,
new forms of corporate governance, new ways of looking at corporate
performance—that build on both free-market and democratic principles.

Hardcover, 300 pages • ISBN 1-57675-125-2 • Item #51252-391 $24.95

Macroshift
Navigating the Transformation to a Sustainable World

Ervin Laszlo

Preeminent futurist Ervin Laszlo confronts the global
crisis and shows how we can shape our future.
Macroshift informs readers about the dangers,
opportunities, and choices we face—in business, in
politics, and in our private lives—and motivates
them to make informed and responsible lifestyle, civic, and professional
choices. Laszlo expertly combines insights into the science of rapid and
irreversible change with practical guidelines for managing that change.

Hardcover, 200 pages • ISBN 1-57675-163-5 • Item #51635-391 $24.95

Berrett-Koehler Publishers
PO Box 565, Williston, VT 05495-9900
Call toll-free! **800-929-2929** 7 am-12 midnight
Or fax your order to 802-864-7627
For fastest service order online: **www.bkconnection.com**

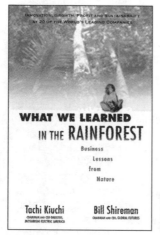